More Praise for *Desert of the Heart*

A beautiful and soulful book. I especially love Chamberlain's reflections on solitude and wilderness. Her vivid descriptions of her life on a desert ranch reach deep into the heart of what truth, creativity, and transformation require of us and bring the reader to a deep meditation on what it means to be alive in a world we simultaneously choose and cannot choose.

LINDA SCHIERSE LEONARD, Ph.D., author of *Witness to the Fire, Meeting the Madwoman, Following the Reindeer Woman,* and *The Call to Create.*

This is a searingly honest and affecting memoir of one woman's journey into solitude. What Chamberlain discovers at Horsethief Ranch is the transformative power of silence, which not only teaches her how to attend to herself, the animals in her keeping, and the land around her, but also to hear the music at the heart of existence. Gracefully written, exactly observed, and filled with surprises, this book asks the reader at every turn to take heed of our brief walk in the sun—to take care.

CHRISTOPHER MERRILL, poet, journalist, and author of *Things of the Hidden God: Journey to the Holy Mountain.*

[This book] transports us into the intimate, wild, challenging, and gorgeous world of a woman seeking solitude...Beautifully told and unstintingly truthful, Karen Chamberlain's story is not about loneliness, but about freedom. It opens our hearts to the consolations of horses and lovers, to the darkness of nature, and to the light of self-knowledge amid the great layered canyons of time.

ANNICK SMITH, author of *Homestead,* producer of *Heartland,* and co-editor of *The Last Best Place: A Montana Anthology.*

Doing what so many of us only imagine, Karen Chamberlain moved her life into a remote corner of the high desert, leaving a busy resort town for a home canyon as self-contained and physically demanding as an isolated monastery, and as rich with experience. In the company of a wild landscape and its creatures, her dog and horses, and occasional human visitors, she finds the space and silence, the shared solitude, to hear herself think.

ANN WEILER WALKA, poet and author of *Walking the Unknown River*

Desert of the Heart

Sojourn in a Community of Solitudes

Wishing you
good days!
Karen Chamberlain

Karen Chamberlain

G R p

Ghost Road Press
Denver, Colorado

Library of Congress Cataloging-in-Publication Data.
Chamberlain, Karen. (1942 —).
Desert of the Heart.
Ghost Road Press
ISBN 0-9771272-4-9 (Trade Paperback)
Library of Congress Control Number: 2005937308

This book is a memoir based on the author's recollections. Some
names may have been changed.

Ghost Road Press, Denver, Colorado
ghostroadpress.com

Acknowledgments

Many people helped put this book into your hands, and I am grateful to all of them. In particular, I wish to thank Michael Behrendt for his vision in purchasing Horsethief Ranch and allowing it to remain the uniquely special place it is. I also thank Michael for permitting me to use his meticulously compiled book, *Horsethief Ranch: An Oral History*, as a source of material on the history of the ranch.

Carol Houck Smith deserves credit as instigator of this project, and I thank her for her support. Living at the ranch, as well as writing about it, was greatly enriched by the friendship of Bonnie Jo Benson, Stephen Haan, Ken Reiche, and Hiram 'Duce' Deneuser.

Bruce Berger, Bill Ellzey, Bill Kittredge, Ellen Levine, Fred Ramey, Lito Tejada-Flores and Linde Waidhofer each read early chapters of the manuscript; their enthusiastic responses encouraged me to continue. Lynne Arundale, Carol Bell, Gail Holstein, and Claire McDougall—all writers of large talent and insight—were the supportive core of the Aspen Writers' Workshop during the time I was working on the book's midsection. Their suggestions have been invaluable.

I'm very grateful for the time taken by Pat Conway, Carol Ehrlich, Dee Bales Gepfert, Su Lum, Marilynn Milmoe, Nancy Starbuck and especially Hensley Peterson to read and critique the bulk of the manuscript. I particularly thank Kirsten Dehner for her trenchant comments, as well as for her strong encouragement. I greatly appreciate the focused attention and apt advice given to each of these chapters by members of the Glenwood Springs Writers' Workshop. And working with Matt Davis and Sonya Unrein has been an author's dream.

I owe a deep debt of gratitude to Carol and Orlyn Bell, and to Tom and Kelly Dodd, for generously inviting me to share their homes during a difficult period of illness and loss. Their friendship and hospitality enabled much of this story to be written. And finally, the story would remain unfinished without the generous, loving support of my husband, Robert Chamberlain.

Contents

Preface

Space. Silence. Solitude. The generosity of unmolested landscape. Have such qualities become rare because they are so difficult to commodify? Or are we ourselves losing the desire to infuse our lives with these graces because we have become so inured to the constant noise, busyness and crowding of a commercialized world?

In the middle of my life, I found some ways of thinking about these questions at a remote ranch homestead tucked away in a Y-shaped canyon in southern Utah. There I had the good fortune to spend four-and-a-half years as sole human resident, without benefit of electricity, phone or near neighbors. I did this because I had long been in love with the redrock desert, and wanted to experience it the way previous generations had—that is, with a maximum of those quiet qualities.

My time at Horsethief Ranch, however, was no idyll. I went there as caretaker, and took my job seriously. The work was hard, the pay abysmal, the rewards extravagant. Because the ranch is a private retreat for the owner's family and friends, and by implication those of the caretaker, those rewards cannot be purchased. But they can be shared. I went there, as I had gone elsewhere, in the belief that home is where you create it. I went there to find a nebulous essence of the West that had magnetized me since childhood. I went there to find that childhood, and how it informed my adulthood. I went there to share, then and later, what I found.

What I found was a rustic, funky, transformative oasis with more than its share of quirks and contradictions. Many of these evolved over geological eons. Others accumulated during its brief human history. Still others were added by contemporary caretakers and visitors. From the cold-water spring to the hot tub, from lilting silence to luminaria-lit suppers with strangers under the ancient apricot tree, what I found above all was the enduring nature of surprise.

I went to Horsethief to learn how others might have lived in the past. What I learned were ways to live with myself and others, human and non-human, in the present. I thank the reader for letting me share what I found.

This book is dedicated
to the land
the creatures
and the people
in it

Once in his life a man ought to concentrate his mind upon the remembered earth, I believe. He ought to give himself up to a particular landscape in his experience, to look at it from as many angles as he can, to wonder about it, to dwell upon it. He ought to imagine that he touches it with his hands at every season and listens to the sounds that are made upon it. He ought to imagine the creatures there and all the faintest motions of the wind. He ought to recollect the glare of noon and all the colors of the dawn and dusk.

— N. Scott Momaday, *Man Made of Words*

Moon and sun are passing figures of countless generations, and years coming or going wanderers too. Drifting life away on a boat or meeting age leading a horse by the mouth, each day is a journey and the journey itself is home.

— Basho, *Oku-No-Hosomichi*
translation by Cid Corman and Kamaike Susumu

Chapter One

Un-Settling

ctober wind rattled the kitchen windows in their frames, blew the darkness in. Dim light from a propane lamp threw back my distorted reflection from beyond the panes: an eyeless, mouthless, dead-faced woman. A hammer was handy—I drove a nail to hold the window steady against its channeled frame. But wind still moaned over the sill, quivering the unputtied panes. And if I looked out into the night, the shaken reflection remained.

Surrounded by boxes, I reached for the knife and sliced open yet another carton of books. Then sank down into a creaky captain's chair. Koa, my longtime shepherd-husky-lab companion, made his way around the boxes to nudge my hand with his nose. Let's do something fun, he seemed to say. Let's go somewhere. I rumpled his soft black fur and took a deep breath. Koa, I told him, I'm afraid we're already there.

We had been here, cleaning and unpacking, for three days. Moving had been a nightmare of treacherous vehicles and unreliable friends. I was quickly learning one of the primary laws of ranch life, the rule of threes: for every task undertaken, you will need to back up through three other tasks to make the first one possible. Yesterday, for example, in order to split a few logs for the fireplace, I'd had to re-wedge the axehead onto a new handle; to do that required de-rusting the vise and replacing one of its bolts; to do that meant unclogging the spray nozzle on a dust-caked, near-empty can of WD-40. I considered myself lucky not to have had to drive the thirty-five miles to Moab for a new can of lubricant.

Yesterday, too, in a fit of despair, I had attacked the kitchen cupboards, which sorely needed cleaning before I could put anything in them. The upper ones, with latching doors, were solid and sealed off, and so were merely dusty, grease-stained, sprinkled with dead flies and spiders. Easy. I scrubbed and rinsed. The lower ones, though, with their wobbly sliding doors, gave me the willies. Dark and deep and hardly mouseproof, they were impossible to see into without a flashlight, even in daylight. No guarantee that whatever I was reaching for wasn't guarded by something I wasn't—something living or dead or trapped halfway between.

Last summer, while visiting, I had watched the previous caretaker remove his sandal and smash a large scorpion scuttling across the kitchen floor. Two summers ago I'd come into the back hallway blinded by sunlight and nearly stepped on a bullsnake napping on the cool concrete floor. Black widow spiders nested under the lid of the indoor toilet tank and under the seats of the outhouse. Why wouldn't such creatures be equally at home in a dark, cobwebby cupboard whose mud-encrusted floorboards were all that separated pantry goods from desert sand?

Rags and spatula in one hand, flashlight in the other, I wormed my way in, bandana-masked, head first and began scraping away at layers of mud and mouse droppings. When I finally finished, it vaguely occurred to me that this fierce cleaning was not mere obsession, but that going into the dark places was requisite for living anywhere. *The darkness is still there,* I scratched in my journal, *and it's neither comfortable nor comforting. But I know it now. It's* my *darkness.*

But that was yesterday. Right now, tonight, it didn't help the heartsick pressure in my chest, nor did it dispel the sense of a vast surrounding darkness invading the house. The legs of the captain's chair skreaked loudly on the cement floor as I stood up, trying to avoid the apparition in the window.

What was I doing here?

I'd left home. I'd run away again, as I'd done so many times as a child. I'd abandoned the magnificent mountains that had drawn me west, the high country where I'd grown, if not up, then at least wiser—or so I'd thought. Traded snow-capped peaks for a drought-stricken desert. Quit a town, Aspen, in which I'd lived for most of twenty-five years, a town that, despite my dismay at the direction of its growth, was still unique, a mini-city in the mountains, a little oasis of culture. And moved to a seven-acre homestead in the middle of nowhere, thirty-five miles by mostly rough road from a strange town where I knew no one. At the security-seeking age of forty-something, divorced and childless by choice, I'd left not one but two creative, challenging jobs to caretake a place that didn't even qualify as a working stock ranch—or even a dude ranch. I'd gone from an earning potential of fifty thousand a year to an income that averaged out, in a short month, to a little over twelve dollars a day. I'd sold a comfortable, convenient condominium in which I'd hardly had to change a light bulb, to scrub mud out of rickety cupboards in a crumbling stone house with a leaky roof, no electricity or phone, and nobody else to fix things when—not if—they went wrong.

Definitely a case of downward mobility.

What was I doing here?

I'd thought I'd known. I'd come here to write, first of all. To write for myself after years of writing for hire. I'd come here to live at a sane pace. To have time for absorbing and reflecting instead of merely acting and reacting. To get to know myself again, both physical self and inner self, and if possible, to match the two of them up. To spend time outdoors, with Koa and my horse Aquila. To grow strong and fit. And yes, to learn another landscape—one that, along with the mountains, I'd loved since I came west in my teens.

For the past six years, every chance I could make, I had visited the ranch. I'd been here in autumn and in spring, the two best seasons to visit the desert if you go by the guidebooks. I'd pulled weeds in August and split firewood in November. I'd spent a week in the heat of July and two in December and January, when the thermometer groveled between sixteen and twenty-four below zero at night and showed no inclination to rise above ten degrees during the day. Over recent years, in fact, I'd spent at least a few days here in all twelve calendar months.

I thought I knew what I was getting into.

But it wasn't the season. It was me. I wasn't a visitor any more. Like it now or not, I'd chosen to live here. Work here. And, by agreement with my friend Michael Behrendt, Horsethief's doting but absentee owner, I was committed to it for at least a year.

Too daunted to cry, I kept cleaning. Mouseproofed the insides of the cupboards with boards and painted them white. Ditto the cavernous closet in the bathroom, thick with sand and packrat droppings, shreds of fabric and swatches of sleeping bags, bits of mummified garbage and rusted trinkets. Ditto with the back bedroom, the caretaker's room—*my* room—heretofore known as 'the pit.' I took a stiff broom, leather gloves, face mask and several large trash bags into the root cellar, emerging as moldered and dust-smothered as it had been. I went into all the nooks and crannies I'd feared, spaces alive with an active darkness that reached forth whenever I opened a door. I repaired and mended, hammered and chiseled, swept and dusted, scrubbed and painted, wondering how many lives I was reorganizing besides my own.

Tentative as a cat crossing a stream, I moved in. Lugged out the teetering three-legged chair, the swag-bellied table, the listing hat-rack and rusting plant-stand, all the useless, charmless, space-consuming junk that had long cluttered the rooms of the main house. Rearranged some items in the bunkhouse, stored others in the chicken coop, tossed the dregs into the bed of the ranch pickup for a dump run. Arranged my own modest furniture to best advantage for Michael's guests as well as for myself. Unpacked my clothes and carton by carton unloaded my books and aligned them along their shelves. Set up my writing table facing a blank wall in the middle room—hardly the view I preferred, but the only place where I could work and be warm year round.

All the while screaming inside, wanting to run the movie in reverse, wanting to go home.

If coming here to live was, as it appeared, a mistake, I might as well examine what exactly was wrong. Obviously some adjustment was needed to go from being surrounded daily by phones and co-workers, to being surrounded by hundreds of miles of unpopulated silence. But I'd foreseen that, had lived with solitude before and welcomed it. Loneliness was not the problem. That I felt drained by six years of overwork was also expected, as was my uncertainty about which ranch tasks to tackle first, and how to go about them. But this sense of having taken a wrong turn, a major step backward, was a daunting surprise. And homesickness? As far as I could recall, I'd never been homesick in my life.

What did I miss? Not my condo, that much I knew. It had functioned as little more than office and bedroom space. Certainly not the hype and glitz of Aspen. And above all, not the tidal waves of deadlines required by two full-time jobs. I did miss my friends, but that was nothing new: my hectic schedule had kept me from full enjoyment of their company for years. What I missed, I suddenly felt, was my whole grown-up life, everything I had learned to do as an adult, all the social and organizational, technical and professional skills in which I had taken pride. None of that seemed worth a hoot here. And it was too late—too late to start again as an independent writer. I'd grown stale writing formula film-scripts, promotional copy, grant proposals. Was too out of touch with myself, too far behind my own dreams of what I wanted to write. What was I going to do with a notebook, a half-dozen legal pads, a clackety old portable typewriter?

I tried to take refuge in what had given pleasure before. I walked through the large garden, its raised beds of vegetables decimated by drought, choked by weeds. But saw only the work it would need come spring. I soaked in the redstone hottub—but only once, after realizing how much wood it took to heat it. I threw sticks for Koa, but ended up tossing them on what little was left of the woodpile. I rode Aquila, my gray Arab mare, out for sunset rides, but the sun was always setting too soon. Such short days. So much to be done. So little time before winter.

One chilly afternoon, while trying to force the bathroom window shut, I jammed the point of its latch deep through my thumbnail. As I washed and bandaged the throbbing digit, I recalled another reason for coming here: to learn to be careful. Care ful. You're the caretaker here. Care taker. I repeated the words, speaking to myself as to a child, chiding, reminding. Re minding.

I reminded myself that I had come here because I loved the desert and loved this place. That everything which had kept me so skillfully busy had also kept me from the dream of living on my own creative terms. That much of what I needed to know in order to live here, I had probably learned as a child growing up in the rural Connecticut hills. *Rest*, I wrote in my journal. *Don't fight it. You know you are supposed to be here. Rest and wait. Let the land do its healing. Let the place do its work.*

Over the next month I began to learn the rudiments of standing still, of taking three steps backward gracefully, of watching, waiting, anticipating, accepting. But resistance was strong, and habit was worse. I had no time to be a child, to earn my life over again. I had to keep at it, had to get things done.

And everything, it seemed, needed doing at once.

What Jean Paul Sartre called facticity—the unarguable state of things— and refined by adding an ominous "coefficient of adversity," prevailed. The state of most things at the ranch, including me, was breakdown. To get through winter meant stockpiling at least three cords of firewood and three tons of hay. It meant insulating windows and doors with sheets of transparent plastic, which meant getting rid of accumulated cobwebs and wasps' nests, replacing broken panes, and washing them inside and out. It meant cleaning the velvet-sooted chimney, getting the two propane tanks filled and their valves and regulators in working order, and draining most of the water system—a system that though ingeniously engineered, was to me an underground mystery of pipes and junction boxes, conduits and drains and valves. Its flow from the spring depended on gravity, but other than that I knew as much about it as I knew about heart surgery.

Meanwhile, there were the more leisurely tasks. Repair the numerous leaks in the roof, put garden, greenhouse and orchard to bed, rake the weeds, mend the gates, de-worm the horses and trim their feet, keep the sheets washed and the house clean for guests, should any show up. Not to mention the everyday chores.

And always, the rule of threes.

Of hay I had four bales. Of firewood, a few dry-rotted, sand-impregnated cedar logs—a stash of which the laziest urban cub scout would have been ashamed. The ranch owned an old Chevy pickup, the only vehicle that might work for transporting hay or wood. It hadn't run for years—hadn't been needed, since Chad, the previous caretaker, had used his own truck. It functioned mainly as peacock roost and junk repository, its bed accumulating such debris as rusted buckets, non-recyclable car parts, snarls of barbed wire, and a couch whose sprung springs and wadded upholstery had long since become skeletal, if not sculptural.

With vehicles, of course, the rule of threes is multiplied exponentially. Sixty-nine, 144, 300, right up to the gong. No mechanic myself, I hired a local friend of Michael's to tackle the basic repairs that would make the truck as dependable as any other twenty-year-old rundown vehicle. It was also agreed that, between repairs, he would use the truck to go up into the La Sal Mountains and transport at least a cord of firewood back to the ranch. His help lightened the urgency of the multiple tasks at hand, but everything I was doing still seemed stopgap. I was taking care, but I wasn't really living here.

Beyond the everyday work, there was an eeriness about the place I hadn't felt before. I was getting used to moving around outside in the dark—feeding the horses, locating tools, going for walks—without a flashlight, adjusting my eyes to the ambient light of stars and moon. I found myself using a kind of 'sixth sense,' which perhaps incorporates hearing and balance, and even vision or touch, but which in any case is acutely sensitive to the *presence* of objects, their nearness or impendingness. One night while out walking, for instance, I ducked to avoid a face-level strand of barbwire I couldn't have seen, or known from memory was there.

I reasoned that in a humid climate the air itself has more substance, and thus 'dampens' (in both senses of the word) this starkness of presence. But perhaps because the high desert air is so thin and dry, and objects themselves so few, the sense of their presence is accentuated. Even more so during a drought, I speculated, and two years had passed without sufficient moisture in any season. That no rain had fallen for four months was evident one morning when the thermometer registered 24° F. It had been well below freezing that night, yet the only frost was in the garden, which I had watered the day before. Elsewhere the ground was dry and powdery as cold talcum, without a trace of rime. Eerie.

Not only did objects possess this impending presence. Shadows, too, appeared to have substance as well as surface, depth as well as texture, especially at night. Walking around in the dark, I half expected to hear a sound as I brushed past, or through, a shadow—expected to *feel* something. The black shapes seemed extensions of the objects that cast them, or more precisely, their negatives, like black holes. Some nights this sensation was so strong that I hesitated to touch a shadowed place for fear I would burn my hand—or lose it.

Sounds, also, had eerie extensions, afterlives, shadows. Echoes, little rasping whispers, as if the intensity or clarity of a sound would cause it to burn for an instant with its own unique pitch. The squeak of saddle leather, the scrape of a screen door across its sandstone threshhold, my now-callused hand sliding across a sheet of paper, even the lightest bird-wing flushing the air—every sound seemed intensified by dryness, possessed of a penumbra of sibilance. Several times, out walking or running, I halted in mid-stride to see if I was being followed. I was—by the sound of my own footfalls. Disconcerted, I trudged through golden light, exquisite autumn days, absently performing tasks that had been expected to give pleasure. I felt displaced from myself, a negative, my own off-set shadow.

One afternoon I and my hammer were in the living room, repairing a giant map of the surrounding canyonlands. The map had been hung where it could be damaged, but was too fragile to move without first stabilizing its frame. As I straightened up from pounding a nail, Koa woofed in warning just as a movement outside the window caught my eye. Startled, I turned to see a man coming toward the open door, his face hidden in the shadow of his hat. Hello? I said sharply. "Hi, Karen," came the cheerful reply. Immediately I recognized the voice of an unexpected friend. Remo! I let my breath out with his name in it, huffing that he hadn't warned me sooner of his presence. "I didn't know where you were," he said reasonably.

Relieved and pleased to have a first visitor, I took him on tour of what remained of the garden: a few raggedy herbs and hundreds of miniature cherry tomatoes, the tangy-sweet kind, still clinging like red marbles to their withered vines. Among the herbs were some leathery leaves of basil, a few sprigs of parsley, some wisps of thyme. I grabbed a basket and we pulled the last of the pungent Spanish onions, discovering nearby two sweet yellow peppers tucked under a shrub of marigolds. It so happened that I had bought a package of pasta and a wedge of parmesan on my last trip to town. And my friend definitely had Italian taste buds.

A simple supper, white plates on a dark oak table. Candleflame counterpointing the dim glow of propane lamps, a fire crackling in the fireplace. Conversation as reaching as the Dvorak tapes we played, as light and limpid as the Schubert. Though he'd lived in Aspen even longer than I had, I did not know Remo well, knew little beyond that he owned land in the desert mountains a hundred miles south and spent his spare time there. Our talk, seasoned with stories of how we each had discovered our affinity with the desert, raised a glimmer of hope that I might find contentment in what I was doing, and introduced the notion that, despite my isolation, I might not be the only person doing it. There were others who loved living with the landscape, loved solitude, yet cherished friendship as well. Perhaps, I thought, leaning back from the table and swirling the last of the wine in my glass, perhaps the world is not so far away after all.

That visit cheered me, and meanwhile another friend was trucking in the horses that spent the warm months on trail rides in the mountains, then returned to our range for the cold season. Since the weather was still mild, Jack Snobble, my old horseman friend, urged me to forget chores for a few days and accompany him on a pack trip. "Come on," he said, "it'll all be waiting for you when you get back." I groaned. That much was true. But the invitation was tempting—to explore the nearby canyon country with a teacher who was a trained geologist, geographer, and anthropologist—and who knew the slickrock desert like a bighorn.

I was about to let chimney sweeping, roof patching, window insulation, and all the rest take a back seat when Michael's truck-repairing friend brought in a load of firewood and with it two items of fairly urgent news. One was that my widowed mother was ill for the first time in her nearly eighty years, and had been hospitalized for tests to determine the cause of severe anemia. The other was that the cows were coming.

That the horseback trip would have to wait was bad enough. That I felt almost relieved at not having to go off and relax for a while was not an encouraging sign I'd left my workaholic habits behind. I drove to town and consulted with my two sisters by phone. One of them had agreed to go east to be with our mother during her hospital stay. I would then fly to New Jersey to help her at home for a week, after she was well enough to be released. I worried about diabetes and leukemia, but there was nothing to be done until test results were analyzed.

That left the cows.

Rule of threes. Let me back up and explain about grazing rights. Although Horsethief itself comprises only seven acres of private land, it leases nearly 14,000 acres of public land in two contiguous parcels from the federal Bureau of Land Management (BLM). One of the two parcels covers almost eight square miles of Horsethief Mesa; the other stretches five miles along the bottomlands of the Green River and its tributary canyons. For each BLM parcel, there are two types of grazing permits: large livestock (cattle and horses), and sheep. Horsethief holds both permits to the bottomland: no one else may graze any animals there. It also holds the original permit for cattle and horses on the mesa.

Combined, the two permits allow the ranch to graze up to sixteen cows or horses a month over the course of a year, except in spring when the desert grasses green up and re-seed. The aim of BLM policy, of course, is to protect rangeland from overgrazing. Unfortunately, its effect has been so restrictive that no one has been able to sustain a living solely from the ranch. But that's another story, another three steps backward. Suffice it to say that Michael's policy has been to use the range allotments as little as possible without forfeiting the permits.

In any case, Horsethief Mesa had seen no sheep for several years, the last sheepherder in these parts having let his permit expire. That permit had been redeemed by a cooperative of cattle ranchers from northern Utah, who, as BLM rules allow, translated it into a permit for cattle, at the rate of one cow for every five sheep. All of which meant that just about the time I was going to leave for New Jersey, one hundred and fifty head of wily cows would be turned loose for a month on the range surrounding the ranch.

Why would this be a problem, since they would have several thousand acres of grassland over which to roam and graze? It was a problem because, other than the taut boundary wires that divided Horsethief's thriving rangeland from the grazed-over pastures to the east, the only fence the cows might encounter was composed of the rusted strands and weakened posts that protected the canyon's orchard, garden, and recently acquired stack of drought-expensive hay. It was a problem because, being cows, they would go out of their way to test that one frail fence, hay or no hay, orchard and garden or not. Cattle are notorious for getting on the other side of anything. They are especially clever—preposterously dextrous, considering their bulk—at getting under, through, or over fences. Even well-maintained fences, which this one was not.

Overweight and wretchedly out of shape after years of driving a desk, I puffed up the steep west slope of the canyon, pockets bristling with nails and wire-staples, hauling pick, shovel and posthole digger. Trip after trip, I trudged up and down with a thirty-pound post setter, a forty-pound spool of barbed wire, bundles of steel fenceposts and cedar bracing-logs balanced on my shoulders. Belted and bandoliered with hammer and fencing pliers, I dug holes, set posts, stretched wires. Where underlying rock prevented posts from being set in the ground, I, Sisyphus, propped them upright with piles of boulders and slabs of sandstone wrestled up the hill from the gully below. I started as the first rays of sun cleared the canyon wall and finished two evenings later by the light of the first-quarter moon.

I'd grown up with cows and hoped I could still out-think them. But by this time I had despaired of out-thinking myself, of discovering a single positive reason for submitting to such strain. There were yet pipes to be drained and windows to be insulated before I could leave to go east. I'd traded one crazy rollercoaster of endless work for another, and this one was a rougher ride. I was, as my punster friend Bruce Berger would later say, completely cowed.

Three days later, blistered, wrenched, sprained and numb, I gimped up the ramp of a 747 bound for Newark International. It was the sixth of November. The hay was safe, the orchard was protected, the garden couldn't be harmed, the pipes wouldn't freeze, the house would stay warm. And I couldn't care less if I ever saw any of it again.

I was away for ten days. During my absence, the previous caretaker, Chad Malone, who was camped nearby studying Anazazi ruins, kept watch on the ranch. The doctors were unable to discover the cause of my mother's anemia. Instead, like her usual spunky self, she simply determined to get well. In New York I visited a writer friend, Kirsten Dehner, who had once spent six weeks at Horsethief, and from her gained support and perspective. I felt revived and strengthened by the ambivalent tonic of distance. While in the city, I mentally peered east into the wooded hills of Connecticut where I grew up. I didn't miss them, didn't want to visit. The return trip included a stop in Aspen, where vacant mansions and jammed-up traffic appalled me still. There's no such thing as home, I thought coldly. Therefore, I can go home.

In the rearview mirror, the orange fins and blood-red buttresses of Arches National Park. A curve, and then the great barn-shaped buttes called Monitor and Merrimac, where I imagined all the animals yet to evolve being kept. On the left, swirls of petrified dunes leading to a pocked wall of white-gold stone, gleaming in the late afternoon sun like the ruins of an ancient city. On the right, the jagged gash of Mineral Canyon snaking out like a scar of fossilized lightning. Straight ahead, afloat on a purple horizon, the snow-capped peaks of the Henry Mountains. In between, a hundred miles of canyonfold and mesa, of mystery and distance.

Jouncing back to the ranch along the Horsethief Trail, I found myself ambushed by the same wild eagerness I'd felt driving in so many times before. In Moab I'd collected the mail and read a letter full of cheers from Michael, Horsethief's owner, his yacht anchored in Singapore. Turning into the driveway, I stopped abruptly as ten horses appeared on the nearby ridge, then wove down through the sage to greet me. I let Koa out of the car and he raced ahead, barking, leading the way, joyous to be back. As I dragged open the front gate, I noticed faint, day-old spattermarks in the sand. Rain.

Chad, my stand-in caretaker, had already left; a note on the kitchen table wished me luck. I filled a glass with spring water from the tap and savored its clean stony sweetness. Then, unwrapping several new audio-tapes I had bought, without looking I clicked one into the tape player and turned the volume up. I was pulling luggage from my car when suddenly my hair stood on end, as E. Power Biggs on the Reisinger Flentrop organ assailed the canyon walls with Bach's toccata and fugue in D.

I looked around at the horses listening, ears pricked, outside the front gate. At Koa waiting expectantly with a stick in his mouth. At the eroded, echoing walls of the home canyon, the squat stone house nestled between them. Dropping my suitcase to the ground, I let a fierce gladness run free.

Chapter Two

Confluences

Once there was a child who lived in a house with her family, and roamed the nearby woods and fields. She did not have a wicked stepmother, but the mother she did have fretted and nagged, and the father she looked to with love often turned on her with harsh words and a heavy hand after puttering in the basement with his tools and his bottle. She and her mother and sisters never knew when they might be beaten for something they didn't know they'd done, and in the house was the feeling of ropes strung taut across doorways, halls, and rooms.

Few people came to visit besides tired uncles and gossipy aunts on lazy baseball Sundays, and no children lived nearby except her two sisters and some boys who played by fighting. One sister was too disabled to play; the other was too young. Grown-ups played rules, not games. The sounds in the house made no sense to the child, and held no peace. But outdoors, the world was boundless, stimulating and steadfast, drawing her deeply into its trackable patterns.

So perhaps it would be better to say this child lived not in the house with her family, but alone in the fields and woods. There she went to evade her mother's disapproving eye, her father's threatening voice. Often she ran away, gliding among trees to the upland cliffs, feeling welcomed by the unknown. And often, as when she hugged her way up a mossy boulder or climbed high in a resinous pine, came a sense of joyous release.

She played at being quiet, at studying blades of grass, petals of flowers, spirals of empty snail shells. She watched a spider sidling along a branch trailing its silk, a bluebird mashing a caterpillar in its bill. She followed tracks of rabbits, foxes, deer, and sometimes startled with her quietness the animals themselves. She played in elm groves among standing rocks and fallen logs, and of the ways they stood or fell imagined homes with sitting, sleeping, and eating areas. To go upstairs she climbed the foxgrape vines, gazing out across river meadows to a range of western hills, a home beyond home. Her life had no friends in it, but she felt apart from nothing.

She sat in sun-dappled grass beneath a pasture oak and played with acorns, crushing the shell of the nut between her teeth and spitting out the bitterness. She played with the nubbled acorn caps, the gray ones fallen from their corns, the new ones red-brown and smooth inside as she tugged them from the nut. She cleared spaces in the dirt and placed the caps like huts among pebbles and tufts of grass. With tooth and thumbnail she notched the rims of the caps with tiny doors so the people in her mind who lived in them could go in and out. She made circles of caps into villages. Older people lived in the gray caps, children in the red-brown ones. Always she placed gray caps among the red. Fingerpaths led among the huts, and circles of tiny stones outlined firepits for cooking, set with bits of dry leaf and twig. Near the firepits were stick benches for the people to sit on, and spore-cups of moss for them to drink from. Some acorns she smashed between stones to make a pastebread for the people, as her mother made bread in the house.

The child at that age knew about Pilgrims, but thought them much less interesting than Indians. As she began to read and visit the library, books themselves became houses. She lived in them as she traveled through them, then wore them as clothing into the next book. She read about animals as she studied the animals themselves—her sisters' cats, the canaries her mother kept caged in the kitchen window, the wild creatures she knew in the woods, and horses wherever she could stay long enough to greet them. She read about Indians as she built a lean-to under the deepest trees and snuck out of the house to sleep in it. She read about explorers like Daniel Boone as she climbed higher up the cliffband above the woods, where the view fell away west and forests and pastures became mere shapes and textures. She designed continents in her mind as she read about faraway places and people who seemed strangely familiar.

When she was eleven, she announced to her parents that with the money she had saved from gifts and chores and working at the polo stable, she'd bought a horse. It was stabled in the neighbor's sheep-shed, and the neighbor said it could stay there, but it needed grain and hay. She had plenty of money left for that; please could they drive her to the feed store? Stunned, the reluctant parents consented to let her keep the yellow horse. When the schoolbus dropped her off, it came neighing to the gate, and soon they were off bareback across the river, following trails that led toward the sun as it set beyond dark hills.

At night, after homework, after the bedtime stories her father sometimes told, she read by flashlight under the covers. The Oregon and Sante Fe Trails, the plains tribes and the bison. Lewis and Clark, A. B. Guthrie, J. Frank Dobie, John Muir. The library became the frontier. School was miles away in town, where most of her classmates lived. One March of

Dimes Day the quiet, dark-haired girl who got good grades but never screamed for Elvis rode her horse to school, sold rides during recess, and gave the bag of dimes to the principal. Her disabled sister had learned to walk and run. So could others. The classmates rode the horse as novelty, amusing each other with their antics. The girl remained silent and unamused. Deeply shy, immersed in her books and notebook and her outdoor world, it took her years to learn to talk to those her age, and to find a friend who loved poetry as much as she did. The last her classmates heard, she had gone away to college, somewhere out West.

*

At age fifteen, Art Murry left home in Oklahoma and lit out for Wyoming, where during the harsh winter of 1910, with Haley's comet smearing the frigid night sky, he broke horses and drove freight wagons for his board and keep. After a couple of decades of mule-skinning in Wyoming, running wild horses in Colorado, and cowboying in Nevada, he figured he'd batched it long enough, and decided to settle down.

Returning to the Green River area of Utah, he picked up where he'd left off, working cows and breaking horses for Joe Biddlecomb at Robber's Roost, once a hangout for Butch Cassidy's Wild Bunch and lesser known outlaws. There he met a girl whose first pony he'd once trained. Muriel, now a woman with mettle to match his own, soon became his bride. By then he had a herd of cows and was looking for a place to run them. In 1929, Joe died and his widow lent Art cash to buy rights to pasture across the river, up on Horsethief Mesa, so named because, rumor held, some horses had been stolen there by one of the men who'd sold Art his rights.

Herding the cows across the river and up onto the mesa, Art and Muriel found themselves smack in the middle of a range war. The area Art had bought the right to graze his cattle on was already crisscrossed with the tracks of several cow outfits and at least one sheepherder. Art pushed farther west, onto Horsethief Point, where he and Muriel found a spring in a side canyon, surrounded by slickrock and pastures of waist-high bunchgrass. After a season of camping under ledges and raising a crop of fat calves, they decided to stay. The spring obviously had been used for centuries; it would support their needs.

Tree-shaded and hidden, the camp at Horsethief Spring was just off a much-beaten track—the outlaw trail that led west past Robber's Roost and on north to Montana and Canada. In 1930, after the birth of their first son, Art and Muriel and Muriel's brother built a two-room house with a tamped dirt floor and a tar-paper roof. For the walls, huge slabs of red sandstone were sledged in from adjacent bluffs, levered and stacked in place with primitive hoists, and sealed with red adobe from nearby clay pits. Enormous cedars were hewn, stripped of their shaggy bark, and hoisted up as roof beams. Crossboards for the roof and windows were liberated from a mine shack down by the Green River. By hook and by crook, the place was literally raised out of its surroundings.

Meantime, around them the range wars flourished. In addition to cowmen jostling each other for territory, there was overt hostility between cattlemen and sheepherders. One day Muriel stepped outside to see a stranger with a rifle silhouetted on the rimrock above the canyon. When Art went up, unarmed, to investigate, he found seven sheepmen with guns and knives. "We're here," they said, "and we're stayin'." Art bided his time until the sheepers had split up their herds and set up separate camps. Then, still unarmed, he paid a visit to each camp, one on one. Though he had little use for guns, he was a big man with a bigger reputation. "Git," he said. And they got.

That winter, a domed, dirt-roofed root cellar was built near the kitchen, and during the next year a storage barn was attached to the house, stout cedar-post corrals were erected, and Muriel, pregnant with their second son, put in a garden. While Art was gone for days at a time with his cows, Muriel laundered and scrubbed, gardened and put up food, one child at her breast and one in tow. The nearest neighbors were twenty miles northeast at Doobinky Well; town was a long day's drive when you could get there. Visits to and from anybody were few and far between. Energized by hope—the Stockraising Act of 1916 promised 640 acres if settled and suitable for grazing—they built and labored and sweated as pioneers had for centuries.

Meanwhile, twentieth-century clouds were piling up on the horizon. For one thing, the eastern bureaucrats who enacted the laws couldn't imagine how *few* cows could subsist on 640 acres of arid grassland. To them, the 5,000-plus acres required to support even the most modest cattle operation hinted at undemocratic practices like baronial Spanish land grants. For another, local land barons were already shaking hands with a new western bureaucracy, whose ostensible purpose was to end the range wars and prevent continued degradation of the land. But the National Grazing Service, established by the Taylor Grazing Act of 1934, was no more immune to politics than was the open range it was now empowered to divvy up. No sooner had Art and Muriel found their own frontier than the frontier as it had been known—a place where "your permit was your nerve"—disappeared forever.

Art, big and quick, and Muriel, tiny and tough, fought drought and heat, disease and flood, rustlers and rattlesnakes, isolation and envy, inadvertently making the very success of the ranch the reason their claim to it was challenged. When they tried to file for water rights on the spring they had improved and encased, they were refused for lack of a survey. After the survey, their application for a grazing homestead was turned down for non-payment of taxes. When they offered to pay taxes on land they couldn't claim, their money was refused. "Wouldn't even accept a donation," Art said.

In time, they bought a farm one hundred and fifty miles away in Colorado, where Muriel lived with the boys during the school year. Art commuted, paid taxes, served on the Fruita school board, and continued to hold his desert ranch against all comers. Finally, broken in health and disheartened by the drowning death of his elder son, he sold a quit-claim deed for twenty years' worth of improvements on the ranch. At age sixty, he packed his family off to begin again in Canada.

The man who bought Art's deed, Ken Allred, was a born and bred Moabite who had little trouble obtaining immediate title to Horsethief's spring and several acres of surrounding land. The new Bureau of Land Management, which had replaced the Grazing Service, even granted him two permits for grazing tracts on Horsethief Point and the riverbottoms below. But even with this boon, the number of animals he was allowed to run was so limited that after six years Ken, too, was forced to give up the Horsethief homestead, along with the improvements he and his wife Patsy had made, and move his family and livestock elsewhere.

He sold to his half-brother and partner, Bill Tibbetts, a sometime horse rustler, cattle-thief, town marshall, and instigator of the original grazing rights deal that had proved so worthless to Art Murry. Bill and his wife Jewel retired to the ranch and hunted prehistoric artifacts for what became the largest personal collection in the state. After six years they became disenchanted with distance, and the ranch changed hands again. By then it was 1967, the year of the summer of love in San Francisco.

Mac and Alice MacKinney had already established their lives locally and raised a family when they decided to retire to Horsethief Point, run a few cows, and live at a relaxed pace off the income. The accident that intervened in their plans could have ruined the chances of any of Horsethief's owners. One cold New Year's Day, Mac loaded a cow recently separated from her calf into the rack on his pickup. Mad and mooney-eyed, the cow knocked Mac from the pickup onto the frozen ground, breaking his back in two places. Alice, tall, strong and gutsy though she was, had her hands full trying to keep the cow from heaving out of the truck and attacking Mac again. After a two-hour battle, she got the cow locked in and Mac under blankets, then drove for help. A Basque sheepherder came to the rescue, and a few hours later Mac was in the hospital under the care of a doctor who told him he would never walk again.

After another year at Horsethief, with the help of a wheelchair, hoists over bed and bath, and finally a cane, Mac was able to lurch around well enough to relieve Alice of some of the chores. The next years were touch and go, with Mac falling almost as often as he walked, Alice supplementing their marginal income by working in town, and each of them doubling the risk of the other by trying to halve it. Alice was at work when Mac suffered another accident—a big gas refrigerator fell on him while he was trying to move it—and only the timely luck of a friend stopping by got him out from under it in one piece.

Alice bought a drafting table and moved her work from town to the dimly lit ranchhouse. Mac bought a bulldozer and leveled space for an orchard he hoped might recoup their drained finances. Then Alice, out herding cows alone, got bucked off her horse and landed on her head. Dazed but unhurt, she realized she'd had it, and convinced Mac to put the place up for sale. Two years later, Mac died of cancer, while Alice, still tall and strong, went on with her memories.

The MacKinneys were the last folk who struggled with, and were ultimately defeated by, the limitations of Horsethief as a working ranch. But no matter the defeat, all of them left reluctantly; all except the Tibbettses would have stayed could they have seen reason or reassurance along that isolated path. Nevertheless, Horsethief had become a home. Though Art and Muriel had been unable to establish clear title to it, they handed on a legacy of endeavor and accomplishment, becoming the first in a series of inhabitants who attempted to settle in and add on, instead of merely passing through.

But those who had passed through also left a legacy. In the beginning were Anazazi and Fremont people, who farmed in the riverbottoms, hunted on the mesas, and wrote their stories on the rocks. In the east y of Horsethief's canyon are several stone storage cysts and evidence of a camp that, from its layered remains of charcoal, bones and stone tools, was used repeatedly by centuries of native families. Later, Ute and Paiute people camped and hunted around the spring, where game animals from rabbits to bighorn sheep were plentiful.

In 1776, while musket and cannon boomed far to the east, Fray Francisco Atanasio Dominguez, Fray Silvestre Velez de Escalante, and members of their Spanish exploration party, edged up from Mexico along the deep, silent canyons and sprawling mesas of this region, becoming the first Europeans to visit "such widespread provinces heretofore unknown." Sixty years later, from the opposite direction, came a French trapper from Fort Laramie, Denis Julien, whose name and the date of his passage *(1836 3 mai)* are inscribed in sturdy Romanesque calligraphy on the wall of a Green River side-canyon below Horsethief Point.

Mormon settlers, fanning out from Salt Lake City, established satellite towns wherever irrigible land could be found to support their dream of infinite productivity. One of the few prophets who foresaw the limitations of this dream was Major John Wesley Powell, who in 1869 and 1871 led the first scientific expeditions to boat through the Green and Colorado River canyons. Powell warned that much of the canyon country would defy development and that the limiting factor would be water. It seems ironic that his name should be applied to the silt-laden reservoir known as Lake Powell.

Mindful recreation has its uses, however, and latter-day owners of Horsethief have received pleasure and instruction from the land, rather than struggling for subsistence. After Alice and Mac moved back to Moab, the ranch was bought by Dick and Nancy Eckert from Illinois, who, with their growing children, spent long summers exploring Horsethief and its environs.

In 1981, Horsethief was purchased by its present owner, Michael Behrendt, and so began another era of dwelling *with* the land, rather than merely using it, of preserving and enhancing its qualities as refuge and retreat, of creating and maintaining a place that an increasing number of guests and visitors consider their home away from home.

*

Hollow click of hooves on sandstone. The long-legged shadow of a horse, topped by a pinheaded nub of a rider, glides up the steeply tiered rock, followed by actual horse and rider. Tongue lolling, a dog trails behind. Beneath the mare's feet, the massive stone glows white-pink in the setting sun. Three stories high and a city block in area, the rock displaces acres of blackbrush and bunchgrass, prickly pear and Mormon tea. It is like riding up the steps of a cathedral. As horse and rider reach the top, warm wind sweeps over the pitted monolith, swirling into its sunken gardens, whistling over benches of broken rock. Near one of these benches, the rider dismounts, drops rein, and gazes around, holding her blowing hair. Panting, the dog flops down nearby.

The June evening is clear; the view is forever. Forty miles east float the prussian-blue peaks of the La Sal Mountains, still streaked with snow. From this distance, their lower flanks green with new-leafed aspen, they appear luminous, unreal, a painted stage set. But the puffy wreaths of cumulus encircling the twelve thousand foot peaks suggest their power: outriders of the Rockies, they are the first to catch the storms that move in from south and west. They create, with their cloud-forming altitudes, the weather that alters this landscape.

Shading her eyes, the woman shifts her gaze north. Sixty miles in that direction, the palisades of the Roan Cliffs line their segment of horizon like books on a crooked shelf. Beyond, low against the sky, lies the Wasatch Range, holding Salt Lake City at bay. Facing south, she views the crumpled chaos of what in recent times has been named and given borders: Canyonlands National Park, its rock slumped and lifted, bristling like mythic serpents turned, like Medusa's head, to stone. This shield-shaped mesa above the confluence of the Green and Colorado Rivers bears names like Upheaval Dome, Island In The Sky, The Empty Triangle. The names suggest the paradox: eternal turmoil petrified into perpetual serenity.

Restless, the horse nudges the woman, who scratches the mare's forehead, then affectionately pushes her away. Sitting down on the rock, she faces west, into the wind, into the sun burning above the horizon a hundred miles distant. North of west rises the stegosaurus-spine of the San Rafael Swell. Then the heave of Capitol Reef, and the high graceful shoulders of the Henry Mountains, partially shrouded by capes of cloud. To the southwest, she scans the sacred hump of Navajo Mountain, the stiff chimneys of Ekker and Elaterite Buttes, the shadowed scars and carbuncles that mark the Maze. The great circle of horizon seems in its expanse to fall away, like the curve of earth seen from a plane.

Sleepy-eyed, the horse cocks one foot, resting its weight on the other three. The dog stretches out on the rock, flat as a shadow, soft black and tan fur ruffled by the wind. The woman, eyes closed, breathes slowly, deeply, inhaling this pulse of lifted mountains, fractured plains, canyon-entrenched rivers. She breathes the land as it jags and wavers through space, as it has risen and fallen, puckered and shrunk and oozed back up through time. She breathes it from beneath shallow seas where it was buried for the millions of years of its forming. Grain by ripple, she breathes in rich-colored sediments, primordial muck. Layer by layer, she breathes them into fire-hued stone, embeds them with shells of molluscs and insects, veins of leaf and seaweed, scales of dinosaurs and fishes, bones of wide-eyed mammals.

Sitting on the wind-exposed rock, the woman opens her eyes to the weather-sculpted land forms around her. Tall spiny pinnacles, fat rounded buttes, tilted caprock mushrooms, flat areas of bedrock sparsely carpeted by vegetation. Letting the sun go on its way, lowering her gaze to the stone around her, she studies what she can see of the wind. Partilcles of sand, blown almost too fine and fast to see, whisk across rock, bounce off patches of leathery lichen, catch on her skin, evolution sifting through the hair of her arms.

When she looks up, the burning ball of the sun is descending beyond the teeth of the San Rafael Swell. The mare stands a few feet away, dozing. The dog, still seeking shade, rests nose between paws in the shadow of the horse. Moments pass, then the last glowing rind of the sun disappears, leaving gilt-edged clouds afloat in a warm red sea. The woman stands and stretches, watching the colors smoke and char. Then turns east to view the blue-red afterglow above the ashen peaks of the La Sals. Her breath stops as she comes face to golden face with June's full moon, looming impossibly large, impossibly close, seemingly suspended in its slow rise above the mountains.

The woman comes often to the great rock to watch the sun set, or rise. Occasionally she brings friends, or guests from the nearby ranch. But few know that this flat-topped monolith has become a sort of secret home, like the homes she concealed in the woods where she grew up. Here, this great white whale of a rock, pocked with sparse gardens of sand, invites her imagination once again to create spaces of sculpted intimacy.

One such area she likes to think of as the living room: a pool of smooth sand containing a live juniper, a dead juniper log, a swag of cliffrose, two snakeweeds, pads of prickly pear, a fishhook cactus, some yellow sneeze-weed and a few bunches of ricegrass. The barrel-shaped fishhook cactus, with its sharply recurved spines, is in full pink bloom. Sheltered from the wind, the woman sits on the twisted cedar log as if it were a cushioned couch, reading the newpaper moon. The mare, not quite allowed in, stands and waits. The dog, who knows to stay off the furniture, lies panting on the sand carpet at the woman's feet.

A wilted breeze sifts past. The woman gazes through the 360-degree window of her house, thinking it should be always so easy to cleanse the panes of perception. Around her, moonlight blends so perfectly with the fading bronze of sunset that it seems night will never come. And so she sits for a while, watching dusk tarnish the gold-red light. Then, with the dog and mare growing restless, she gathers the reins and hops on.

They shamble down the great rock and weave across the rolling mesa toward the ranch, shadows cast in front of them, this time by the moon. She watches her animals: gray-white mare beneath her like a chunk of smoked moonlight, black-tipped ears alert as a lynx. Black and amber dog, tail up, nose to the ground, half-hidden by patches of brush. Horned larks skim the sage like skipped stones, whispering their evening cheeps. Far off the ravens cry.

The tepid air feels the same temperature as her body, though she knows it is cooler. The wind disappeared with the sun, but now, bending at an easy lope around clumps of sage and islands of prickly pear, they create a breeze of their own. Approaching a gully, she eases the mare to a walk and they slide down the bank into a sweet coolness, a bracing draft faintly scented with humidity. Juniper berries come to mind. Tonic, if not gin. Subtle waftings of resin and sap, bird feather, lizard skin, seedheads of grass. Sandsilk, stoneshadow. Ghost-essence of the last rain that passed this way a week ago. Her own and the mare's evaporating sweat.

Then the mare lunges up the far bank and they are again surrounded by a canopy of warm air, leftover day-heat that burns from the direction of the long-set sun, radiates from rocks, hovers in the dusk like moonlight itself. The dog spies a rabbit and gives chase, his hysterical yelps shredding the dusk. The rabbit, as always, escapes. The dog circles back, grinning as if pleased, as if his only intention had been to cause the cottontail to flee.

They come to a two-track trail and take it, following the route Art and Muriel, Ken and Patsy, Mac and Alice, Bill Tibbetts, the sheriff, or anyone else of that era would have used to approach from town. She imagines Art bringing a bunch of cows and calves along the same trail, bovine bawling replacing the sandy chink of the mare's hooves. She imagines Muriel in the ranchhouse, lighting the lamps, never knowing when her man might return home, always with a pot of something on the stove ready for him. Kids fed, back outside playing in the dusk.

Abruptly turning the horse from the trail, they cut across a flat stretch of slickrock and come to the rim of a hidden canyon. Nestled between its walls eighty feet below is the ranch and its outbuildings, inconspicuous as acorn caps. The sloping roof of the ranchhouse glints silver-gray in the fading light, looking for all the world like a slab of slickrock covering a pile of red stones. A rustic bunkhouse, layers of tan paint peeling, blends with the high sandhill behind it. The raised beds of a large fenced garden surround a greenhouse whose glass panes mirror a mulch of pale straw. Only the marine-blue eye of the hot tub, directly below the cliff, seems out of place. Shade trees, orchards, outhouse, woodpile, derelict vehicles, and the circles of upright cedar posts that form the corrals, all appear as shadows looming out of shadow. In one of the corrals a horse looks up like a toy, uttering a plaintive whinny. Otherwise all is still. No Muriel, no kids, no visitors, no one home.

The woman turns the horse toward the moon, picks up the trail, follows it down the ridge to a clay driveway. There, a guardian skeleton presides over this wide spot in the road, a hunkering cowpoke made all of cowbones, arthritic ankles set in battered boots, faded bandana round its skull. The sign beside this scarecrow reads PRIVATE PROPERTY—DEAD END—TURN AROUND HERE. Horse and rider continue along the driveway past a tall piñon shaped by nature into a perfect Christmas tree, hung with silver balls that glitter in the dusk like miniature moons.

Dropping from the driveway into the gully beside it, they follow a brushy trail toward two large rectangular water tanks set in a broad wash below the ranch, brimming with gold-green water. The dog jumps into the upper tank, lapping a drink and half-attempting to lie down. Ripples of broken moonlight wriggle over the water, insects lift off into the squadron of bats flitting overhead like tumbling leaves. The mare lowers her muzzle into the ripples, swashes away the debris of dead bugs and floating algae, and sips quietly. In the next tank, the dog stands dripping, grinning, waving his wet tail. The woman listens to the mare swallowing water, hearing in it the rhythms of her own heartbeat. Around her in the moonlight, the sense of space and stillness is enormous; the earth seems anchored to something larger than itself, the moon tethered like a balloon above. Nothing turning, nothing moving. Again tonight, no doubt, the nested birds will sing all night long.

Chapter Three

Power and Disconnection

During those first uncertain days after moving to the ranch, while sorting out a drawer of junk, I came across a tiny white plastic telephone, something that might hang on the wall of a dollhouse. I dropped it in the trash, and went on cleaning and unpacking. But then something stopped me. Wryly, I retrieved the miniature phone and hung it on a nail by the blackboard, just inside the kitchen door.

Along with the eerie dryness and the demanding workload, part of what was disconcerting about those first weeks was the sense of being un-plugged. The Aspen condominium I'd owned and lived in was sandwiched wall to wall in a hive of interlocking apartments located just up the hill from the center of town. The local power company provided electricity with an efficiency that encouraged one to forget about the source of com-fort and convenience. In addition to basic appliances, amenities included two phones, computer/printer and fax. In winter, I stepped out the door onto a roofed porch and stairwell designed to shed the heaviest snow. A maintainence crew kept sidewalks shovelled and parking lots plowed. Subtle outdoor lighting cast a warm glow over the grounds, defeating the very idea of night—as well as starlight or even moonlight. Groomed landscaping invited neither prowlers nor other forms of wildlife; one felt that even the most modest songbird would have to apply for a nesting permit with rent-check and damage deposit in its beak.

By contrast, I now lived far from the nearest town, connected to it not by water, phone, or power lines, but by a single thread of road, a third of which was raw dirt—when it wasn't mud, snow, or dust. Instead of an airtight, well-lighted apartment, I now dwelt in a dimly-lit stone house riddled with drafts and holes. The roof leaked, wind breathed in, mice, insects and other creatures had easy access via cracks in walls and ceiling or the gaps under the doors.

As a visitor to Horsethief, I'd found the outdoor-indoor aspect of the place appealing. But living with it was something else. My childhood had been spent outside as much as possible, and as an adult I considered myself a seasoned outdoors-person, a hiker who preferred to camp without a tent when weather allowed. But this was a house—a structure intended to separate the wild world outside from the human world inside. How could such thick stone walls be so illusory? It was unnerving to feel so much intimacy with so vast an out-of-doors. Wind, blowing from the far Pacific or the Arctic, ghosted around doors and windows. Night, co-extensive with the darkness of the universe, was held at bay only by the complicit glow of a few propane lamps. Coyotes howled, owls hooted, bats flew, bugs crawled. I felt as if I were dwelling under a roof without walls, or within walls that had no roof.

Since there was so much darkness out there, I thought I should reacquaint myself with it. I began to take night walks with Koa, whose eager presence was steadying and whose senses seemed extensions of my own. From the rimrock above the ranch, I'd look up at a sky crowded with stars, then out across hundreds of square miles of darkened landscape, unpunctuated by even the tiniest pinpoint of light. One evening as the rumble of a midnight jet broke the silence, I thought about that self-contained world speeding past overhead, stewardesses serving meals, handing out headsets, pillowing their passengers into movietime or sleep. Then I looked back down into the home canyon, where a small square of lamp-light shone from a single window.

The plane, by comparison, seemed a city in the sky, a hurtling, horizontal skyscraper, temporarily insular and self-sufficient, but above all connected—contiguous, in fact, with both ends of its journey. Whereas here I felt not only disconnected, but exposed, vincible. The house seemed a shell, useful but illusory; by living in it I had opted to be the sole mediator between it and the encroaching world outside. *I* was the walls and roof, heat and light. *I* had to light the lamps, keep the propane tanks full, the pilot-lights lit, the house insulated, the pipes thawed. I was all that would keep the oncoming winter, if not at a distance, at least outdoors.

True, one of the reasons I had moved here was to experience a different set of living conditions, to understand what earlier generations had made do with. While I was under no illusion about returning to 'the simple life,' still there was something romantic about the notion of propane lamps, splitting firewood, being snowed in. At least there was until that first fall, when those vague notions became the conditions under which I lived.

But human nature thrives on mitigating conditions. Anticipating that being snowed in might be a real possibility, I stocked cupboards and freezer with extra provisions. I had the propane tanks filled, and asked Bill Parmenter, the kindly, competent delivery man, to show me how to light the pilots on the old Wedgewood kitchen stove, the old monster-size

Servel refrigerator, the old water heater in the bathroom, the old stove-pipe heater that warmed the core of the house, and the equally ancient gas appliances in the bunkhouse. I split and stacked fireplace wood, the living room's only source of heat. I patched the roof.

Perhaps self-reliance breeds tolerance. As I made myself less vulnerable to the elements, I found my affection for them increasing. Stapling the last sheets of clear plastic insulation over the windows, I felt a twinge of regret about shutting out the wind and the critters. They were, after all, my roommates. They'd done me no harm, and they made life interesting. I was, in fact, beginning to feel a kinship. Carrying in an armload of firewood, I watched a daddy-long-legs spider step delicately from a log onto my sleeve, as if drawn to warmth. I stacked the logs on the hearth and shooed the spider safely beneath them. Later, sitting by the fire, I journaled:

> There is little but these flames between me and wind and cold. Yet precisely because the elements are so pervasive, so eternally powerful, I don't want to be wholly protected from them. I don't know how to invoke them in my being here—but I do ask that they be part of it.

Later, in bed, after turning off the gas lamp, I scribbled a footnote by moonlight:

> With the lamp off, there is only the moon and this stone house in all this wide terrain, and the house for all the world like a stone, a capped rock. And within, I curl into sleep like a coyote or kit fox, like any creature in its den, surrounded by the moonlit land.

I was becoming more at ease with my surroundings—but I was not a kit fox or a coyote. I had yet to come to terms with my disconnection to the human world, to my own kind. Miniature dollhouse toys aside, the most significant discontinuity was the lack of a telephone.

The kitchen blackboard, of course, proved more useful for relaying messages than the tiny toy I'd hung next to it. Or than the full-size plastic wall phone a friend of Michael's gave me later as a joke. Glued to the wall between the two seats of the outhouse, its fake push-buttons, cord and headset fooled many visitors who knew the ranch had no phone, but also knew technology could change that in a twinkle. "Why didn't you tell me you'd gotten a phone?" my friend Remo complained during his next visit, tongue in cheek. "I would have called to say I was coming. You could have baked me a cake."

Before moving here, I had mulled over telephone options while patiently listening to my friends. True, people have lived for centuries without telephones, they argued, but they lived in groups or communities or at least as couples—whereas I would be there most of the time alone. I argued that living alone wasn't unusual: many back-country people, including previous caretakers, had lived without human companionship—and without a phone. My friends' arguments were reasonable but irrelevant. A cell phone signal would not reach in or out of the canyon, and in fact I'd have to drive most of the way to town to get within range. Besides, after working two jobs that had kept my ear glued to a receiver for hours a day, the idea of doing without was appealing. Even more so was the prospect of living as people had lived for most of human history—and still do, though not often by choice. I had the choice.

In the end, I decided to take my chances. To the extent that I wasn't careful or that circumstance negated precaution, I reasoned that accident or illness was possible anywhere, anytime, and that many people have died with a phone or even a doctor at hand. I was lucky. On only three occasions did I regret the lack of a phone. Otherwise, its absence was a blessing for me and a relief for most of Horsethief's visitors.

While not having a phone increased the feeling of disconnection between the ranch and the rest of the world, it was only one factor in what might be called a 'barrier of conditions' that made the distance to town seem farther than its thirty-seven odometer miles. Granted, thirty-seven miles isn't normally a strenuous commute; but ten-plus miles of that distance is a rattletrap dirt road, a nameless dotted line on most maps. Depending on the condition of that road, the drive to town can take as little as fifty minutes or as long as two days. And except for the outskirts of Moab, there is nothing in between but landscape. No other ranches, no towns, not even any homes. And in winter, almost no traffic.

The English language has no synonym for the word neighbor. Friends may live in another country, acquaintances come and go, but neighboring has to do with geography, with being nearby. Even this is relative. My nearest permanent neighbors lived at the ranger station at Dead Horse Point, a twenty-mile dogleg away in the opposite direction from town. My nearest impermanent neighbor was a professional cowboy who managed a large cow-calf herd from fall to spring. He usually set up his camp about a dozen miles away, near the paved road. Since these were my only neighbors, and since the distance between us contributed both to the barrier of conditions and to a sense of community, I should introduce them.

Duce, given his nickname by army buddies in Germany, was born in San Diego and came east to get west. Like Art Murry, he hit the road for

Wyoming at a restless young age, and has guided, cowboyed, and outfitted from Montana to Mexico for most of his sixty-odd years. Leather-faced under his gray beard, pony-tailed under his battered hat, slim-hipped and barrel-chested, he might seem a bit short until you get to know him. By then you don't notice. Competent and concientious, crackling with humor or temper, he gives good weight, stays sober because "it's too easy not to," doesn't own a gun because "sometimes those dang cows make me so mad..." He keeps track of more or less eight hundred cows belonging to six owners, knows which cow belongs on which side of several fences, what illnesses it's prone to, when it's due to calf. He can repair the differential on a water truck or put an orphaned calf on the teat of a cow whose calf has died quicker than most nurses change bedpans. He knows the lay of the land like the palm of his roping glove, and gives directions guaranteed to end you up lost. He's lent me some of the best novels I've read.

Because the cattle cooperative he works for has a grazing lease on Horsethief Point, I'd been acquainted with Duce since I began visiting the ranch. After I came to live here, we saw each other more often—once a month or so—and became friends. "You're fun to watch," he chuckled when I dropped the butt of an axe on my foot while we were chopping ice off a water tank. Speaking of a recalcitrant cowdog, he called it "dumber than a bucket of rocks." Of a former partner: "He was smart, smart like tractor." We do most of our visiting on horseback, though once or twice a year he'll accept an invitation to supper. More is "too much socializing."

I met my neighbors from Dead Horse Point about the same time they met each other, a few years after I'd begun caretaking the ranch. Stephen, darkly handsome and cheerfully competent, was on an open-ended odessey from the Pacific Northwest to the next stage of his life, when he parked his red school bus at the Dead Horse Point visitor center and encountered the ranger on duty. Bonnie, her wheat-blonde hair swinging long over the service revolver at her waist, was equally enchanted. Believers in unicorns as well as dedicated pragmatists, they proposed to each other in Horsethief's hot tub and were married a few months later. While Bonnie pursued her professional duties, Stephen worked at odd jobs, including a stint with Duce's cow outfit. He designed about one workable invention a month, and also blessed the ranch with occasional but essential help. They both figured greatly in my life after I met them.

Since Horsethief, like Dead Horse Point, is not on the way to anywhere, I seldom saw these neighbors more than once or twice a month. But in the West, where distance is an integral part of community, more would be less. We enjoyed each other's company, but respected each other's time and privacy. And we communicated by keeping a 'mailbox' at the intersection of our roads, a three-pound coffee can with a weatherproof lid, hidden by weeds and wired to the base of a signpost to keep it from blowing away. Big enough for notes, borrowed tools, even homemade cookies—until we discovered that Duce was stealing the cookies. Streamers of survey tape tied to the post served notice: blue indicated a message for Bonnie and Stephen, orange signalled one for Duce, red meant one for me.

But the mailbox helped us communicate only when we could get to it. For Bonnie, Stephen, or Duce this wasn't a problem, since the highway was paved all the way to the Park. But the ten miles of dirt trail between ranch and pavement could be treacherous with snow or mud. Several times I slithered out with difficulty, to find later that I couldn't drive back in. A sleeping bag in the car is a given; vehicle problems or impassable conditions may mean camping in it overnight, and if one does make it to town, it's nice to bring your own bag when requesting an overnight stay on a friend's couch.

Such precautions aren't unusual, of course—anyone who drives off-highway faces similar hazards. But such conditions do contribute to the distance between the ranch and the rest of the world, a stretch not quite overcome by a friend's plane buzzing the home canyon, or a BLM helicopter kicking up clouds of dust around the shredded windsock outside the front gate. While such events are welcome novelties, daily reality at the ranch unfolds beyond a baffle of potential—and sometimes potent—circumstance. If conditions are marginal, one simply stays put. But on a couple of occasions, I couldn't leave when I needed to.

Tucked away in a side-canyon a half-mile from the Horsethief Trail, the ranch is invisible to passing traffic—when there is any. One Sunday morning in December, I'd arranged with Bonnie and Stephen to rendezvous at our mailbox at nine a.m. to carpool into town for brunch with mutual friends. At eight-thirty, I went out to start my car. Click. Nothing. Click. Not even the slightest grind. I left the key on, dropped the gearshift into second, coasted down the mild grade of the driveway past the house, and popped the clutch. Still nothing. Totally dead.

Normally, this would not have been a problem. I would simply use one of the other ranch vehicles—the jeep or the truck. But the rule of threes applied that morning, and both the other vehicles were in town for repairs. In fact, one reason I was meeting Bonnie and Stephen was so they could help ferry the truck back to the ranch.

Hoping my friends would drive in to see why I hadn't showed up, I brewed a cup of tea and waited. When they didn't come, I donned my warmest clothes and filled my pack with what I would need if I got to town—including a book I was reading, *Whiteout*, by Ted Conover, a writer I knew who'd become an Aspen taxi driver in order to research the book. Then I took a folding chair from the breezeway, whistled to Koa, and with me toting the chair and Koa his customary stick, we walked out the driveway to the Horsethief Trail.

The winter sky was overcast and still, but hardly warm. I set up the chair and sat there absorbed in the book, by the side of a desert road running thin and red across the rolling landscape. Every half-hour or so, I'd put down the story about taxi driving and look up hopefully. Scan the silent horizon, stare up the empty road. West. East. Every hour or so, Koa and I would play stick to warm up. After five hours, playing stick didn't help. With an hour of chilly daylight left in which some weekend hunter, miner, or intrepid winter camper might yet happen along, I decided to risk missing a ride while I ran back to the house for a sleeping bag to keep me warm while we waited.

I left the pack beside the chair, and as Koa and I trotted back to the house, brooded about whether to walk or ride horseback for help the next morning. In December, a Sunday afternoon was the most likely time to catch ride. On Monday, I was sure there would be no traffic at all, and none likely the rest of the week. Best to do something about the situation while the weather was holding. It occurred to me that this was a time to be even more careful than usual.

Still brooding, I tucked the sleeping bag under my arm and started back out the driveway— when along came Bonnie and Stephen in Bonnie's pickup. "Is that your *chair* out there?" they asked as we greeted each other. My car was parked inside the front gate, hood up and jumper cables waiting, so it took only minutes to get it running. Nevertheless, by the time we finished telling the day's stories and laughing over mugs of mulled wine, it was dusk. While Bonnie and Stephen soaked in the hot tub, I charged up the battery by driving out to retrieve pack and chair. No new tracks in the dust on the road; no one had come by.

Such a tentative thread, the road.

And yet, how protective I became of my claim to risk, or at least to distance. How perversely dismayed I was, for instance, one January day when, after making first tracks out with the ranch jeep through a foot of heavy snow, I returned after dark, tensely anticipating the churn back, the possibility of spending the night in a sleeping bag with Koa. Nearing the turnoff to the snowed-in trail, I reached down to put the jeep into low range—only to see that the county grader had plowed me a wide, snow-banked boulevard home.

And how affronted I was, during my first year at the ranch, when the paved road to Dead Horse Point was streamlined into a highway, two lanes for vehicles, two for bicycles. For years, the old road had led only to the Parks, and to a few dirt trails like the one to the ranch. But as the Parks were 'improved' to draw more tourists, the old road with its steep grades, tight switchbacks and terrain-hugging wiggles, was deemed unsuitable for large recreational vehicles, watertank-trucks, and the planned-for invasion of oil and gas tanker-trucks.

There are often justifiable and sometimes even fine, non-bureaucratic reasons for building or improving a road; no doubt there's a case for this one. One could argue that its smooth curves and streamlined straightaways shorten the trip to town by a minute or two, save gas and tires and so on. Nevertheless, while the tradeoff enables more people to say they've seen the country, what it does is help insulate and protect them from actually *seeing* it. What's been quenched is the sense of adventure, an opportunity for intimacy with the landscape.

Which brings us back to the ranch, where such intimacy remained quite unthreatened. By spring of my first year, I'd begun to feel comfortable, even somewhat celebratory, about the self-contained world I lived in. Removing plastic insulation from the windows, I realized I'd made it through winter without major mishap. Koa had proved his inestimable worth as fine company, I'd befriended some of Michael's guests, and friends of my own had visited. My first garden was proliferating rapidly. Though the drought continued and the spring remained low, the quality of its water was unaffected. I treasured being so close to the source.

The low roof, thick stone walls, and minimal window area of the house had helped hold heat in winter, and the same design cooled it as the weather grew warmer. Which was good, since air conditioning was as impossible as it was unwanted. On the other hand, I didn't thrive in 110-degree heat, either, which is common in summer. But the desert air is so dry that eighty to ninety degrees is comfortable, and one hundred degrees isn't too bad if one stays out of the sun. Given our body temperature of 98.6°, consider that in the shade, the air might not feel hot, but neutral, an extension of oneself. Or so it was when I came inside, poured a glass of iced tea, and sat reading in a shadowed room.

And so it was driving to town in the pick-up, windows rolled down, hot wind whipping in, skin cooled by its own evaporating moisture. In the rearview mirror I could see Koa, front feet poised on the toolbox, fur sleeked by the wind, leaning into the ride, cooled by his panting tongue. Watching campers and suvs passing on their way to nearby parks, I imagined their climate-control interiors: cool, quiet, smelling of new upholstery. I preferred my way, open to the sun-baked land, knowing how it felt, smelled and tasted at its overheated worst. Faint scent of sage, chamisa, cottonwood. Cool draft from a salt-wash, gunpowder smell of hot rock.

Perhaps it reflects a severe case of technology-deprivation, but I don't much trust the climate-controlled experience. Our detachment from senses other than the visual accompanies our increased dependency on a media-world of manipulated imagery and filtered sound effects. This may not be bad; may even in some way compensate for the spatial refuges and temporal interludes lost to us in an overcrowded, homogenized, hyped-up world. It certainly allows us to distance ourselves from the biosphere we say we are trying to save. It helps us accept what we see on a screen as a substitute for the infinitely richer reality beyond the image, helps us cruise though a landscape of astonishing sensuality and know only what we see through the windshield, our mood enhanced—and our receptivity diminished—by appropriate CD music. We admire the wrapping without thinking to open the gift.

Technological illiteracy aside, my choice not to have a phone did not prevent other media-dependency. Much as I loved my books, what I craved while unpacking them during those first hesitant weeks was not what would carry me into other worlds, but something to link me to the real world I'd left behind. Not escape, not even entertainment, but connection.

While the ring of silence and the chitter of birdsong were preferable during the day, at night the sounds I made against the silence of the house—harsh scuff of sandals, skreak of chair legs, clang of pots and pans—became irritating, almost insufferable. For the first couple of weeks I listened to the classical and jazz tapes I'd brought with me. But I soon ran through them, and not wanting the music to become overfamiliar, I dug out a little shortwave transistor radio I'd brought, and cleared a place for it on the kitchen counter.

I pulled up the aerial, pushed the 'on' switch, pressed the FM button. Nothing. Annoyed, I tried the AM button, then the shortwave bands. Still nothing, not even static. I turned the radio over for an overlooked switch or button, something that might turn it on. Then, three steps backward, I unpacked a carton of glassware so I could move the chair it was sitting on so I could get to the drawer where fresh batteries were stashed.

I replaced the batteries. Still nothing. Silence? or tapes? I asked myself in frustration. I didn't want to hear my footsteps on the concrete floor, or the squeak of sliding cupboard doors, or the dry sharp shadows of any of those sounds. I didn't even want music. I wanted human voices, news. What was happening out there?

I settled for a jazz tape, and ended up playing both sides over and over, just for the impromptu voice that punctuated the riffs. Next morning, I went to town to find someone who could fix my radio. In a garage off the side alley of a back street, I tracked down the local electronics wizard, a man with one green wandering eye and one blind white one, who saw me coming and said it'd be thirty dollars just to open up the radio and check it out. Hesitating, turning the radio over in my hands, I almost dropped it. As I fumbled to catch it, my thumb accidently released the 'on' switch from the 'lock' position I hadn't noticed in the kitchen's dim light, and the radio began playing. I kindly thanked the man's green eye and left.

The little radio became my ear trumpet, my media fix, my incoming connection to the ongoing world beyond the ranch. I depended on it by day for weather forecasts, and at night for news and entertainment. As months went on, this dependency was alternately funny, frustrating, even stimulating. That first forlorn fall, for example, I caught a World Series game on a Los Angeles hispanic station, charmed to hear in Spanish the same familiar sportscaster's drone—the identical modulations as in English—but with more obvious enthusiasm for the game. For a while, I tuned in to 'old time radio' on another L.A. station, amused by programs I recalled from childhood: Jack Benny, Dragnet, James Stewart as 'The Six Shooter,' Orson Welles' 'The Black Museum'—often well-written, always amusing in their innocence. Imagine, in a 1945 'Gangbusters' episode, the brusque indignation with which the narrator reports a then-current crime wave: "Right here in these United States a crime is committed every three minutes..."

Nighttime airwaves were packed with broadcasting from all over the globe. I dialed along the short-wave bands, practicing Spanish with radio Nicaragua, Russian with radio Moscow, English with the BBC. Unfortunately, I couldn't reach National Public Radio, but I did locate a California news station that gave frequent updates on West Coast weather. I found that if I added twenty-four to thirty-six hours of travel time and five thousand feet of elevation, I could fairly accurately predict what weather patterns to expect from the prevailing westerlies.

For a while, one of the interesting things on nighttime radio was the spectrum of call-in talk shows: sympathetic romance counselors, fatherly financial advisors, charismatic preachers, deadly-dudley politicians, even bantering car mechanics. Never having heard a talk-show before, at first I was fascinated. I couldn't call in, but listening to the pander, the slick advice-givers, the self-promoters, the whiners, the dreamers, the pain, ignorance, cynicism and earnest hope of it all, satisfied a need to connect with trends that were shaping the world I still very much lived in.

I had found my incoming media fix, which depended on batteries, as did tapedeck, flashlights, and a few tools and conveniences. Meanwhile, propane powered the basics: stove, refrigerator, heater, and lamps. Lighting a gas lamp mantle with a wooden match took longer than flicking on a switch, but otherwise the lack of electricity wasn't, at first, an inconvenience.

It was my need for an outgoing media fix that turned my attention to electricity.

I'd come to the ranch to write. With hope and trepidation, I had left my computer and printer with my former husband, Rob, and borrowed his Smith Corona manual typewriter in exchange. Hope because writers from Heraclitus to Proust had obviously done without typewriters, much less computers. Trepidation because I'd become habituated to the computer as a means of keeping up with my thought processes, and I planned to work on some essays and a novel.

I tried longhand on legal pads. Fine for poetry, but too slow for prose. I tried the portable typewriter. Somewhat faster and more legible, but still tedious and frustrating. There wasn't enough light in the house to see what the keys were producing on the page, so during the day (weather and insects permitting), I typed outdoors at a rough wooden table. At night, even with an oil lamp to supplement the propane lamp over my desk, it was still a squint to see what I was typing. Finally I resorted to a propped-up flashlight pointed at the page.

John Stuart Mill and Abe Lincoln aside, this was silly. I was getting nowhere. Typing a two-page letter took most of a day. Stories and essays were even more discouraging. Bad enough to halt a train of thought while I scrolled up, down and sideways to erase a single mistake, without having to scroll around in my mind to find where I'd left off. The typewriter, in fact, began to loom as the essence of the rules of threes.

By now I had come to delight in the ranch, and even the work of the ranch. But if it allowed no time for my own work, I would have to leave. In a few months, my first year at Horsethief, and my original commitment to Michael, would be up. There had to be a way to stay.

Even before coming to Horsethief, I'd looked into powering the computer. I'd researched new and used generators, the quieter models, thinking to set one up in the root cellar—near enough to the house to be convenient, tucked under an earth-dome behind a heavy wooden door to muffle its chug. But one expert warned that inadequate ventilation would be a problem, as would winter cold. As would fumes, and the chatter, however muffled, of a diesel-powered machine. I'd have to haul fuel for the mechanical creature and make sure it was properly fed. I'd have to fix it, or find someone to fix it, when, as was inevitable, it got cranky.

The alternative was solar power, which I'd also researched. It was clean, dependable, required no input but sunlight, and emitted nothing but the power needed. But the problem of whether I could run the computer I already had on a 12-volt solar system, or whether I would have to adapt to a less-than-standard model made for photovoltaics, was boggling. Solar modules, gel-cells, deep-cycle batteries, inverters, 12-volt, 110-volt, AC, DC...Where to start?

As it turned out, I started with an abandoned well. Or rather, Michael did. Let's go three steps backward.

The first year I lived at Horsethief was the second year of a serious drought. When Michael parked his sailing yacht on the other side of the globe and came to the ranch for a month-long visit that June, a heat wave had exacerbated the dryness, reducing spring-flow so much it appeared there wouldn't be enough water for all needs of the ranch. Something had to be done to supplement the spring.

Michael determined that Ken Allred's old well outside the front gate was still viable, and over the course of a couple of weeks he created a solar system and pipeline that would carry water from the well to the 5,000-gallon storage cistern—the 'swimming pool'—set into the cliffbase above the garden. The solar pump purred along pumping well-water into the cistern until the drought was broken by a heavy rainstorm. The storm rendered the pump temporarily unnecessary, which was fortunate, since it took that opportunity to quit anyway. By then Michael had returned to his sailboat in Bangkok, but in his log notes I discovered the name of a local person who installed, and possibly repaired, photovoltaic systems.

Robert Soldat. Superior Energy Systems. Next trip to town, I phoned him. Before you could say Please, more rain, Robert had returned the faulty pump to its dealer, got them to honor their warrantee with a new pump, and installed it in the well. Impressed with his knowledge and thoroughness, I asked what it might take, solarwise, to power a computer. He promised to do some homework, and so did I.

Summer went by in a whirlwind of work, then fall with its urgent preparations for winter. Hoping that solar power might after all enable me to get on with my writing, I re-upped for another year of caretaking. But that Thanksgiving came and went before Robert and I put our heads together, opted to install the computer I already had, settled on what would be needed and how much it would cost, and placed an order. Meanwhile I'd heard that the poet Gary Snyder used solar power to run a computer and printer in a similarly remote part of California. I wrote him explaining briefly what I hoped to do and how, and asked if he thought it would work or did he have other suggestions? His return note confirmed the plan. "Good luck," he added, "Don't let your batteries run down."

The day after Christmas. Thermometer peaking around the 10 degree mark during the day, plummeting to sixteen below at night. Robert, black beard hoary with frost, green eyes glittering behind his fogged glasses, hacked a shallow trench in the dirt roof of the root cellar through sandy soil that, had it not been frozen, you could have kicked aside with your foot. In ski hat and parka, long-johns, canvas overalls and thick mittens, he built braced frames for four solar panels, set them in place atop the root cellar, and secured the panels to them.

We couldn't have chosen a colder time in a colder year. I kept tea, hot soup, and the fireplace going while Robert connected the solar modules to one another and ran insulated copper wire along his trench, under the wrecked roof of the breezeway tool room, and through the cinderblock wall of the back bedroom. From there, at least, we could work inside. Good thing. No sooner were the outside hookups complete than a major storm dumped a foot of snow on the desert. Another day and the project would have had to wait until spring.

Meanwhile, Robert had constructed a sturdy plywood cabinet to fit in the bedroom closet and hold three deep-cycle, rechargeable, 'starved electrolyte' batteries. A voltage meter on the front of the sealed cabinet allowed me to keep track of how much power the batteries were storing and releasing. On top sat a small black metal box—the clever little inverter that would make the whole thing work, translating 12-volt direct current stored in the batteries into the equivalent of standard household alternating current.

While bitter weather continued outside, we ran wiring from the inverter along door-jambs and ceiling to the middle room where computer and printer sat waiting on my writing table. Robert mounted a four-plug socket on the wall below the table. Then, not wanting to risk damage to the computer if something wasn't working right, he plugged in a 60-watt test bulb. Flash! Suddenly the dim room was lit up brighter than an operating table. With the ancient cedar roofbeams, the battered propane heater, and the startled spiders in their cobwebs as witnesses, we plugged in the computer, turned it on, and watched as familiar patterns emerged on the monitor screen. We typed gleeful messages on the keyboard, and—sure enough—printed them out. Horsethief—!z@*#%&z*!! —was electrified.

Although solar power ran only the computer, that was the tool I needed. Now I had it at a press of the inverter's tiny button. Even on gray days, even during a month of winter fog, I found no limit to the number of hours I could operate this system, and often worked late into the night without, as Mr. Snyder warned, letting my batteries run down. *Tell the ravens and the coyotes,* I noted in celebration, *tell the deep buried frogs & hibernating lizards, the crouched cottontails & highstepping deer, everything that yelps and yawks, croaks and sings, leaps and skitters and soars: now I will tell your story...*

Autonomy. The freedom to choose and create one's life. I once listened to the Russian poet Joseph Brodsky talk about his youth in the oppressive climate of Stalin's Soviet Union. Inspired by what they could know of the West by reading American literature—especially Mark Twain, Willa Cather, Jack London and other writers of the frontier—Brodsky and his friends held to a belief in what he called "the autonomy of the individual." By this I believe he meant not simply political freedom, or the liberties of entrepreneurial economy, or even values like self-reliance. I think he meant even more the right to creative fullfillment based on the freedom of one's own intellect and imagination.

Installing a solar-powered computer system might be seen as a matching gesture toward a place that already nourished such a rich sense of individual autonomy. I happen to believe that everyone has a right to breathable air, drinkable water, unpoisoned food. Gratis. Not *if* they can affort bottled water, organic produce, or a shot of oxygen from a machine—but free from the political and economic manipulation that turns basic needs into consumer products. At Horsethief, while half the population of my country breathed polluted fumes and munched on genetically modified snacks, I treasured the essentials of clean air, pure untreated water, a healthy organic garden, and a house that held warmth or coolness against the temper of the seasons. In addition to these basic bounties, I could claim the luxuries of space, silence, solitude and meaningful labor. I had the gentle companionship of my animals, and now, finally, the means to pursue my chosen livelihood.

Autonomy. One cold morning I got up, put on a robe and shivered into the kitchen. As I was about to light the stove burners to take the chill from the room, Koa dropped a ball at my feet. We bounced and chased the ball around for a couple of minutes, wrestling playfully. When I stood up, the kitchen was much warmer. I lit one burner to boil water for tea, instead of the four I'd been using to heat up the room. After that, when I'd find myself standing by the heater rubbing my icy hands, or easing timidly into cold clothing, I'd remind myself to *move*—grab the broom, play with Koa, jump up and down. I could, if even so slightly, alter my surroundings.

And yet, without connectedness, autonomy is self-righteous smugness. For me, the first connection had always been to what makes life possible—the Earth itself. Living at the ranch amplified that irrefutable connection hugely. And though I did without many things friends considered necessities, gradually I discovered fresh ways of connecting with what is vital to human life. Not just physical basics, but fundamentals of civilized existence: books, music, art, science, and above all, friendship.

His Holiness The Dalai Lama speaks of three kinds of suffering: physical and mental pain, the suffering of change, and the pervasive suffering of conditioning, which happens when one is under the influence of a contaminated process of causation. Indeed, we seem to be rapidly evolving toward a global corporate oligarchy whose highest value is media-glorified consumerhood by the many in service of endless assets for the few. What will that mean for our ties with Earth and with each other? Will the ideals of creative autonomy—independence and diversity of thought, and especially tolerance and truthfulness—disappear like the dodo? Will we who take pride in supposing our lifestyle perpetuates a maximum range of choice, discover that we have fewer options than ever?

One autumn morning as I awoke, I felt something clinging to my fingers. Blinking, I focused on my hand, curled inches away on the pillow. Wisps of spider web led from three fingers to the wall above the bed. The web-spinner was nowhere in sight, but as I looked up at the oiled cedar beams, then outside at the golden light suffusing the overgrown garden, the bowed heads of the sunflowers, I had no need to ask what I was connected to.

Chapter Four

The Substance of Shadows

Sitting at Horsethief's kitchen table, my friend Mike Moore swirled the ice cubes diluting his glass of George Dickel and peered at me over his rimless spectacles. "I don't care what you say, it's a gritty thing you're doing here," he intoned. Then added, "But I think you should get rid of that revolver before something happens like the incident in Alaska." Unused to hearing such direct words from his taciturn voice, I simply nodded and went on chopping vegetables for dinner, thinking about the issues Mike and his wife Susan and I had been talking about.

Our discussion had grown out of a story Susan and Mike told about a neighbor in their Vermont village. The neighbor, who taught a firearms safety course for young people, had taken a group of friends and students on a bear-hunting trip to Alaska. Two men, later determined to be state wildlife officials, arrived by motor launch at the dock of their riverside camp. For no clear reason, the neighbor and his friends took exception to the newcomers' plan to camp there. The two men did not identify themselves, and the neighbor's party became suspicious that the men intended harm. The following morning the neighbor and his friends instigated a confrontation during which the two men were shot, one of them fatally.

Mike and Susan declared the shooting an act of murder for which the neighbor bore primary responsibility, and we talked about other means of self-defense, including negotiation or even abandoning camp themselves, that should have received priority from the neighbor's group. This led to the question of whether I had a gun at the ranch. I did, though not by preference. A visiting friend of Michael's had thought I should have some "protection," and insisted on leaving me with a loaded .45 caliber revolver, plus a box of flares, mirrors and other emergency signaling devices. I thought most of it quite silly, right out of a cult mercenary catalogue. But I'd allowed him to leave the revolver (from which I later removed the cartridges) on the sad chance I might need it to put down an injured horse.

A gun is a weapon no matter what purpose it has, however, and I had to agree with Mike and Susan that having it around for "protection" was counterproductive, if not downright stupid. Especially since I was so irked by the question that came with it, a question that, in the frequency with which it's asked, speaks all too clearly of the fear we're taught to live under.

Aren't you afraid, living out here all by yourself?

It's one of the first things visitors ask. Sooner or later even some close friends hint at it, as now. The only people who know better than to ask are other back-country folk—climbers, skiers, cowboys, river rats, field scientists, voyaging sailors—friends who by profession or inclination spend considerable time alone or at risk.

The answer, of course, is yes. And no.

Let's take "no" first. For me, living alone at Horsethief requires nothing special in the way of courage. When I think about Art and Muriel and other homesteaders who struggled with Horsethief's isolation, or about the hair-raising stories I've heard from my cowboy friend Duce, I might as well be selling insurance. A brave person is someone who faces fear, not someone who doesn't have it. Brave, to me, is facing not only your own fear, but the potentially violent irrationality of others, whether those others are individuals, groups, or institutions such as governments. Brave is dealing with rape, addiction, abuse. Brave is an inner-city teacher, a labor organizer in the Brazilian rainforest, a Tibetan nun.

I don't think I'm a particularly brave person, simply because I wasn't born with the same set of apprehensions other people live with, or saddled with the same set of circumstances other people live through. But I feel fortunate to count among my friends and family some exceptionally courageous people. To a far greater extent than I, they have met fears forced on them by a world in which physical and emotional brutality are almost as common in reality as in the media. Thus my own family's respectable, religious, rural, hardworking history includes wife-and child abuse, child-rape and sodomy, alcoholism, attempted murder and successful suicide. All within one small clan of ordinary, middle-class citizens, living what we once called sheltered lives, free of the violence suffered by citizens of other classes and other countries.

Meanwhile, our public reasons for fear loom daily more impersonal and all-encompassing. One day on my way to town I picked up a teenager hitchiking from Seattle to Miami. I asked him what he and his friends were thinking about. "Hey, we're pissed," he said. "There's nothing left. Even if nobody drops a bomb, everything is spoiled. You know, like, there's no place to go, nothing you can do about it." He turned away to stare out the window.

Aren't you afraid...?

During my first year at Horsethief, my response was to look around, shrug, and reply that I couldn't imagine a safer place on earth. But after being asked so often, I started to think about it. I knew what was implied—or did I? Now when someone asks, I offer the question back. What is there to be afraid of, I ask? What would you be afraid of, if you lived here?

One visitor, an eight-year-old girl named Maureen, answered, "Wild animals."

Wild animals. I wish. Most large mammals in this region—wolves, cougars, bears, bison, pronghorn, bighorn sheep—were eradicated to make room for humans and their livestock. Though transplanted bighorn sheep have made a comeback, predators lie low. The only carnivore that could possibly pose a threat would be one of the few remaining cougars in the area, and while these cats have occasionally attacked humans in more populated areas, it's unlikely I'd encounter one here, where space and prey abound.

Coyotes are the only other sizable predator, and while I might go out of my way to see them, the inclination is hardly mutual. Unless rabid, coyotes are far too smart to bother Koa or me. Or maybe they have too keen a sense of humor. On a recent trash patrol along the Horsethief Trail, I found a bullet-riddled beer can on which had been deposited a neat turd-pile. The size, shape and bits of bone and fur in the pile made it obvious who'd made the deposit.

Wild animals. If there were any around, they might be a problem, since I wouldn't try to avoid them. Growing up, I was one of those insufferable kids who tried to pet the bears in Yellowstone, and who once caused a zoo bison to smash its fence out of sheer disdain for my attempt to feed it a few blades of grass. I also admire wolves. I wouldn't mind hearing some of those splendidly complex canines around the ranch, though I know this isn't a realistic notion.

One autumn afternoon, two Moab townsmen stopped by while they were out hunting. Since both were kin of former owners, I invited them in. Talk got around to unusual animals, and one of them recalled seeing what must have been one of Utah's last wolves. "It was back in '64, I reckon. I was drivin' truck for one them mining outfits down by Monticello, and it was winter, snow on the ground. I come round a bend through the trees and there it was, just a-standin' in the road. Big 'un. Didn't run, didn't even move. Just stared. There I was, a-settin' in the cab, heater blasting away and him just lookin' at me. Yeller eyes. Sure was glad to have that cab around me and the door closed. Didn't have no gun or nothin'..."

The man's response was interesting. Beyond the given that if he'd had a gun, he'd have shot the animal—would have felt duty-bound by heritage to shoot it—was the admission that he'd been afraid of it. I don't think I would have felt that way. No doubt my heart rate and nape-hair would have perked up, especially if I'd been afoot. But hair-raising excitement at the presence of a wild animal is not the same as hair-raising fear that it will harm you. Which makes me wonder how many wild creatures are killed because what we fear is our attraction to them.

Maureen accepted my reassurance that no wild animals would harm her at the ranch, but then her curiosity reasserted itself. "Well, what about snakes?" she persisted, top-knotted ponytail bobbing above her head like a question mark. "Deserts have rattlesnakes."

Yes, there are snakes, I said. But the rattlesnakes here are very small. There are also bullsnakes, which are bigger but not poisonous. Besides, bullsnakes eat rattlesnakes, and do a lot of good by gobbling up mice. And there are patchnose snakes, with pinkish stripes like a pretty ribbon, and an extra scale on their nose like a bandage. Maybe that's why they're so shy.

"But what about the rattlesnakes?" Maureen ignored my ploy. Nobody wants to hear about good snakes.

No rattlesnakes had been sighted in the area for a decade, until my first spring at the ranch. My friend Bruce Berger and I were hiking out on the mesa in shorts and sandals. We walked around a clump of blackbrush and abruptly parted company as a shrill hissing rattle emanated from the shrub at our feet. Bug-eyed, we stared from our suddenly respective distances as the feisty little creature seethed and vibrated. Then, despite its posturing, we cautiously stepped closer, and I recognized it as a midget faded rattler, an adult, though scarcely two feet long. Big enough to poke two holes in a bare leg. But the bite of a rattler is seldom fatal to a healthy adult. Even if I'd been alone and been bitten, I'd have been able to walk or drive for help. At worst, I'd have been sick for a few days.

During that and subsequent summers, I encountered midget faded rattlers—the only endemic species—fairly often. My biggest fear was for Koa, who had no fear, and for the horses, who could be struck on the nose as they grazed and die from asphixiation. While most horses are savvy enough to avoid snakes, Aquila tends to treat them like wind-up toys, shying at first, then following them, nose down, as they sidle away. So far she's been lucky. During one July, we came upon rattlesnakes on five consecutive evenings while out riding. Wherever I stopped the mare, a disturbed snake gave warning. The closest call was while riding home along the driveway at night, an unmistakable whirr from right under Aquila's legs. Vaulting off, I shoved her away, grabbed the biggest rock I could find in the dark, and lobbed it at the noise. From the way the tone and tempo of the rattling got bent out of shape, I must have hit the snake, but when I raced back minutes later with flashlight and machete, it was gone.

When no snakes have been reported in an area for years and then become quite common, it's natural to wonder why. One reason that comes to mind is that two years before Bruce and I sighted the rattler, a federally-employed trapper illegally took forty-seven coyotes, plus numerous bobcats, ringtails and kit foxes, from Horsethief's mesa. It's known that coyotes eat snakes, including rattlesnakes. For nearly two years, the wild dogs who had serenaded the ranch since I'd come here were not heard. But we began seeing more snakes.

Maureen still thought rattlesnakes were scary and coyotes weren't much better. We agreed that if we found a rattlesnake near the house, we'd kill it. But if we found one out on the range we'd let it alone, since it has as much right to a peaceful home as we do. Harmless snakes we would also leave alone. (I didn't tell Maureen that I catch bullsnakes sunning on the road, and release them in the garden.) We looked at field-guide pictures of rattlesnakes, and I showed her the snakebite kit—which so far remains handy but unused.

Then we talked about scorpions and black widow spiders. Since both have been found in and around the house, I wanted my young friend to know about them. Black widows have spun their taut, amorphous webs above and below the kitchen table, over beds, next to front and back doors, behind the toilet, under the outhouse seats and beneath the dashboard of the jeep. As Maureen and I looked at field-guide photos of this elegant, ebony spider with a red hour-glass on its abdomen, I explained that black widows hide from daylight and don't like rain. They do like dry, shadowy places, and come out at night to sit in their webs. They won't attack you, but if you touch one you may get bitten. And yes, it would hurt: the poison affects the nerves, causing acute pain, muscle cramps, vomiting and fever.

"But wouldn't you be afraid, if it would hurt?" Maureen needed to know.

If I got bitten, sure I would be afraid to hurt. I don't like spiders crawling over me, either, but I can't say I'm afraid of them. I don't kill every spider I see. I do kill black widows where they're a threat. After that, being bitten becomes just another risk—in the same category with rusty nails, appendicitis, or being hit by a semi in town.

Scorpions are another hazard, though the sting of the local variety is said to be only slightly worse than that of a wasp. (This is not true for the sting of all scorpions, some of which can be fatal.) One day while working in the garden, I reached for the trowel and nearly grabbed a poised stinger curved over a segmented, wax-yellow body. I and the three-inch scorpion eyed each other warily for a few moments. Then I got a jar, punched nail-holes in its cap, and scooted the bristling creature into it with the trowel. I kept it as a display for a family due to visit the next day—a family that included freckle-faced Maureen. Initially repulsed by the scorpion—"Oh, yuck!"—by the end of the day she was fascinated. We took the creature for a walk (in its jar), and she watched wide-eyed as we let it go and it sidled away. Walking back, we looked around the spring for milder-mannered creatures to put in the jar, like butterflies or tadpoles.

During her visit, Maureen's natural curiosity and playfulness overcame her apprehension, and we didn't need to talk any more about being afraid. But there was one animal we didn't mention. That one, I believe, is what most people mean when they ask their question. The twenty-first century has dawned even less civilized than the Dark Ages, when travelers could expect to be beset by thieves and beasts, and city dwellers who could afford them lived behind locked doors. We've eliminated most of the beasts, but otherwise the situation seems appallingly like that of a thousand years ago.

Where I grew up in rural Connecticut, the doors of our house were locked only while we were away on vacation, when the key was left under the mat. Even in Aspen, that potential mecca for thieves, I locked the door of my condo only when I would be gone overnight. At Horsethief, a lock on the door would be ludicrous—not only because it would be so easy to circumvent, but because it goes against the neighborhood rules, the tradition of hospitality in remote places.

Part of that tradition is based on strong respect for private property. Stepping onto someone else's land without invitation or permission is considered trespass, whether or not signs are posted. One summer evening, a pick-up loaded with kayaks and, by inference, kayakers, jounced in the driveway. The gate was open, so they drove in and asked for Chad, the former caretaker. Upon learning he no longer lived here, they apologized profusely for "trespassing." Despite my invitation to have a glass of water while I wrote down Chad's forwarding address, they roared out the driveway as if I had threatened to call the sheriff.

The other part of the tradition is that if someone really needs something, it's there to be used. A rancher's line camp was often unlocked and stocked with food; a cowboy or traveler whose day had gone off course could help himself, replacing the items later if possible. Even today, in many places it's understood that a cabin or corral, whether on public or private land, may be used by whoever needs it. I learned this one day when Duce apppeared at the gate on his rangy roan, herding two stray cows. "Okay if I throw these critters in your corral while I go get the trailer?" he yelled. As I helped corral the cows, he explained that to have refused would be a breach of manners. I told him that sounded right by my upbringing, and reminded him of the keys left under the seat of each ranch vehicle. "If I come home and the truck's gone, I'll just figure you misplaced your gas money," I teased.

If risk is implicit in the back-country, so are these traditions. Horsethief in its rough history has seen its share of roost-robbers, but since I've lived here, only one person has driven through the front gate without an invitation or connection to the ranch. Even that person was one of the stockmen whose cows Duce managed, a hard-bitten, arrogant old geezer with a reputation for being "nosy," as Duce put it.

That day the front gate happened to be open in anticipation of a guest's arrival. Mr. Geezer drove right in, something not even Duce would do. When I came out to see whose fancy pickup had driven up to the front yard, the man leaned out his window with a leer and asked if I'd seen any cows around. Since it was summer, Duce's cows hadn't been 'around' for months, and Geezer knew it. His attitude was rude at best. The two Latino cowboys with him in the cab averted their heads in embarrassment, especially when the man said pointedly, "Don't guess you ever get lonesome out here." I turned for the house with Koa at my heel, replying with disdain, "Sure don't. Not for the likes of you."

Angry about what felt like rudeness to the point of trespass, I mentioned the incident to Duce. A few weeks later he reported back. "Y'know, I told Gerald, my boss, about his partner Ray drivin' in on you like that. So Gerald calls up Ray when he knows Ray ain't home, and he leaves a message on his machine. 'Ray, this is Gerald. I got a phone message here, some lawyer feller down in Moab tryin' to get ahold of you. Wants to talk to you something about sexual harrassing. Now what in hell's that all about?'"

Duce and I laughed, and I felt better for knowing his outfit patrolled their own. But it brought all those questions home.

Aren't you afraid?
What if somebody came with a gun and was going to rape you?
What would you do?

Okay, let's get down to it. First of all I'd try not to be here. That may sound odd, but it's a good start. When you're used to all the sounds that whisper from the walls of the canyon, you can tell when a vehicle is coming in the driveway. Sometimes Koa hears it first and woofs, sometimes I warn him. If I'm not expecting anyone, I go outside (if I'm not there already) to see who's coming. If it's dark, I take a flashlight but don't turn it on. That way my night vision is clear, while whoever is driving in is still seeing by headlights and dashlights.

Any advantage I might have when a car arrives is short-lived, however. Even if a stranger or strangers showed up, I would meet them outside and ask their business, as I did with old Ray. If they seemed threatening, I'd tell them to leave unless they wanted to talk to my husband. If they didn't leave, I would go into the house, ostensibly to send out my husband. Inside, I'd watch and wait, or ease out the back door to jot down a license number. If they entered the house or attempted to find me, I might, as circumstance allowed, walk, ride, or steal their car and drive to the nearest phone. That is, if it wasn't winter, when death by exposure might be a more certain fate than anything that might happen at the hands of strangers.

Now look at all those ifs and mights. That's vulnerability, which means fear is probably close behind. In any event, I'd have to respond as best I could to whatever a situation demanded. I'm as susceptible to harm as any urbanite—but no more so. I can't phone for help, but most people who are attacked don't get a chance to do that anyway. I can run, I can ride, I can reason, I can shoot, but that's all horseapples. You can't know what you'll do until something happens.

But what if you couldn't get away...?

It could happen that way. It could happen that, remote as it is, somebody with ill intent does find this place. Let's even pretend there are two of them. I'm working in the garden, naked. Koa and I hear a car coming in the driveway. Koa barks, I quit hoeing, pull on tank-top and shorts and meet them at the gate, carrying the hoe. They're driving a low-slung, late model sedan, a sleek road car that looks all the more out of place for its veneer of red dust. They get out, one of them takes off his sunglasses, blinking in the blaring summer light. Las Vegas types, the smaller one all polyester and brush-cut hair, the bigger one in a lime-and-pink Hawaiian shirt, dark pants, greased ducktail. Ordinary as salesmen, road-sticky, game-wise, comfortable with cruelty.

Something I can do to help you folks?

They say their first names, Al, Ed, then mention something about being friends of a friend of Michael's brother, who lives in Vegas. Okay if they take a look at the place?

I nod and start to show them around, hoe in hand, Koa following. Bunkhouse, garden, hot tub, Aquila in the corrals. All the time aware they're looking at me instead of at what I'm showing them. They ask none of the usual questions. They glance at each other every so often as if they know something I don't. I feel a twinge of apprehension. I suddenly think I want to show them as little as possible. Especially the house.

I guide the tour to the front yard, where I invite them to sit in the shade of the apricot and have a glass of spring water. Sure, they say, why not? I lean the hoe against a post and go inside. I think about going straight through the house and out the back door, then decide against it. After all, nothing is implausible. Nothing except the tightness in my face, the cold creep at my nape. I am gathering up the glasses of ice-water when I see the men at the kitchen door, about to enter.

Balancing the bunched glasses in my hands, I shoulder the screen door out toward them. Polyester holds it open for me, but Hawaii blocks my way. Okay if we see inside?

It's kind of a mess, I say. And my friend is taking a nap...

Aw, come on, ain't nobody else here, Hawaii grins. What're you holding back? Polyester reaches out and touches my hair. Terror crawls up me. Unable to think or speak, I push forward, clutching icy glasses of water. Polyester lets the door slam and catches me around the waist. Let go, I yell, twisting aside. Wet glasses slip from my hands, smash-splatter on the stone patio. Hoe falls, clanging. Koa barks, then growls low. Hawaii reaches under his shirt, draws a pistol from a shoulder holster. I scream as he blasts at Koa, who yelps pitifully, then lies twitching. I am howling No, No, trying to reach my dog, sweaty arms dragging me back. Through stark horror, I hear Polyester say something about having a little fun in the house. Then I hear clearly: Come on, lady. You don't want the same thing to happen to your horse. I kick, writhe, bite the hairy arm locked around my neck. Then a bone-jarring crack on my head as I am dragged inside.

A case of too little fear too late, you might say. But I do think about these things every time I hear about another grim rape, another gruesome murder. There-but-for-the-grace only counts until it happens to you. Someone could come to Horsethief to do wrong. The odds are small, but the bell curve is wide. It only takes once. So there is no smugness in saying that something long ago must have chosen for me not to live in fear. And I am grateful that nothing so dire has happened to me that I must live otherwise. Which is good, since fear creates its own climate of danger. By drawing awareness away from the present, where it may be needed, into a vaguely threatening future, where it may not, it saps attention and promotes over-reaction. At the ranch, dwelling on what-ifs is a waste of healthy paranoia. Living apprehensively interferes with living carefully, with paying attention to real dangers.

Such as?

Such as Aquila falling while we're out for a run, me breaking a hip or dislocating a shoulder. Such as hoisting a hay bale wrong and slipping a disc. An axe in my foot, like Chad did once. The list is as long as the day's chores. The real danger in living here is circumstance: the little treacheries of timing, tools, one's own body. Accident or illness can happen anywhere. Here the danger is compounded by isolation and distance.

The phrase 'healthy paranoia' wasn't meant facetiously. On the contrary, it's the flip side of the rule of threes: being attentive, prepared, careful. You take three steps backward before you start, you look ahead to see what might go wrong, and you do what's necessary to prevent accident or minimize consequence. Silver spoons aside, no one is born with an insurance policy in his teeth; precaution can't prevent mishap. But keeping one's thumb out of a halter buckle while haltering a horse, say, not only lessens the chance of losing that thumb if the horse acts up. It also reduces the chance the horse will misbehave, since a trained horse knows how a halter should be put on and is likely to respect a person who does it properly.

On that subject, it might be noted that of all the hazards of ranch life, horses are among the worst. My horseman friend Jack Snobble says "they can find more ways to hurt themselves, or you, than any other animal." Even well-mannered horses react violently to fright, are prone to accident, and are subject to herd hierarchy, which may mean sudden biting or kicking. In the corrals or in the saddle, the more horses around, the closer attention one pays.

One Easter Sunday afternoon after guests had driven away, I decided to de-worm the three horses we had been riding. I tied them to stout posts in separate areas of the corral so they wouldn't hurt each other if any of them struggled. I chose the first mare, Shasta, because she knew the routine and was calm. Sure enough, she tongued down the syringe of worming paste I pressed into her mouth. The second horse, tall red Moriah, had been at the ranch for only a few months. I had never wormed him, so didn't know what to expect. He jerked his head up as I pressed the syringe into his mouth, but made no further fuss.

Then I took a deep breath. Aquila. The sweetest-tempered mare in the world. Except she hated to have things stuck in her mouth. I knew it would be a fight, even as I spoke to her gently, snubbed her lead rope tightly to the post, then tried to insert the syringe. Next thing I knew, something whacked my forehead and Aquila was above me rearing and yanking at her halter. As she came down I jammed the syringe into her mouth and squeezed the plunger. Only then did I realize I couldn't see for the blood running down my face.

My hand came away red from my forehead. Stunned, not knowing how badly I was hurt, I turned each horse loose. No reason they should suffer if I passed out. An hour of ice packs and cold towels later, I peered in a mirror and figured the wide gash bisecting my forehead must have been made by the clip of the lead rope as Aquila reared up. I considered driving to town for stitches, but by the time the bleeding stopped, I decided it would heal on its own. With daily salve massages, it did. But until she grew calmer with age and experience, subsequent de-worming or doctoring sessions with Aquila took place while other people were around.

Author Barry Lopez speaks of paying attention as "the basic law about everything." And so it is here especially, where the word "paying" implies a sort of dues, an awareness tuned to possibility, a severe respecting of con sequence, of the relentless, sometimes helplessly swift ordering of things. It has to do with fear only in an ancient, tribal/biblical context: thou shalt fear the gods. Thou shalt revere, thou shalt stand in awe and readiness.

Paying attention also implies a transaction, a potential return on one's investment. There is no guarantee of this. Caveat emptor.

One warm, wet January, the desert thawed a month early, and rain on top of melting snow turned the Horsethief Trail into an impassable quagmire. Coincidentally, a feeling of pain and tightness in my chest that had bothered me occasionally for a few months suddenly became acute, until I feared heart attack, a leaking aneurism, some life-threatening crisis. My heart pounded sorely in my chest, blood thudded through valve and ventricle, every irregular beat magnified by an ache that subsided only with rest. Whatever was wrong, it felt serious.

Meanwhile, rain continued to fall, snow continued to melt. No one could get to the ranch, nor could I leave. And of course by choice I had no phone. Even if the road was marginally passable, I feared the effort of wrenching the jeep through ten miles of mud would bring on whatever crisis was impending. The first day I tried to side-step the threat and live normally. By the evening of the second day it could no longer be ignored. I went to bed and stayed there, for the first time in my life mortally afraid.

Though lying down helped ease the pain, inactivity fed my fear. I needed help. There was no way for help to come. No miracle was possible, and for those hours I breathed with more fright than I had ever felt. With the horses turned loose on the range, I set out extra food and water for Koa, who showed his concern by staying close beside the bed, where I imagined friends finding my body come spring.

Around midnight I slept for an hour or so, then was awakened by more rain. At three a.m., the rain turned to snow, and despair gave way to dim hope. Praying the snow would continue, I dozed until dawn. Snow was falling heavily through the gray light, with three inches on the ground. The chest pain had subsided a bit with rest. Veering between relief at the possibility of escape and panic at the prospect of driving out, I packed what Koa and I would need. The day could only get warmer. We had to leave now.

Stiffened by slushy snow, the mud was chilled just enough to provide some traction. With the jeep in low range, we managed the long slither, mostly half sideways, to the paved road. In town, I contacted a doctor in Grand Junction and drove there for an immediate appointment. To my great relief, my heart checked out fine, and a second doctor diagnosed the condition as costochondritis, an inflammation of the cartilage between ribs and sternum. "Not life-threatening," she declared, "merely a medical annoyance." I resented the phrase, but was mightily grateful for what it covered.

I have a longtime dear desert rat friend, Jim Fulton, who lives under similar circumstances two hundred miles south. No phone, ten miles to the nearest neighbor via a dirt road that makes the Horsethief Trail look paved. One winter morning, Jim was in a hurry to get to town, ran upstairs to grab some papers, missed the top step on his way down, and plunged head first to the bottom. He knew when he got up that he wasn't going to make it to town that day, and that if he didn't quickly re-locate his shoulder, he might not make it at all. With his good arm he spread his sleeping bag on the couch in the main room next to the propane heater. He next went to the outhouse and emptied his bowels. Then, built like a barrel of nails and twice as tough, he braced the dangling arm with the one that still worked, and shoulder first, took a flying run at a sturdy door-jamb. It took three tries, but he managed to pop the head of the humerus back into its scapular socket before losing consciousness. Hours later, he woke, took a handful of aspirin to get him through the night, and next morning wrestled his stick-shift pickup to the doctor's office to have the gash in his head sewn up.

There are other ways, such as a rope around the wrist and steady traction, to re-locate a shoulder, but the point is, had Jim been unable to reverse the dislocation before the surrounding tissue swelled up, things would not have boded well. The pain of a dislocation is such that it would have been nearly impossible to drive one-handed for help without lapsing into shock and passing out at the wheel. His neighbor might have driven in to check on him after a week or so, but by then it would likely have been too late.

I think about Jim and shake my head, knowing I haven't his courage, much less his strength.

Aren't you afraid...?

Why do we do these things? Why would any sane person put him or herself at such risk? I think the answer has to do with freedom to explore ourselves in the world, to expand beyond the givens, to become one with something larger than ourselves. No one would choose to live in a state of fear. But many people, from rock climbers to stock brokers, choose to live at risk. We opt for jeopardy—physical, intellectual, aesthetic—out of willingness to commit ourselves to what we think we can match, what might draw the best from us, what we are willing to forfeit in return. Always it is a gamble, always it is the loving of the game: the beauty of the substrate, the terrain, be it vertical rock, high altitude paragliding, or wide open sea.

To the extent that risk invokes fear, it can be a means of facing and perhaps overcoming one of the fears natural to human beings. Some ranch visitors, for example, fear getting lost. In many areas, losing one's way is more inconvenient than life-threatening. You will always come to a paved road. But here most roads are seldom-traveled dirt trails, offering few clues which way or how far it might be to a house or town. One might wander through a maze of gullies and canyons until thirst, heat or cold took its toll. Walk a hundred yards from the rim of Horsethief's canyon, turn around, and the canyon has disappeared—you cannot tell it is there. The terrain mocks you with intimacy, appearing endlessly familiar in all directions, yet endlessly strange. Which way is home? Did it ever exist?

I was blessed with a fairly dependable sense of direction; being lost is not for me a fear. Nevertheless, I've occasionally come up out of a gully with my orientation at least ninety degrees askew, baffled that mountains that should be straight ahead are behind my shoulder. And it did happen, one overcast autumn evening, that I got lost. Koa, Aquila and I were out under thick, low-hanging cumulus, watching the last light fade. On the way back. I stopped to let the mare graze while I reclined on her bare back, resting my eyes in cloud-softened darkness. Now a horse while grazing turns every which way, reaching for bites of grass, and after some while I realized I had no idea which way we were facing. It was completely dark—no more afterglow, no moon or stars, no breeze, just a low ceiling of cloud. Neither Koa nor Aquila were any help. To my plea of "Let's go get some supper," Koa fetched a stick, ready as always to play. And Aquila, with no horses in the corrals to draw her home, was content to go on grazing. Dark shapes of junipers loomed everywhere alike, and above I felt the mute, mapless clouds. Feeling apprehension rise, I took a deep breath and urged Aquila somewhere, anywhere. Her horse sense soon brought us to the driveway a few hundred yards away.

Darkness itself can be scary, especially in a strange place and especially when one is alone. For ages it has harbored very real terrors, and still does. For many people it is the most frightening thing of all. Night was a spooky time for me when I first came to the ranch, and occasionally I still find myself uneasy for vague but perhaps ancient reasons: I don't know what's out there, and have only this thin skin for protection. But having reaccustomed myself to it, night has become comfortable, even comforting, as it was when I was a child and snuck out of my bedroom on warm nights, leaving my pillow propped under the covers. Sometimes I would stay away until dawn, camped out in my lean-to. And sometimes, for the sheer joy of it, I would run and run for hours along the rural roads and bordering fields.

It was during one such run that I met every child's nightmare. In the neighborhood lived a tall, gangly handyman named Red, who earned his way doing chores for the wealthy folk who lived on the hill. Red, too, enjoyed taking the night air—maybe because it was the only time he didn't feel self-conscious about being seen. Afflicted with St. Vitus's Dance, he didn't so much walk as quake and vibrate. He also stuttered badly, though he managed to perform his tasks to the satisfaction of his employers.

But Red coming down the road with the moon behind him was something else. His violent tremulations seemed aggravated by a footloose pleasure in walking free. Or maybe he felt no need at night to keep them under control—if indeed he could. But the first time he came toward me out of darkness, I darted into a field and headed straight cross-country for home. Not that Red meant the slightest harm, poor man, or even jolted a step in my direction. On the contrary, I recall him turning as I swerved past—possibly I startled him, also?—and in a gargle that contorted his rough-whiskered face, uttering something that sounded like Huh huh huhllo.

Several times after that while night-running, I encountered Red and came to recognize his quavering shape with equanimity. I'd slow down and say hello, and he'd say it, too. Once he even got out a whole sentence that sounded like Huh huh hope I d-d-don't s-s- scccare you. I hope I told him he didn't, and wish I could tell him now I'm grateful to him for showing me that many monsters exist only in our own minds.

The desert darkness is especially comforting when I visit the corrals around midnight to check the horses. Feeding them a quartered apple, I savor their dark silhouettes against the stars, their bony faces etched by a moon-white sky. Often I find them staring intently into the west canyon beyond the corrals, and I wonder what they sense is there. The cat? An owl? A coyote? Or perhaps a presence only horses can know. Could it be one of the reasons we fear darkness is because deep down we still believe in ghosts? Walking outside at night, I think about the native people who once camped and hunted here, and wonder in what sense they might still inhabit this place. I believe in spirit they do, and that if they could see what I and my kind have done to their homeland, they would be bewildered or angry. But rather than fear they might mean harm, I envision them by the glow of a stone-pit fire, surrounded by the same night that surrounds me, eating, talking or peacefully asleep. I cannot help but include them in what by the nature of time is already theirs, can only hope my thoughts might bring ease, to them and me.

What is there, then, to be afraid of?

Nothing I'm likely to encounter at Horsethief—which should end this chapter. But just as I've turned the question around and asked it of others, so I must ask it of myself. If I lack the capacity for certain fears which trouble other people, I must admit many things I'm afraid of don't seem to bother whole segments of the population. Millions of people, for instance, can watch a horror movie and laugh all the way to the credits, whereas I clamp my hands over my eyes if the music even hints that the headless body or the bodiless head is about to appear.

But there are other fears, the little and large despondencies that gnaw us awake at four in the morning, the raw material of personal nightmare. Let's imagine, as it is easy to do at Horsethief, a world from which institutional and even personal violence has been removed. No war, no murder, no coercion. What would be left to fear? Would our lives become slack, devoid of drama and tension? Would our adrenal glands become as useless as our appendices? I think not. The capacity for fear runs as deep as human nature, and mortality would still be a given. We would watch loved ones die, we would face death ourselves. Wouldn't that be enough?

But even the fear of death is not the final fear. There are also questions of right living, and the fears that arise when I become mindful about this. Let's call these civilized fears, as opposed to the barbaric ones of the violent world we just imagined null. But by civilized I don't mean numbing or vague. Some of these tame fears, while not immediately life-threatening, can be as heart-stopping, blood-pounding adrenalizing as encountering the Monticello wolf was for that ore-truck driver, or as coming face-to-fang with a rattler might be for young Maureen.

For instance, I'm often stricken with acute shyness, and 'stage fright' is a euphemism for the sheer green terror that can grip me in public speaking situations. Obviously there is no fear of being hurt. Rather, there is the wholehearted desire that my words will honor my audience, will honor language itself, will be worth the silence they negate. Wherever there is whole-hearted desire, fear is the shadow.

What frightens you most, then?

Living in this remote, peaceable place allows me to fear above all the gun-happy mentality of that vacationing bear hunter in Alaska, which, carried by political extension to its current extreme, is the same mentality that can speak with a straight face and a self-righteous heart about nuclear 'victory' or 'life-saving' bombs; pander to the strangulating, inhumane network of global capitalism and the 'rights' of free-trade organizations; and dismiss outright the facts and relevance of environmental destruction and global warming. I fear what that kind of thinking has already done to my planet, and what it will do to the world my friend Maureen must inherit. I dread and loathe such distortions of mind and language, and I am frightened and angered by the concommitant homogenization of human cultures that makes my life here so peculiarly rare.

When I first moved to the desert, darkness was how I grew into it. To walk out at night was to become intensely aware of its mystery and beauty, its invitation, its breath on my skin. The shadows were stern and deep. I felt I could enter their darkness as one would a door into the unknown. And since childhood I've thought of the unknown as a gift, a womb of rebirth that we enter not to be held, but to be set free.

But freedom itself is risky business. Like the dry desert air, it contains little—no flags, no givens, no laws on the books. It demands we create ourselves from it, often a fearful prospect. Yet fear can be a compelling ally, can help us inform passion with caution, action with attention, courage with compassion. The shadows are not empty, they do have substance; all around us are frightfully real things. To live only in the light is to be blinded, to bask in ignorance is to dwell asleep. I think the shadows must be entered: their substance is the ground we stand on.

Chapter Five

Solitude and Vertigo

Over the mantel of the stone fireplace in the living room hangs a pastel drawing, a large abstraction whose bold lines, sensuous shapes and earthy colors speak to me of a woman looking out through the cave of her own body at a landscape of green and golden light. Blocks of magenta, blue and ochre compose her stillness as she contemplates the arc of her body as the architecture of the land, the space around her as the space within her.

I'm astonished at how many people tell me that of the things they would encounter at Horsethief, solitude would be the hardest. During my second year at the ranch, I visited my mother in New Jersey and attended a luncheon given by one of her friends. As we sat around the table, the questions that fluttered over the teacups and custard pie made me feel I'd come from another planet. "You live there *alone*?" one lady intoned, eyebrows raised as if to suggest I was living in sin. "Land sakes," exclaimed another spirited woman, blue-gray coif unruffled by her mannered vehemence, "I can't even stay off the phone for a day, much less go for a week without seeing anybody." "You can't even stay off the phone for an hour, Mabel," taunted one of her friends, and laughter went round the table as the ladies turned to each other talking of sons and daughters, neighbors and friends upon whose company they depended. "Since my Charlie's retired, you know, he drives me crazy," confided the candid matron on my right. "But I'd be crazier if I didn't have him around."

Another woman I know, a sophisticated New Yorker and intrepid traveler, put it this way. "I don't like being by myself. When you're alone, you *disappear*."

In a way, I understood what she meant. Before moving to Horsethief, my days and often my nights were filled with phone calls, meetings, consultations with co-workers, a constant stream of voices. Even when I wrote, composing filmscripts, promotional copy, grant proposals, it was usually with other people around. And when the day was over, my head was still busy with people, evaluating, preparing for tomorrow. When, infrequently, I took a break—went for a hike, sat on a rock—I didn't know what to do with myself. With my busyness peeled away, I didn't quite know who I was.

But solitude had been a great part of my childhood—one of the best parts. And I had known it during other times of my life, always with a sense of reclamation and relief. It was one reason I began visiting the ranch, and a primary reason for moving there. Who was behind that mask of busyness? What would happen if she just *stopped*? I found an answer of sorts one evening during an early visit to the ranch. Sitting on a ledge at sunset, I found myself holding hands with the bare branch of a juniper. Time disappeared, as did whoever it was who had been so busy. When I let go the branch and stood up from that rock, I knew I did not stop at my fingertips.

Aren't you afraid of being here...*all by yourself?* I had spent enough time alone to know what solitude is not. It is certainly not alienation, nor even simple isolation. It is not loneliness, nor the anxiety I felt when I first moved to Horsethief and confused my identity with the things I had given up or left behind. It is not resentment of the time I spent being so infernally busy, for I was myself then too. No rancor or umbrage drove me here, but rather an odd contract between exhaustion and eagerness. There was no desire to be separate or isolated, only to inhabit a quieter self whose periphery I knew well, but whose core was a mystery.

Perhaps that is why I took to the night. In the same way I'd been at home in the dark as a child, I gravitated into desert darkness. If I could again be comfortable in its fathomless presence, perhaps I would find in it a deeper, more centered self. What I found, of course, is that darkness is not always fathomless. It is full of things you stumble into or trip over. At first I carried a flashlight, but unless I was using it to spotlight something I was doing close at hand, it made me nervous to have my vision limited to a single cone of light. So I did without, using starlight and moonlight and the sixth sense of proprioception.

And gradually, I learned to see: the shadowy shape of a horse coming toward me, darkness forming out of darkness, taking on depth and night-color until it became a solid horse standing in front of me, extending its head, its muzzle, its breath, and I could reach out and stroke sparks from the silk of its coat. To be able to write, finally:

Darkest of dark nights, cloud cover and no moon, and yet it is possible to distinuish gray cat from gray-black night, to watch Mouse as he prowls along the corral posts or weaves, tail twitching with pleasure, among Koa's legs—shadow without a source.

Since desert sky is seldom covered with cloud, its darkness is anything but total. Starlight alone is bright enough to outline horizons and silhouettes and give them some detail. A slice of quarter moon not only throws distinct shadows, but provides enough light to see my way around with confidence. And the full moon, reflected from colored sand, or especially from snow, creates a landscape so brilliant as to be surreal, like day-for-night in film, except one sees it in its spectrum of dusky colors, and its shadows have more contrast.

As a child I was fortunate in having an Uncle Louie, a gentle, learned man whose passions were stars and birds and the telescopes he made to view them with. I recall the highbush blueberry days of summer, my uncle walking along sunlit paths in the piney forest, whistling the call of a wood thrush while yellow butterflies bobbed around his straw hat. And I remember the firefly evenings that followed, squinting through the telescope at a nondescript star that had suddenly resolved itself into distinct red and blue twins, while my uncle stood by in the dark, contentment in the puff of his pipesmoke.

Thanks to my former husband, Rob, a deepwater sailor and amateur astronomer, I still knew some of the stars and constellations, and loved their litany of ancient names. But many of them had slipped away along with my keenness of vision. During my second spring at the ranch, I decided to relearn what I had forgotten. Over the months, studying the charts by flashlight and the sky with my distance glasses on, I became familiar with the zodiacal constellations parading along the southern and western horizons on their way to intersect the sun's path, and began to connect the bright dots filling in the rest of the sky. Draco. Hercules. Pegasus.

One September midnight, while scanning the great bowl above me and naming constellations as I walked back from the corrals, I suddenly felt quite unmystically at home. Not just down here in the dark, but up there in the sky. *Presto!* I wrote:

Now I put on my glasses and those floppy white roses up there shrink to clear and burning pinpoints of light. I can't name many individual stars yet, but the Perseid meteor shower the last few nights has been a real show—by Horsethief standards—starballs whizzing and blazing

in every direction, while the Milky Way ever so slowly pivots and
wheels our galaxy edgewise into the void.

Aldebaran. Lyra. Regulus. As the nights became filled with benevolent particulars, so did the daytime hours. Above all, there was the work of the ranch to attend to, so I was eased into solitude by my habit of busyness. During adolescence and early teens, my closest companions had been a horse and a dog. In re-entering that pattern, I found the decades had allowed a bit of humor to replace the innocently shared solitude of childhood. "Whadaya think, guys?" I might say while haying the horses. "How 'bout we go over to the mall and see what's happening?" I wroaked to the ravens, who often answered, then answered again, building an absurd dialogue in which at least one of us didn't know what the other two were saying. Though the ravens were the only creatures who responded aloud, I sensed that other creatures listened.

I also polished the art of talking to myself, rehearsing internal speeches or writing letters in my mind, listening to myself with the ears of the recipient of my concern, frustration, or anger. Desert space makes a fine sounding board: talking aloud helped me discover the motives, preoccupations and conditions faced by the person to whom I was speaking—who was often, indeed, myself. Sometimes the process was fierce, but the result was a detached empathy, relieved of tension. When I met the maker of my mood, I was prepared rather than pent-up. I could give room to another point of view. Or I could more coherently present the case I'd been rehearsing. Or, stress having been released aloud, I could say nothing and let things be.

During my first year at the ranch, I usually enjoyed the surprise of unexpected guests showing up. But as their numbers increased during the following year, I became less sanguine. One blustery evening in early spring, I was sitting on a belltower-shaped rock from which I could see the Horsethief Trail. While Koa hunted rabbits, I stared with negative anticipation at a cloud of dust rolling down the dirt road toward the ranch. Uh oh. So much for peace and quiet. Wonder who's coming now... When the dustcloud veered off the road onto the open range, I stood up and began cursing the driver for tearing up the desert with his vehicle. Then, as anger cleared my wind-whipped vision, I saw there was no driver and no vehicle, as a swirling dust-devil petered out over bare slickrock, then spun into fresh dunes and resumed its whirlwind route across the range.

Relief on two counts. But the experience revealed how much I had come to enjoy being alone. On the other hand, I enjoyed good company equally. The resistance seemed to be toward changing gears—a lack of flexibility rather than ambivalence toward either solitude or human contact. I was seldom eager to go to town, for instance, but once there, occasionally the reverse was true. Often by the time errands were done it was evening, the hour of sunset and silhouette, of gathering together for companionship as night came on. Usually I was eager to get home, but when social encounters had been insignificant or disappointing, I resisted hitting that long lonesome highway, reluctant to immerse myself in solitude again without having made contact with someone who confirmed, enlarged or pivoted my sense of perspective.

One August evening while I was trying to decide whether to spend a second year at the ranch, I was driving home at dusk after a frustrating day in town. A third flat tire on the truck, a long round of calls to message machines and unanswered phones, nothing in the mail but bills, ads, and a disturbing, taunting letter from Remo, to the effect that if I was looking for a boyfriend, he already had "other women" in Aspen. As I turned onto the highway west, I noted the line of headlights coming toward me, tourists returning from sunset-watching at Dead Horse Point or Island In The Sky. Returning to town for a pleasant dinner with friends or family, a comfortable night of motel TV and air-conditioned sleep. Returning, eventually, to the security of normal lives in normal places, refreshed by a visit to the desert and its eternal scenery. As I imagined conversations in the passing cars, I felt a perverse nostalgia for a life I'd never lived. I wanted to be going somewhere normal, too.

But as the road rose up over the mesa, my breath caught at the sight before me. Dark clouds floated like rags in a green-turquoise sky, exquisitely banded with pink and orange-gold at the horizon where the sun had set. Hovering among the clouds was the thinnest scimitar of moon, upright as a listening ear. As I stared at the limpid beauty before me, envy collapsed into confusion. I thought of the passing cars headed east for town, unable to see what I was seeing, unable ever to live where I was going, and found myself trying to sort through a complexity of emotions. By the time I turned onto the Horsethief Trail, I realized the sunset hadn't erased the day's frustrations, nor the gibe of Remo's letter. But it had popped me back into my own life, had recentered me, sad or glad for the moment, in my own fortune.

Russian writer Joseph Brodsky defines a prison as "a lack of space counterbalanced by a surplus of time." The reverse can also be true—an abundance of space rendered inaccessible by lack of time. Worse, space can become crowded with the same things that reduce one's time. For better or worse, my solitude gradually became filled with more and more guests, both mine and Michael's. For whatever reasons—because a woman's touch had made Horsethief homey, because canyon country had become trendy, because humans are ever more needful of wild retreats—people were showing up at the front gate at an increasingly startling rate.

Wonderful people, almost without exception. I was glad to see them, glad to visit, garden and ride with them, glad for their indispensable help. But after a four-month period during which I could count on one hand the days I'd had to myself, I was as drained as anyone would be from a perpetual house-party whose guest list was neither predictable nor controllable, and whose hapless hostess also functioned as maid, handyman, wrangler, guide, gardener and sometimes chef and chauffeur. Guests would disappear down the driveway waving goodbye, I would swing the front gate shut, and quietude would immediately close in. But as I gathered laundry and tidied up, I'd be bracing for the next car. I began to kill more spiders with less remorse *(bugs moths beetles ants all those hardshelled flying things there are just too many of them I'm fed up to here with too many of anything),* began to have less patience with recalcitrant horses *(Shasta refused to be led today so backed her all the way around the corral Aquila & Moriah looking on wide-eyed ears pricked in disbelief),* began to talk more to myself, less to Koa *(need time time to myself crave it like a drug a lover am going to scream if anyone comes tomorrow where is my* LIFE*).*

If there can be a light-headedness in too much solitude, for me there is an out-of-balance despondency in too much company. I lacked time or space in which to write. I lacked, indeed, any life of my own that did not center around guests and the work of the place. In May of my second spring, with Michael visiting for a month and his guests arriving in droves, I requested a two-week leave of absence. My friend Bruce Berger, off visiting Spain, had invited me to use the house he'd recently inherited in eastern Arizona. I knew only that it was located on the edge of a wooded golf course, and promised a cool, quiet and possibly productive interlude.

Loading Koa and my computer into the car, I drove south across the Navajo reservation blooming with clusters of ivory yucca and orange globemallow, silvery needle-and-thread grass rippling like hair in the wind. In east-central Arizona, approaching a range of forested peaks, I passed through the sleepy farm town of St. Johns, thinking I might very well be comfortable in this part of the country.

Imagine, then, my dismay when forty miles later I turned a corner into the bustling mini-metropolis of Show Low, malled and McDonalded and blaring with billboards, and from there trailed bumper-to-bumper traffic from stop-light to stop-light along a corridor of real estate offices and restaurants, car dealerships and shopping plazas, to the combined town of Pinetop-Lakeside. Combined because you couldn't tell where one town ended and the next began.

Culture shock. This could be Anywhere, USA. California's Camino Real, New Jersey's Route 22, some misplaced suburb of Phoenix. Koa, where are we? There must be some mistake. Ah, but maybe the house itself...

Following Bruce's directions, I drove out of town and turned onto Fairview Drive, where an enormous landscaped sign announced "Pinetop Estates." Uh-oh. Sure enough, designer blacktop curved cleverly through a plucked forest of ponderosa pines, among which were set several large resort complexes strung together by fairways lined with more or less assertive homes.

Pulling into the gravel driveway of Bruce's house, I felt a bit reassured. Through the spindly pines were a lime green fairway and more mini-mansions, but at least the house at which I'd arrived was rustic and unpretentious. Besides, I'd come to work, not gawk. I unpacked the car, explored the house, and set up shop next to Bruce's grand piano in the living room.

So far, okay. But something strange was about to happen. Much as I tried to ignore it, I felt anxious, isolated, *lonesome*. I began next morning to balance myself by writing a few letters, but going to town to mail them only intensified the sense of being out of place. Returning to the house, I arranged my notes and set to work, but found concentration difficult with the whispers of golf carts and voices going by. Nor was my estrangement dispelled when I took Koa for a walk that evening.

A maze. We were in a piney labyrinth of countrified streets and clipped fairways sedately lined with vacation estates and lots for sale. Signs along the greens prohibited dogs and non-members with annoying regularity, faux-colonnaded houses sported semicircular drives and three-car garages, yards were paved with volcanic gravel, even the pine forest was thinned. And this monotony prevailed in all directions as far as I cared to walk—usually a few miles each evening. I couldn't see the forest, or the sunset, for the roofs and trees.

Despite all the houses, there were few signs of life. Once I met an older couple strolling, once a child playing in a yard. But no one mowing a lawn, taking out trash, washing a car, and except for a few prominently displayed flags on Memorial Day, no hint of community. Yet everywhere permeating the air on those evening walks was the smell of meat being charred over an indoor gas grill. Not once did I see anyone tending an outdoor barbeque, much less tossing a softball or slam-dunking a basketball in front of one of those multi-car garages. A ghost resort.

Bruce had told me that hardly anyone lived there year round, so I guessed the resort season wasn't yet in full swing. But the peculiar sense of isolation clung. In other towns and cities, I'd loved walking the streets, absorbed by all the bustle. But this was a desert of a different color, a no-person's land where the only humans were unapproachable folk buzzing about in golf carts.

For shame, I scolded. You're in a setting that ninety-five percent of the world would consider idyllic and you can't adjust. The sky is blue, sun gleams on ponderosa needles, wind sighs through them, squirrels play, and you're edgy and homesick. Though I stuck it out for a week, I felt relaxed only when I was writing or playing with Koa. Even then there was an underache. How strange to be in an inaccessible landscape, among people with whom one has no contact.

I didn't exactly flee, but I did leave early, partly to explore some nearby catacombs of the early Mimbres people. Leaving the area by a different route, I found that if I'd driven a few miles east of the resort instead of staying within it, I'd have discovered the mountain woodlands of the White Mountain Apache and felt much more at home. As I retraced my route north, angst drained away and I felt like a fool, like someone who'd encountered a personal Bermuda triangle and let herself be swallowed whole. I'd learned a simple truth that I would relearn again under grimmer circumstances: solitude is what you have when you're alone and at peace with yourself and your surroundings. Without that peace, it quickly becomes isolation.

Home, in any case, is where you sometimes have to get away from in order to gain perspective. Instead of returning to the crowded ranch, I sought refuge with Remo, who was camped on his land in the foothills of the Abajo Mountains a hundred miles south of Horsethief. There I hoped to find a solitude that was neither absolute nor isolating, and perhaps re-balance our friendship.

If I understand Thomas Merton correctly, physical solitude is a state of being comfortably alone, and inner solitude is a state of being in harmony with oneself and one's surroundings whether or not one is physically alone. I think there is also such a thing as mutual solitude, which, like inner solitude, perhaps exists on several levels. At least so I've experienced it with three different friends who each came to the ranch several times a year, often for a week or two at a time. I always looked forward to their visits.

One of the three was Dick Dorworth, a long-time friend who spent his days rock-climbing and his evenings writing. In between, we hiked and enjoyed good talks over supper. Another was Ken Reiche, a young friend of Michael's whose keen appetite for exploring mindscape as well as landscape eventually made him a close friend of mine. A skilled gardener and builder, he would often work all day around the ranch without intruding upon my time or space. The third friend was Remo, with whom, even before we became lovers, I grew to be at ease whether we spent days hiking and exploring together, or being apart for months at a time.

On one level of mutual solitude, let's say, two people are absorbed in different tasks or activities with little or no awareness of one other. Their parallel energies reinforce each other almost impersonally, humming along without meeting or interfering. Ken, pruning vines in the backyard or constructing a stone patio for the bunkhouse, not only didn't disturb my work, but fed it by his rapt attention to his own project. On another level, the resonance is more personal, with increased sensitivity to the other person's presence, but without strain or self-consciousness. Because Dick was also a writer, my awareness of him propped on pillows in the living room, immersed in his journal, quickened my own desire to write.

On a third level, the sparking energy derives from sheer harmony with the other's presence. As Remo and I grew closer, I delighted the more in my own work knowing that he was baking bread in the kitchen, tinkering in the breezeway, or reading in the living room. And if he chanced to touch my shoulder as he walked by my chair, it was as if the universe softly said Yes, and the smile within me would focus rather than break my concentration. Indeed, there were to come times when my solitude felt incomplete without him.

No doubt there are other degrees to which one can participate in mutual solitude, but the point is that one's own activity or quiescence is enhanced by the activity or presence of the other, and that harmony pervades. With other guests and friends, there were moments of intertwined solitude, or even separate solitudes, but not that sense of vivifying affinity. Ken, Dick, and Remo were each at peace with themselves, at ease with what they were doing. They filled their own space without excluding mine.

But not all of solitude, mutual or otherwise, is sweet inner peace. That is where the vertigo comes in, the all-and-nothingness, the Todo y Nada of Saint John of the Cross. For with solitude comes awareness of our individuation, of our mortality, of the unknowable core that is our deepest self. Out of imagination and memory, yearning and uncertainty, ambition and desire, we create ourselves or are created. But aloneness is a condition of life. No matter the support we receive from those who love us, it is how we grow, age and die. And sometimes the sense of being alone can place us vertiginously next to Nothing.

Winter on the desert, I learned, is the season of sternest solitude. In the warm months, songbirds sing, voracious hummingbirds dive-bomb the feeders and each other, lizards scuttle in the garden and among the rocks. At night there are the crickets and the crews of bats, not to mention, in May and June, the mockingbirds that sing all night long, raucous and giddy, from the gully below the home canyon. Solitude? The horses whinny for attention whenever they hear the squeak of a screen door, hardly a week goes by without guests, and always there are the busy bugs and flies. More like living in a city than a desert.

But in winter the sense of being alone is stark and sometimes harsh. Gone are the campers, bikers and hikers, the jeeping and rafting brigades. Rarely does anyone visit, and there is little outdoor work to be done. The lizards are asleep, the horses turned loose on the range, leaving only Koa and me and sometimes the ravens to entertain each other. Trips to town are few, and often slowed by snows that blanket the ground and muffle the silence. In late December or January, the dry desert fog creeps in for a week or a month, shrouding the ranch in a gray-white cloud and coating everything—trees, grasses, fencewire, weeds, the withered remains of the garden—with an elegant ermine of hoarfrost. It is then that the stone house in the hidden canyon seems most secret and remote, a dream one enters through tunnels of drifting fog.

While all else is dormant, this is my time for reading, writing, reflection. A time for letters, for connecting with distant friends. A time of translating physical solitude into the pacts I've made with myself, into a lasting peace. It is also the most exacting season, with pipes to keep from freezing, firewood to keep dry and stacked, roaming horses to keep track of, vehicles to keep running. A cold, rigorous dreamtime, it was not at first my favorite season.

One chill, brittle evening during my second winter at the ranch, I rode Aquila to the great white rock that overlooks the mesas and canyonlands. It had just snowed, and we loped along with Koa through clouds of sunset-pink powder, the mare's hooves kicking up a hiss of snow, our breaths puffed out as frost. But by the time we reached the rock, the sun had set without trace in a greasy, darkening sky, and the wide landscape was somber and bleak. I dismounted, but the sunken gardens of my outdoor 'house,' cowled in white like sheet-covered furniture, did not invite me. Nor did the distant horizon, nor anything between. Nothing looked alive, or even real—everything had lost its presence, receded into vague blotches of juniper strewn like so much trash over gray undulations of snow. Staring out over the deadened land, I became acutely aware that I was the only human being for dozens of miles in any direction, and that no one in the world knew where I was. Even my dappled mare looked dull, faded, a ghost-horse the color of...what?

For those moments, my presence on earth was as frighteningly meaningless as I have ever experienced it to be. Something opened up and I teetered on its edge, overwhelmed, dizzy and falling—into emptiness, into the abyss of myself, into that place where my city-bred friend disappeared, that place where we all disappear, where emptiness is not the ground of freedom and choice and becoming, but is simply and totally groundless and empty. And I was afraid, suddenly, of being...*all* by myself.

And yet sometimes when we cannot place ourselves in space, along comes time. Or we have a dog who shakes himself and snuffs and reminds us that it's possible, advisable, and maybe even pleasurable to do something else. As I absently stroked Koa's cold fur, I mused on how often I'd wished to view this land with the eyes of the first person ever to see it. And those were the eyes I was given. There was no one else out there, anywhere. From all signs, there never had been. Yet I was there, and so, somewhere in the dusk, were browsing deer, hunting coyotes, soft-pelted cottontails hiding under snow-bent bunchgrass, a living world suspended for moments, for months, in its own dormancy. From here it was possible to look upon a vast landscape bounded only by the horizon, and feel neither ownership nor dispossession, nor even now estrangement, but rather a severe belonging. I live here. I live here, too.

Shivering, I rubbed my hands, numb in their gloves, and following Koa, soberly led Aquila down the rock, walking to get warm, walking to find my feet on the ground beneath the snow.

Many people, including some nature writers, claim that encounters with natural grandeur— with imposing landscapes or large wild animals—make them feel small, insignificant, humble. This is not the feeling I experienced that evening on the white rock, nor have I ever felt quite that way. What triggered my dizzy apprehension of emptiness was not the vastness of the winter landscape, but the frightening perception it *wasn't* there, had receded, faded, died. For me, it was the dread negative of a bedazzlement I knew well, wherein one perceives a world so full of itself—so present, so full of otherness—that edges between it and oneself are erased.

Perhaps because I grew up quite literally in the woods, it took years for it to occur to me that I might be out of place in a landscape, or that I was other than the creatures I stalked and watched in the Connecticut hills. It seems to me that if we approach nature's immensity with the notion that we have a rightful place in it, if we dismiss our puny arrogance and gawky self-consciousness and allow ourselves to be as much an aspect of landscape as any other element, as much a part of the spectrum of life as any other creature—*but no more so*—then instead of feeling reduced, we might feel exalted at being one among such a magnificent array, at being a jot in the weighty evidence for the creative nature of the universe.

"Desire is the desire of the other's desire," says Roland Barthes. We—you, I—are part of nature's desire for itself. Maybe it's the *but no more so* that we find humbling. But if we switch to Meister Eckhart's perspective that "The eye with which I see God (nature) is the eye with which God (nature) sees me," we are popped back into a universe in which we have a rightful place—in which our right derives from being part of, of having power *with*, not over. We may still be awed, but we need not feel small, for we are expanding inside with what we see.

I ponder the supposed emptiness of deserts, of my desert here, and can no longer find it. The silent distances, the spires and canyons, the eroding rocks themselves, seem as close to eternal as I will come. Their shapes seem not to change, yet they often seem *about* to change, to reveal, to move or speak. Some days I can walk out and see simply sandstone—Navajo, Kayenta, Entrada, sediment pressed into rock, eroded into thin-lipped ledges, cavernous overhangs, lichen-covered slabs, scoured cubbyholes. And some days I walk out and see runes, alphabets, signs and messages whose significance drives me to distraction because I cannot read them. Once, among exfoliating layers of a ledge, I found a flake of russet stone roughly shaped like an enlarged human heart, with a crack leading to a hole in its center. Whose *is* this?

> *Today the rocks surged up at me again, their caps of snow like break-ing surf, utterly still, looming nonetheless. I am surrounded on this desert by mirrors of my own becoming. I am the rupestrine woman in the pastel drawing, dwelling among rocks, reflected in their shapes, their gestures, their posture: here a flung arm, there a half-buried thigh, here an angled hip, there a rounded breast, a throat tilted back to sing.*

Even the colors of the rocks are the colors of skin, pale pinks and ochres, smoked blues and chocolates, tans and burnished reds. I feel the shapes and poses of the rocks as the bones in my body, a veer of yearning sliding beneath the surface of dream, utterly sensuous and incomplete, so that staring at a rock I feel it suggesting something I must become, something achingly close to orgasmic, something whole within itself, potent yet unfinished. That is landscape: not a place you live in, but a place that lives in you.

Above the east canyon there is a vertical gash in the cliff shaped exactly like what I felt when at age fourteen my parents ordained that I must sell my closest companion, my horse. I know it so well I no longer need to look at it. The cleft was formed by centuries of frost and root and running water, its edges rounded and softened with moss and lichen. But I am not fooled: I knew it when it ran raw and sharp and burnt deep as a crack of lightning.

I don't know how to experience emptiness or nothingness for long periods. I do know that what I beheld that winter dusk was a gift, and I'm grateful to whatever it is in the nature of mind or protoplasm that lets us enter such rips and holes in the fabric of our everyday shroud, and to *in corporate* what we find there, *en compass* it, like a swim bladder or a direction finder. What I see now when I visit the white rock is a silent fullness, and I am stunned not by emptiness, but by the enormity of time, its vastness and bulk, as if time were what space is filled with.

The desert silence is not empty either, but rings, vibrates with what is too small to see, too high to hear, sings and wheezes with the speech of particles and waves and streaming ions, the music of galaxy and cosmos, the whispers of light and darkness commingling. And whether this is indeed an audible music of the atmosphere, or whether it is due to the keening of our own blood through ears and brain, what matters is that the silence is alive. It breathes and hums and aauuums—not busily, but vastly, as if what it brings to our ears is a keyhole, a leak into the infinite inersecting of past and future, dead and living and yet-to-be, intimately known and barely imaginable, skin-enclosed and incomprehensibly distant.

One mild Thanksgiving afternoon, my visiting sister Nance, niece Malli, and nephew David saddled four horses and rode to the rim of Taylor Canyon. We tied the horses to cedar limbs while the kids, ages twelve and nine, began to explore the brink of the 800-foot canyon. As Nance and I caught up with them, David was lobbing the biggest rock he could lift over the edge of the cliff. Now I can stand quite comfortably with my toes at the lip of a canyon, but I have an acrophobic terror of other people falling, especially children. By way of saying Please be careful, we cautioned David that pushing rocks off cliffs isn't real cool. You can never tell who or what might be down there. What if you hit a bighorn sheep? David shrugs, looking sheepish himself. For all his energy, he is a gentle child, and the intention of hurting even a spider is not in him.

But I know there is no one below, not even an exposed lizard. Rather, in the lump of vertigo I've just swallowed is the absurd fear he'll crush the shadows—a fear that expands when both kids start shouting for echoes, screaming nonsense names—Blue Turtles! Sky Pie! Froggie Weirdo!—across the gap of Taylor. In seconds, the echoes return, *doh*

doh doh and we squeal with laughter, and the laughter laughs back. Yet I want to beg us to stop for fear our shrieks will pierce the silence like arrows, rend and shred it, damage it permanently, allowing the sounds of the mechanized world to seep through, first as echo, then whisper, then insistent murmur, then creaking, grinding, groaning, whining blasting bleeping honking shrieking *noise.*

Vertigo. Kqanisquatzi, world out of balance. Never to be silent anywhere again. And yet, of course so far the silence returns, though even here it grows increasingly shy, wary of the buzzing inroads on all sides.

After exploring ledges and caves and potholes and finding a packrat's midden, we rode back lazily in the short-day sunshine, arriving at the ranch in time to relieve my brother-in-law, Dave, of basting the turkey. A merry meal was enjoyed by all, the kids playing echo with each other across the table over pumpkin pie *eye yie yie yie.*

A rock falls in the desert just as a tree falls in the forest, whether or not we and our prized, empedastalled and severely overloaded consciousnesses are there to perceive it. Thank God they fall—and sprout, grow, age, decay—without us. For me, *Cogito ergo sum* is false, or at least extremely limiting. Rather, I am because I am *here*, in this place, on this outcrop, looking across this canyon to those buttes, that salt dome, those mesas. Because I am here with these children. Because I empty myself into the landscape with them, or alone, therefore am I also here. As in the I and thou of love—because you are, therefore I am—it is the intimate otherness of this world that confirms my own being in it.

I walk out to the mesa at evening, sit on a ledge and offer my hand to the bare branch of a half-dead juniper. The hand rests easily in the curve of the branch, as if accepted. Through my fingers I feel the tree's life: air moving against its bark as against my face, sap flowing slowly like my blood, roots penetrating the rock beneath me, minutely absorbing water as my skin breathes, both of us held to the earth around us, metabolizing time back to sprout, to seed, to sand, to nothing, to the enduring momentary something that nothingness is always becoming.

But still, friends ask, *isn't it hard, being out here all by yourself?*

It's hard to be anywhere, including here, all by oneself. By that I mean not that solitude is a hardship, but that it's sometimes difficult, for me at least, to locate a state of being solitary. Voices, not always one's own, fill in. Imagination is an astonishing social director. Even one's breath is full of others' being. Yes, I've been lonely at the ranch, but far less often and less acutely than I have been lonely in the arms of a lover with whom I could not communicate, or with friends when our lives swept us past each other without true recognition or exchange.

His Holiness The Dalai Lama speaks of "the poverty of a solitary peace." I am no cenobite or hermit. I didn't come here to live simply. I came here to live out my complexities among the complexities of others, to recognize and live with otherness, to find a peace that doesn't exclude but connects. I believe it was Oscar Wilde who said that any map was worthless unless it contained a utopia—which may be why Horsethief is not on many maps. I didn't come here to find an isolating utopia, but to learn and communicate out of the one messy, incurable world we have. I think of solitude as a door through which I step into, not away from that world. When I walk out on the mesa to sit with my juniper, I think of my friends with love, not loneliness. I think about them in the Spanish sense, *pienso en tu*: I think *in* you. I like to imagine them as they go about their lives, watching them from my mind like a ghost of the solitude I know we share in moments when we are most ourselves.

Chapter Six

Creature Comforts

One June day while working in the garden, I heard one of the ravens uttering a peculiar cry as it winged up the gully toward me. It sounded irritated—outraged, in fact. I looked up as it flapped by about forty feet away, flying low, the whisking sound of its wings reflected from the cliff, wroaacking as if persecuted.

Sure enough. Riding on the raven's shoulder, clinging to the feathers between its beating wings, was a smaller bird, gray, with warm-colored breast and darkish tailfeathers. As I watched, incredulous, the little bird let go, fluttered along on its own for twenty feet or so, then dug its tiny talons fiercely into the raven's feathers and resumed its ride. Still complaining loudly, the raven made another pass over the house, then cleared the western rimrock and headed out over the desert. The little bird alternately hitched a ride for a hundred feet or more, briefly let go, then grabbed on again. Last I saw of them, the gray bird was still clinging like a winged bur.

The next day it happened again, only this time there were two small birds, one riding, the other flitting along making angry peeting cries which were almost lost in the raven's offended croaking. Again I watched the avian circus until it was out of sight. My Peterson's field guide had identified the hitchhiking bird as a Say's phoebe—a prairie and desert-dwelling member of the flycatcher family. It said nothing about the bird's habits, but I concluded that the resident pair of ravens had been threatening the phoebes' nest. In later inquiries, though, none of my bird-watching friends had heard of, much less witnessed, such a thing. Chasing, yes—but not riding.

Two days later, I saw a phoebe riding a raven again. Male and female ravens look alike, as do phoebes, so I don't know who was chasing or riding whom, or how many times the birds might have performed this act when I wasn't watching. In any case, after that the phoebes' activity subsided, while the behavior of the ravens became all the more interesting over the course of the summer.

Maybe it's the tarnished Poe romantic in me, but I've always been fascinated by these large black corvids. Over the years, I came to know Horsethief's pair quite well. In early spring, before tending to their nest, and later in the fall, they would often follow along for miles during horseback rides, circling above in playful courtship patterns, or floating from juniper to juniper intent on what Koa might scare up. Clever opportunists, they eked out winter by gleaning grain from the corrals, raiding the garden compost heap, and by other means, I'm sure, known only to them. In late summer, nothing was more entertaining than watching them raise their young.

One August afternoon, again while in the garden, I heard insistent croakings from a ledge below the west rim. Hmm. Three ravens: two ruffled adults and a sleek fledgling. Well, almost fledgling. As I watched, it became evident that the parents were dealing with a problem child. Taking turns, or both together, the adults would fly out over the canyon, then return to the ledge, hoarsely demanding that the youngster try it. Wroaaack, come on, it's fun, it's easy. But their recalcitrant offspring merely stood there on the ledge, head cocked as if to say Who are these people? while the parents screeched and scolded and flew and coaxed.

Finally, croaking with what sounded like exasperation, the adults flew off into the west canyon, where I heard them talking in more relaxed voices with what I presumed was the second and possibly more willing fledgling. Meanwhile, the youngster on the ledge uttered several juvenile, questioning croaks, cocking its head for long minutes in between, as if waiting for a reply or listening to the conversation going on upcanyon. The last I saw, the reluctant youngster was trudging with what appeared to be great determination along the rimrock toward the sound of its parents' voices.

Actually, it was not the last I saw; at sunset the whole family of four floated back down the canyon on the way to roost for the night. During the next week, I watched more flying lessons as the parents demonstrated finer points of banking, ledge-landing, cross-winds navigation, even loop-di-loops and other aerobatics, with the keenest sense of space and timing. Later, as September's gold light slanted toward fall, I eavesdropped on a soft, burbling lecture given by one of the parents to one of its young. For over an hour, the two birds faced each other in a cliff alcove above the hot tub. The adult did most of the talking and wing-fluffing, preening the young bird's feathers with its beak, while the juvenile cocked its head and occasionally uttered a questioning croak. Call it anthropomorphism, but it looked and sounded precisely like mom or dad giving serious advice to an offspring about to fly off into the world. Soon after that, both youngsters were gone.

The adult ravens remained consistently interesting, amusing, mysterious. One blustery fall day, when the wind had been blowing too hard to let the rain fall, I heard both ravens fussing angrily about something up by the corrals. Thinking it might be just a domestic squabble, I hesitated to get involved. But the ruckus went on, so I went to check it out.

Both ravens were perched unsteadily atop a juniper snag in one of the corrals, feathers askew in the wind, wings lifting to keep their balance. Both faced the same direction, wroaawking fiercely at a large white bird who perched with equal unsteadiness on top of a corral post about twenty feet away. From its windswept crest and yellow bill, I recognized the visitor as a cattle egret, definitely not a local resident, likely blown off its migration course by the wind. To the ravens, the egret was intruder, not visitor, especially when it dropped to the ground and began to glean tidbits of grain from the sand. Raven voices rose in outrage as they took over the egret's fencepost and shrieked down at the silent stranger, who ignored them in favor of food.

The ravens' protests became so near-hysterical that I wondered if territory was the only issue, or if the egret's size, strangeness, or even color, intensified their reaction. My sympathies leaned toward the wind-buffeted egret, who matched the ravens in size, but whose slender elegance contrasted with the ravens' burliness. In hopes of preventing an outright attack, and also to provide for a stranger, I broadcast several handfuls of grain around the corrals. "See, there's plenty for everybody," I scolded the ravens. They went right on hurling hoarse insults, paying no attention to me or the grain. By sunset, the wind had abated, the ravens had disappeared down-canyon, and the egret seemed content to roost in a juniper near the corral. In the morning, it was gone, but I didn't see or hear the ravens for days.

Along with lizards and bats, the ravens were the most familiar of the many wild creatures that enriched my 'community of solitudes.' Although they didn't, that I'm aware of, talk *to* me, I'm convinced they talked *about* me. They watched me attentively as a source of food, and often appeared when I came outside to work, play with Koa, or ride. In their coal-glitter eyes, in their expressive voices, gestures, and flight, I saw agile intelligence and an appetite for play. Though I enjoyed all birds—the blue scrub jays, the soft summer songbirds, the bright spring and fall migrants, the winter chickadees and juncos, and the occasional owls, hawks, and eagles—I felt the ravens might, if I could listen well, have the most interesting things to say.

Certainly more than the peacocks.

When I moved to the ranch, the livestock whose care I inherited included a single, fully-plumed peacock. The incongruity of such exoticism—this georgeous irridescent bird with teal-blue body and bronze-green tailfeathers, fanning its argus-eyed plumes against red slickrock, or trailing them like a robe as it highstepped through snow—was appealing. And the poet in me was ready to hear something haunting, if hardly romantic, in its loud screeching call. But Chad, the former caretaker who had brought the peacock to the ranch, had gotten fed up with the bird long before he left, and it didn't take many months to discover why.

I appreciate aggressiveness only in an abstract, evolutionary sense. The peacock, as a stranger in a strange land, had a right to his bad manners so long as they bore some relationship to keeping him alive—or so I felt at first. And I did enjoy some of his antics as well as his beauty. In spring, for instance, he would spend much of the day in front of the only reflective surface available, the glass-paneled door on the north side of the house. Sometimes he would sand-bathe in the shade nearby, but mostly he stood facing the glass door, posing and preening. One day, when my visiting photographer friend Linde Waidhofer set up a tripod and aimed her camera at him, he spent all day responding with pose after pose. As long as Linde was there, he spread and vibrated and rattled his great fan, the epitome of avian narcisssm.

I also enjoyed watching Koa and Mr. Peacock play 'bag'—if not together, then at least at the same time. This game, one of Koa's favorites, consisted in me tossing a large, empty paper grainsack like a frisbee, and Koa either catching it in mid-air or pouncing on it as it hit the ground. He would then run around blindly, the giant bag across his face, growling and shaking it violently. Finally he would bring it back to me for a fresh toss, and so the game would go until the bag was in tatters—just right for starting a fire under the hot tub.

As far as Koa was concerned, it was just him against the bag, with me as assistant. But the peacock must have sensed some competitive edge to this game, and would try to join in, rushing aggressively after Koa and the bag, often leaping high into the air, tailfeathers and all, to avoid being run down by the bag-blinded dog. Koa paid no attention to the peacock, who obviously didn't understand the game, and this seemed to offend the bird further. He would try all the more to interfere with Koa's sport, which resulted in him getting bowled over (tailfeathers and all) when he couldn't leap out of the way fast enough.

Games were one thing, but the peacock was a contentious creature who had to be penned up when children were around. He would chase the horses—including the stallion, Eagle—away from their grain, and I had to threaten the bird with a stick to keep him from flying at the horses' eyes. One spring day, I was on knees and elbows in the back yard, leaning down into the underground waterpipe junction box to turn on a valve.

Suddenly I heard, as Leda must have, the heavy beat of wings, and rolled away just as the peacock landed (tailfeathers and all) on my rump. At that point I decided that if the bird was to stay, he needed a mate.

And so Lady Lou, a modest and proper peahen, came to Horsethief, a gift of Jack Snobble, the geologist, teacher, and horseman who shared our herd of horses for half the year. Lady Lou, dull-as-a-stew, proved a willing mate for Mr. Peacock, but did little to cure his aggression. Instead, it grew worse. Plus now there were two large birds hanging around the house leaving their sizable slime-gray calling cards on the doorsteps. That was when the flimsy poultry pen in the breezeway got re-built, all in one frustrated day, while my favorite waffle-soled workshoes dried in the sun. Mr. Peacock and Lady Lou produced a clutch of nine eggs, three of which the peahen incubated until they hatched into fluffy, peeping, buff-colored peachicks. One was killed by Mouse, the barn cat, but the other two grew enough during the winter so that come spring, they too could make large messy deposits in the yard.

Keeping the birds penned seemed to defeat the purpose of having them around. But in addition to the problems of peacock-poop and keeping the four birds from shredding the garden, the male was getting out of hand. One spring day, Lady Lou and her two maturing chicks were stepping around the front yard eating bugs while Koa and I watched them from the patio couch outside the kitchen door. Along came Mr. Peacock, strutting snaky-necked, edging toward Koa and me on the couch. Suddenly the bird launched into the air, talons aimed straight at Koa's head. I threw myself over the dog, covering my head, and fended him off by batting him to the ground. A few minutes later he tried it again. At that point, I got a stout stick, gathered three guests from the hot tub, and together we held Horsethief's first and last official peacock round-up.

Through Robert Soldat, the solar expert who had set up my computer system, I learned of a woman who raised large birds and might want the peacocks. In fact—aha!—perhaps she would be willing to trade: a peacock and three peahens for several of the wild turkeys Robert said she raised. I could let them go in the east canyon beyond the spring, where they would be somewhat protected from predators, have plenty of food, and...

And so it happened that Anne Fry, a skilled bird-lady, came with Robert one evening and took the peacocks. A few weeks later Anne and Robert returned, the cage in the pickup filled with eight wild turkey chicks, still in their baby plumage. "They've started to roost," Anne explained, "which means they're old enough to be on their own." This was something I hadn't thought of. The turkeys were old enough to roost, but were they, I asked, big and smart enough to avoid being caught by Mouse? Anne and I looked at each other, nodding slowly, and decided to keep the chicks in the pen until they had grown enough to discourage Mouse.

So began one of the more frustrating periods in my sojourn at Horsethief. The turkeys grew rapidly on mash and pellets and the insects they gleaned from their open-air pen. In three weeks they were large enough to be turned loose. "Don't worry," Anne had said, "they won't hang around. They really are wild." And so I chose a July day when my friend Susan Obermeyer and her sons Bill and Tom were there to help. We herded the turkeys up into a grove beyond the spring, where I'd placed a bucket of water and a tub of grain. The birds commenced pecking around, cheeping to one other, appearing quite content with their new lot.

Since Susan and the boys would be caretaking while I was away for a week, I encouraged Bill and Tom to chase the turkeys—"Seriously!"—if the birds came into the yard, so long as they chased them up beyond the spring and left them alone there. "You can do anything you want to make them afraid of people—just don't hurt them!" I warned. The boys grinned.

A week later I returned to find all eight 'wild' turkeys roosting on the now guano-coated gazebo in the back yard, pecking around house, yard, and breezeway for food, leaving filth everywhere. We chased them, pelting the ground around them with stones, back up past the spring. The boys said they'd done that every day, but the birds always came back.

After Susan and the boys left, I moved the water and grain farther up into the east canyon, naively hoping they'd stay there. When the birds came back to the yard, I hissed and shrieked, pelted them with gravel, whirled a long stick over my head—and after a week of such exercise succeeded in getting them to roost in a tall juniper all of fifty feet farther from the house. Still they came pecking around like barnyard fowl. Still I had to suspend everything else to be sure they roosted in the upper canyon. No evening rides or hikes, no end-of-day gardening.

Plus with all the chasing, the turkeys were getting smart. At least three times a day, hissing and yowling like a banshee, I herded them up through the spring grove and over the berm into the upper canyon. At first they stayed together as a flock, peeping reassurance to one another as they scuttled along, letting themselves be herded. But soon they learned to split up, hide quietly in the underbrush, and double back after I had passed. The canny birds *wanted* to be tame—or at least wanted to remain in the vicinity of their first roosting perch in the pen. And they used all their wily wits to do it. I, on the other hand, was the one who was going wild.

After ten days of this, one evening the whole flock doubled back and cut across into the west canyon, away from their roost. Hissing and winging stones, I herded the now-mature birds all the way through the canyon and up onto the mesa. Grabbing rocks on the run, I chased them farther and farther west, chucking stones, dirt, anything to head off potential AWOLs, until all nine of us were exhausted and only Koa was still up for the chase. By then we were a mile from the ranch, at the last large juniper before slickrock woodland gave way to blackbrush dunes.

The sun had set. Dusk was gathering. It was long past time to roost. "Okay, guys. That tree is your last chance. It's coyote time. Take it or leave it." I waited, stones in hand, until they took it—one by one flapping up into the limbs of the juniper. But then one tried to double back around a patch of prickly pear toward home. I pitched a fast stone and heard it thud against feathers as the turkey slumped in a heap among the cactus. "Oh, no," I thought. "I didn't mean..." But I was dead weary of chasing birds that wouldn't behave-and-go-wild, and just about ready to sacrifice them to animals that *were* wild. I felt awful about the bird—but then, as I turned with Koa toward home, the downed turkey righted itself, shook its feathers and flapped dizzily onto a juniper limb.

"Well," I thought as we walked through the August twilight, "maybe that's that."

Next morning, however, the turkeys were back even earlier than usual, cheeping under my window before dawn. Of course: the sun rises on the mesa long before it reaches into the canyon. Once more, without feeling, I chased them up past the spring. My sister Nance and her family were due to arrive the next day, and that settled things. Time for a wild turkey roundup. And so, with niece Malli, nephew David and brother-in-law Dave as outriders, Nance and I herded what must have been a puzzled flock of turkeys down through the spring grove, across the back yard, and with only a few bewildered attempts at escape, into their breezeway pen.

I closed the door to the pen feeling even worse than I had when I'd stoned the turkey out on the mesa. I liked these birds. I was tired of their persistence, but I had come to respect them. They weren't aggressive like the peacock, and they were anything but stupid. As individuals they were easily flustered, but as a flock, which is how they were meant to be, their instincts were amazingly clever—especially considering that they were all the same age and had no older birds for guides. I had hoped to have turkeys in the upper canyon, wild and wary, a surprise to anyone, including me, lucky enough to catch sight of them. I didn't care if they 'escaped' out of the canyon and onto the mesa, I just wanted to know they were around, as their ancestors had been for countless generations. What was I going to do with a flock of penned-up birds?

Anne agreed to take back six of the eight 'tame' turkeys in trade for five full-grown wild ones. These we would turn loose in the juniper- and brush-choked gully below the ranch, where they would have plenty of food and cover and no prior bond to a roosting site near the house. If they discovered the upper canyon, fine. If not, that was okay too, as long as they stayed away from the house. Two of the tame birds would stay in the pen until Thanksgiving.

But the best intentions pave ill routes. On turkey-exchange day, Anne and Robert didn't arrive until after roosting time. Released after dusk beneath a huge juniper in the gully, the five travel-shocked birds scooted into the underbrush instead of flying up into the tree. Checking the gully early the next morning, I found clumps of feathers, drops of blood, and coyote scat. No turkeys, no turkey prints, no sound of turkeys. On foot and horseback I searched the gully for signs of the remaining birds. Not a track, not a dropping. A few days later, my friend Ken found another clump of bloody feathers. Though I looked for a week, that was the last trace.

So much for game management, although with what I know from my mistakes, I'd try again. Even penned, the first flock of birds had been interesting. If they weren't raving beauties like the peacock, their alert brown eyes, warty red-blue heads, dangling wattles and smoky chocolate-black plumage posed subtler evolutionary questions. Although they prefered to walk or run, even as juveniles they were amazingly fast fliers. Omnivorous, they turned over rocks and even their grain tub to gobble up beetles, worms and sowbugs. They patrolled the stone wall of their pen for insects and spiders and were quick enough to catch flies in mid-air.

As a flock, their stealth—their ability to suspend audible communication while hiding in the underbrush, then gather without signal at a specific place—was as astonishing as it had been frustrating. I'd been unable to perceive a flock hierarchy or pecking order, but there were distinct alliances. One large tom, for example, seemed to favor one of the smaller hens. They fed together, dustbathed together, even roosted side by side.

Before dawn on the morning after Anne had taken the rest of the flock (including the above pair), I awoke to bereaved calls from the two remaining toms, high plaintive cheeping with a note of protest in it (cheep CHEEP cheep cheep cheep cheep—*Where* ARE *you you you you? Come* GET *me me me me...*) Later, when I returned from errands in town, the call of the two toms had changed to a hollow warble with no weak note, no protest or question in it. Instead, their mournful, guttural dirge made me question deeply why I was keeping them.

I was keeping them to eat. I was keeping them because, dear as animal life is to me, I was not totally inclined toward vegetarianism. I avoid red meat, but do enjoy fowl and fish. For several years of my life, I had respectfully hunted and fished for most of the flesh I ate. But that was long ago. It was time to re-establish a personal link with the creatures who fed me.

On the Monday before Thanksgiving, Anne came to help. Though a vegetarian herself, she had grown up on a farm and was willing to teach me what she knew of humane killing. It was a gray, mild afternoon, sun slanting through the clouds and silvering the fallen cottonwood leaves in the back yard as we set up a bench, bucket, and barrels near the gazebo. The two young toms had grown impressively large, but they weren't hard to catch. After being swung by their legs gently, heavily, upside down, they went into a trance and did not struggle.

Working quickly, we strung the first turkey by its feet from the gazebo, me holding up the bird's weight with both arms around its body. "Hold tight," Anne said. "They're really strong —you'll be amazed at how much strength they have—and you don't want them to flap around, or it will be a mess. Now," she added, "we'll think good thoughts. Now—" as she plunged a small sharp knife up through the bird's throat into its skull and swiftly scrambled its brain. Then, with the turkey senseless and brain-dead, she slit its throat. "Hold on," she warned, and I hugged face into feathers, feeling the turkey's heart thudding harder and harder as its lifeblood drained away, its blood pressure dropped and the unconscious bird struggled mightily against its death.

I was that death, I who held the huge bird's body so tightly. I took the turkey's life, but in that moment also received it, felt it given over to me, vouchsafed. I had admired this bird, had chased it, fed it, watched it for hours, respected its life even while I had reluctantly directed it. There was no way to rationalize my choice as controlling human; no justification, spiritual or otherwise, for causing death. I did not 'deserve' the life of this bird because I had known and respected it. Rather, it was, as all food is, a gift, for which I was doubly grateful because I was able to receive it so directly, and because I had witnessed the life of the giver.

As Anne and I quickly plucked the turkey's dark feathers from its still-warm body, I thought about how the bird had lived. I felt far worse about the other five turkeys whose demise was unintended. Not just that they had died, but that they had died accidentally, in a strange place, scattered, probably terrified, and possibly slowly, of thirst. What is the dream of wildness, that it must be 'managed'? The bugs the birds ate were wilder than the birds themselves. I wanted the turkeys wild not only because as yardbirds they'd have been as messy as the peacocks, but because as a human I knew their long history as a successful native species, and desired to help that history continue. I still do, but would not attempt to play a role in it again without radically improved planning and timing. The goal, after all, was to leave the birds alone.

If the ranch could not have wild turkeys, there were many other wild creatures to appreciate—creatures which, if not exactly companions, enlivened my days and nights. They made of the home canyon and the surrounding desert an ecosystem as wild as any on earth, interacting with each other and with the land in myriad overlapping circles and cycles, of which I could perceive little more than the surface.

One evening, sitting at the kitchen table jotting notes in the logbook, I felt an odd sensation, as if I were being watched. I turned around, and sure enough: perched on the counter behind me, almost on my shoulder, was a huge green praying mantis. Triangular head cocked as if inquisitively, the insect's bulbous eyes seemed to stare right at me. Whatever did I look like to that multi-faceted vision? I thought of the Hindu pantheon of gods, millions of beings reflected in facets of colored light. Playing, I offered the creature a pencil, then my little finger, to see if it would take either one in its upraised front legs. It ignored the pencil but held my finger lightly, then jumped onto my wrist. Moving slowly, I carried the mantis outside and let it go in the darkness of the garden. "May you have many healthy children," I said, thinking about insect pests. But I appreciated the mantis for its own sake and felt glad for its gentle presence.

Another encounter of the six-legged kind happened one night in late summer. I'd been reading in bed, and had just turned off the propane lamp. From under the stack of books and journals beside me came a scratching and rustling. Flicking on a flashlight, I discovered in its beam a mouse-sized grasshopper fully four inches long, with finely tapered wings streamlining its abdomen. "Hello there. You're beautiful," I said, "but you go out." Fetching an empty coffee can, I herded the strong-legged creature into it, clamped on the lid, and punched holes in it.

Thinking to study the grasshopper more closely in the morning, I set the container outside the back door, went back to bed, and tried to sleep. No way. It probably can't breathe, I thought, and it has nothing to eat or drink. I took the lid off the can, went back to bed and slept. Next morning, as Koa nosed me awake, I saw the huge hopper clinging to the inside of the screen door. It had come in through a hole in the screen, but like Koa, seemed to want out.

Things happen fast. I opened the screen door, Koa trotted out, I shooed the grasshopper off the screen, it sailed into the sunlit yard to be struck midair by a jab of blue lightning, a scrub jay. Both creatures crashed to the sand as the jay tackled a hard-shelled rocket half its size. As I stared, the jay righted itself, pinned the hopper to the ground, dismembered and devoured it.

I'm not comfortable causing death, accidentally or at all. It was a fearsome thing to kill the two turkeys—before, during, and after. But I didn't regret it then, nor do I now. Awed by the huge life-strength ebbing from the dying birds in my arms, yes, and by taking part so directly in the process of killing in order to eat. But grateful for that gift and unremorseful about being its recipient. I would kill again for food if I had to. No doubt jays don't think about such things; this one's only difficulty was swallowing the meal I had inadvertently provided.

That fall, in the frost outside the door I found a monarch butterfly, stiff but alive. Taking it gently inside, I set it among blossoms of a store-bought bouquet. Later I spied the butterfly on the windowsill, revived but listing to the side of its half-missing leg. There it stayed for several days, black-orange wings breathing slowly, antennae tips touching the glass. Paying no heed to the lid of sugar water I set nearby, it faced outside, as if there were still a place it wished to go. Twice more it tried to fly, stained glass wings afire in the dim daylight of the kitchen. But then one afternoon I found it tilted on its side in the window, still facing outdoors. I touched the arc of its wing and ever so feebly, like dying lips trying to speak, the wing lifted in response. Lazarus. Was it cruel, or just silly, to keep the creature in a warm kitchen, to offer it sugar water—to prolong its death? Only the cut flowers in the vase might have answered.

A great deal of my time at Horsethief was spent outdoors, where I savored the company of creatures I didn't necessarily interact with. Along with the ravens and other birds, foremost among these were the lizards, each of whom had its own territory and returned to it after winter hibernation. As soon as the weather, rocks and ground warmed up and worm and insect populations began to move around, out came the lizards to eat them. Since the appearance of these reptiles coincided with the beginning of gardening season, I quickly developed an affection for them as allies.

But I would have liked them anyway. Tree lizards, marled with patterns of brown, black and tan, were to me the handsomest. Sagebrush lizards, similarly mottled but with shorter tails, were more shy. And the checkerspotted whiptails, streamlined and very fast, went about their business so efficiently I sometimes wasn't sure, at the end of a day, whether I'd really seen any, or dreamed them the night before.

I came to like each species, and each individual, for its antics as well as its usefulness. The lizards were most active in the relative cool of morning, hunting and feeding on insects—which of course led to territorial encounters and chases. In the hot afternoons, the lizards kept to the shade, panting to lower body temperature or doing 'push-ups' as a territorial display. At first, working in the garden, I was startled by sudden rustlings in the mulch-straw at my elbow. But as I observed the scurrying noisemakers, I learned that I could expect to see the same one in any given area—unless it was chasing or being chased by one of its neighbors.

In late summer, baby lizards would appear. Often less than two inches long from nostrils to tailtip, they were otherwise replicas of their six-to-twelve inch parents. One day, after letting the hot tub drain, I returned to clean it and found a tiny tree lizard resting on the lip of the tub. So small a falling blackberry might have crushed it, it dropped into the tub as I approached, landing unfazed on the wooden bench two feet below. But before I could rescue the little thing, it fell into the scum at the bottom of the tub, where it lay motionless.

Picking up its soft, flattened body between thumb and forefinger proved tricky—so easy to squish it—but I managed to lift it out of the muck and set it on a flagstone, where I could watch it at eye level while standing in the empty tub. It still didn't move, and its eyes were rolled up under their lids as if it had drowned. Gently, I dripped water on it from the hose. Wet and clean, the little lizard's marled brown pattern glistened. So close and vivid was the tiny creature that my eyes could *feel* the texture of its skin, could see its circulation through the skin of its throat. Still it didn't move. Either it's dying or it's just plain cold, I thought—and then, as the stone quickly dried and warmed in the sun, the wee lizard blinked—and was gone.

Gone. That fast. An illusion not just of movement, but of being. Disappeared so quickly it was as if the creature had *almost* been there. At the instant it had seemed most present, most real—luminous to the point of pulsing transparency—it wasn't there. Was this what ultimate reality was about? During the seconds it took me to refocus, everything around me seemed unreal—the blue-painted tub, the red stones of the patio, the cold-running hose in my hand. The only reality was the absent baby lizard.

I'm not sure what this perception has to do with ultimate reality, but I think it does have to do with wildness. Neither the baby lizard nor its larger relatives were what one would think of as paradigms of wildlife. And yet, familiar as the lizards were, they possessed a wild quality of being not-quite-there, seen-but-not-seen, about to be gone, gone.

It's a quality I've experienced with other wild creatures. The coyote I saw while riding the rimrock one winter evening, for instance. Trotting along nose-down through thin snow, weaving among stunted junipers and humpbacked rocks, it seemed unconcerned that a human on horseback was approaching. Sunset reddened every hair of its thick gold fur, its bushy tail was dark above, lighter below, and I could see the moist black nose, even the black lid-line below its amber eye, intent on the terrain. Yet something about it seemed not quite there, as if it could be anywhere, all around itself, where it was going and where it had been, all at once.

More recently, but again during a winter ride on the mesa, I and an architect friend from Aspen, Wayne Poulson, spooked a herd of about two dozen mule deer. Never had I seen so many deer together on the desert, and never any herd so close up. As they stotted and bounded past us, it was like being in a city, everybody running to catch the bus at once. But then they were gone, so absolutely it seemed they'd never been there. A flurry of wildness, a sense of presence so complete it left behind a palpable absence, a mystery Wayne and I both felt.

The most powerful sense of a wild animal's presence I've experienced in the desert happened while driving with friends Mike Moore, Susan Walp, and George Sibley down the Shafer Trail, from Island in the Sky to the Colorado River 1,200 feet below. Needless to say, it's a slow drive—so when we rounded a mass of boulders and saw a bighorn ram standing ten yards from the trail, we had a good look. In fact, to our surprise the ram didn't move, even when Mike drove closer and stopped the car. Tall as a deer, he stood facing us, forefeet close together. His summer coat gleamed metallic blue-gray, his great horns wrapped almost full-curl around the sides of his head, and the golden eyes that took us in through that frame of horn went all the way to the other side of a world we could not know. Mike shut off the engine. The ram stood still as a statue, head high, legs poised, gazing at us with neither fear nor arrogance nor interest. Only his nostrils moved.

Many minutes passed, in which everything but the ram disappeared. When Mike finally re-started the car and drove slowly by, the ram still did not stir. Like offerings to a god, we each spoke quiet words to him. Mike, obviously moved: *Bye, big guy...*Susan, with yearning: *You're so beautiful...* George, as if stunned: *Good luck, fella...*me, awed to the core, *Take care, neighbor...*As we drove away, the ram turned his head regally and looked back over his shoulder, as if to communicate with his herd up the gully behind him. He never moved his feet.

The ram didn't disappear abruptly, like the baby lizard or the bounding deer, nor seem to be everywhere at once, like the coyote. But his presence, his wildness, his life defined in his own mysterious terms, was so overwhelming that he made everything else disappear, including our selves. Feeling small or humble was irrelevant—for long minutes, we weren't even there.

And yet we were, the more so for the ram. As Mike guided the car down the rocky trail and we started to speak about what we had just experienced, what I heard in our voices was gratitude—thanks to the animal for being so completely itself, for staying put, for allowing us to lose ourselves in his presence. I don't know what it is about the wildness of animals that we humans need, but when it is given, it completes something in us we didn't know was missing.

Perhaps it's not even necessary that an animal be wild. Perhaps animals complete us in ways that don't require them to roam free, ways that wildness simply heightens and enhances. I think about the woman I passed once in the rain, on 91st Street between Columbus Avenue and Central Park West in Manhattan, a short woman with short gray hair, wearing an apron under her unbuttoned coat, wearing thick socks and flat-soled shoes and pushing a blue canvas baby stroller. On the seat rested a grimy white hen wearing a poodle sweater, and on the sunroof were perched two slate-blue pigeons, which may or may not have been tethered. My first thought was of birds bought at market and intended for the table—until I focused on the hen's doggy-sweater and frayed, soiled feathers, which gave the impression not of neglect but of overpetting. And the pigeons, the rock doves, perched on a crocheted afghan folded on the sunroof, in the rain. I turned to stare after them, but this sight of wildness, too, was gone, hidden by the woman's flapping coat. What I remember thinking was not "there but for the grace..." but "there *with* the grace..." —meaning that to be old and alone in the world without an animal for company seems to me to be very alone indeed.

Chapter Seven

The Covenant Animals

I first heard the phrase 'covenant animal' from a blacksmith named Britt. Setting down one of Aquila's hooves he'd just trimmed, he straightened up, stretched his back, and complimented Aquila's manners. "She's a keeper," he said. "Definitely a covenant critter."

When I asked what he meant, he ran a calloused hand through his graying hair and replied, "Well, some animals just seem to have evolved as human companions. It's as if somewhere way back, they agreed to be part of the human world in a way other animals don't. I'm mainly talking about horses and dogs, but in other countries it might be camels, or llamas."

"Or elephants...reindeer...yak..." Britt had me thinking globally.

"Yeah—animals that can survive wild, but let themselves serve humans in exchange for food and whatever else they get out of it. Lots of times it's a raw deal, but sometimes they get to live a better life than they would in the wild."

"And sometimes a more interesting life?"

"Mmm," he nodded. "Maybe, when they have a working life built around something they do naturally. Like hunting dogs, or race horses. And probably cowponies and jumping horses like what they do, even if it doesn't come so naturally. Just like herd dogs, or dogs that guide blind folks. They know their place."

"One thing about most dogs and horses is they'll do *anything* for you," I blurted, "as long as they trust you."

"And as long as they understand what you want," Britt cautioned, reaching down as Aquila raised her hoof into his hand. "That's why you've got a good'un here."

"What about cats? Are they covenant animals?" I asked, thinking of Mouse, the gray barn cat who lived wild but accepted saucers of milk and kibble.

"Cats—yes and no, I reckon. Sure wouldn't depend on one to save my life." Britt was ready to nail a shoe to Aquila's hoof. "What I don't get is these people who want to make fru-fru pets out of everything," he said, jamming a bunch of horseshoe nails in the corner of his mouth and temporarily ending the conversation.

I thought about the creatures around the ranch and the extent to which I had a mutual relationship with any of them. Britt was right: only with Koa and the horses did I have an ongoing partnership recognized by both of us. I had known that to live in solitude, at Horsethief or anywhere, I needed animal companionship—Koa, Aquila, even Mouse.

Maybe I didn't need Mouse, but I was glad to have him. More than most cats, he bridged a gap between wild and domestic, independent and attached. One of a litter of kittens who lived with their wild mother under a vacant house in town, he was brought to the ranch and turned loose in the greenhouse with food, water and a little milk. I didn't wish to make a housepet of the gray kitten, but also didn't want him so unapproachable I couldn't help him if he got hurt. Gradually he got used to the place, and though he is fast friends with Koa, he still doesn't know how to get along with humans. He makes himself scarce whenever there are guests, and disappears for days if they bring dogs.

Because I feed him, he tolerates me, and sometimes in winter asks for affection, mraowing under my window at night. Only then does he allow me to pick him up, warm his paws in my hands and sniff his desert-scented fur, while he purrs loudly. Twice on frigid nights I've let him in the house, but the first time he yowled until I let him out, and the second he invaded Koa's bed under the kitchen table, purring and rubbing against his buddy until Koa growled at him. Since Koa's comfort is more important than the cat's, Mouse stays out, keeping mice away from the house, haystack and tack shed where the horses' grain is kept. Healthy, handsome and tough, he's managed to elude coyotes, hawks, eagles, owls, and rattlers, leaving pugmarks I've recognized a mile away from the ranch.

Koa wears no collar except when we go to town, and has never been tied or enclosed. This is because even more than most dogs, his notion of freedom lies in staying close to his owner. In that sense he is very free indeed, since I take him everywhere I go except on airplanes. He's even been sailing a few times. On hikes and horse rides he roams within sight, scaring up cottontails or jackrabbits and chasing them with joyous, hysterical yelps. Even when he was young and fast he never caught one, and now that he's older and stiffening with arthritis, the rabbits can almost relax. He doesn't chase other wildlife or livestock.

I first saw Koa sitting with quiet dignity among six writhing siblings in the free puppy box at Rose Market in Telluride, Colorado. His alert face, calm demeanor and soft black coat trimmed with amber and white, reminded me of Bear, my last dog, whom I still missed. I phoned Rob, my then-husband, and the matter was settled. We'd recently spent a year in Hawai'i, so 'Koa' seemed an apt name, denoting in Hawai'ian the amber-and black-grained wood from which Hawai'ians had hollowed their sea-going canoes, and also 'brave, fearless warrior.'

Koa does happen to be an alert watchdog, but what makes him extraordinary is his intelligence, dignity and innate good manners. Always a prince, never a beggar, he responds best to being addressed in full sentences and courteous adult language. "Stay with me," I ask him when I want him to heel.

Usually, Koa's good manners supercede his appetite for play. He knows better than to interrupt me when I'm busy, but has a clever knack for finding moments to propose a game of stick or ball. "Fetch" is something I never taught him, nor did I teach him to 'throw' a ball by heaving it out of his mouth or pushing it with his nose. However, he's very good at showing others—adults, children, dogs—how to play such games. Once on a beach in Mexico, I looked up from reading to see Koa, far down the shore, surrounded by a Mexican family. As I watched, he pushed a giant red beach ball to each person in turn, patiently waiting for them to push it back.

Like Aquila, he responds eagerly to complexity. The more difficult I can make it for him to retrieve something, the more excited he is when he comes running back with it. Early on, I taught him to "Stay!" while I threw a tennis ball, instead of chasing it the instant it left my hand. When I finally said "Okay!" he raced to locate the ball, returning it with squeals of excitement. Without being asked, he promptly 'sat' again at my side—in hope, presumably, of gathering further evidence that a ball doesn't necessarily vanish if it's not chased immediately.

Another facet of Koa's intelligence is his sense of humor. As a little pup, the first game he made up could be described as "pounce on the ice cube and skid it around the kitchen floor." The first toy he invented was a green plastic flowerpot with a loop of macrame braid attached. He scampered around the yard, dragging the pot by its hemp rigging, growling a fierce puppy-growl, violently shaking the pot back and forth and whacking himself on the head with it. He'd play alone with the pot, but mostly enjoyed putting on a show for company.

Later, when we'd go camping, Koa made a joke out of finding logs the size of teepee poles, picking them up however he could get a grip with his teeth, and dragging them to the campfire, dropping them with a waggy grin. In winter this game is played with clods of icy snow ranging in size from grapefruits to large pumpkins, which he pounces on and pushes until they're scraped down to a size he can carry.

The range of Koa's vocabulary is as impressive as his playfulness and cool urbanity. Though he speaks only when cars approach the ranch, he understands and responds to far more words, phrases and concepts than any dog I've known. Place a stick, ball, frisbee and glove in a row, and he will fetch the item you request. He's familiar with a host of common animal names, from 'bug' to 'kitty' to 'cow,' and with many not-so-common ones, like 'pronghorn' and 'porky' (porcupine). When we're driving at night, he helps 'watch for deer' by focusing intently on the road ahead, whining with excitement if he sees one.

He knows many of my friends' names, and understands the concepts of arrival, destination, and mode of transportation—as in "Koa, guess who's coming tonight—Remo!" or "Koa, we're going to town today, in the truck"—and also time-oriented concepts like 'pretty soon,' 'for a while' and even 'tomorrow morning.' His willingness to accept unappetizing medication for his arthritis reflects a likely comprehension of its effect, and his dourness of spirit when stiffness overtakes him indicates an awareness of aging. He stares and whines after road-killed creatures on the highway, but whether this has to do with notions about death probably can't be determined. He doesn't whine or stare after tire carcasses on highways.

My awareness of Koa's mortality, on the other hand, grows sharper as he ages. I celebrate the days with him while bracing myself against the increasing incapacitation and eventual death of this most excellent friend, who has witnessed and participated in my joy and anger and sadness, and who is a door into my solitude and into the world's wild, unknowable otherness.

For even with our pets, familiarity is but a window. We love them because they are ours, responsive to and dependent upon us. And perhaps we also love them because they offer us these qualities out of their innate, long-ago wildness. They bless us, like angels from the ancient world of tooth and claw, fear and flight and exacting instinct. They are messengers who grace our lives and heal our distance from a natural world in which we can no longer easily abide, and from an historical world which for all good reason we have learned not to trust.

Horses have been a passion since my first pony ride at age two. When I turned five, my father took me for riding lessons whenever he could afford it. From then on, every cent I saved went into a piggy bank, which at the determined age of eleven I raided without my parents' knowledge and bought a palomino horse from the local polo stable where I'd worked summers and after school for three years. The little horse, whom I named Lucky, was my closest comrade and dearest friend until I turned fourteen and my parents decided it was time to put away such childish dreams—the most painful thing I ever had to do. Still, horses continued to draw me until in my twenties I began travelling. Later came marriage and more travel, until the marriage came undone and I began to search my life for what had nourished it before.

Through my job writing natural history films, I met Jack Snobble, retired teacher and skilled outdoorsman, and his two dozen Arabian horses. Among them was a dappled gray filly with a sweet dished face, large wide-set eyes, and a pink nose. Aquila, Jack called her: *ah Quill uh*, she-eagle in Latin, the daughter of Jack's stallion, Eagle. I'd been wanting to have a horse again, though I hadn't considered one so young I'd have to train her. But when Aquila followed me around the pasture, I melted. "Face," I called her: nothing but a pretty face. I spent all my spare time grooming her, handling her feet, getting her used to a saddle.

Because she was too young to ride, we went for long walks, me leading her uphill and down over the roughest country around, sometimes steep enough to bring us both to our knees. I led her through supermarket parking lots, traffic intersections, and suburban neighborhoods bustling with barking dogs, snarling lawnmowers, and kids on bicycles. 'Face' turned out to be more than pretty. She snorted, she danced, she got startled by big dogs and patted by tiny hands, she looked and listened, always with intelligent, trusting curiosity.

That autumn, although it would be a year before I moved there myself, I sent Aquila to the ranch with the other horses Jack was taking back there. The following April, while visiting, I took her for a walk. On impulse, I led her to a rock and eased onto her back. She turned her head and nuzzled my toe, and on we went, me guiding her with the halter rope. And so without fuss, our harmony continued to build. She's proved an exceptional riding horse, satin-gaited and more than willing. The rougher the terrain I ask her to negotiate, the more eagerness she shows. Attentive to voice signals—walk, trot, canter, whoa, stand—she takes pride in responding quickly, as long as I perk her interest.

On the other hand, she has the lowest boredom threshhold of any animal I've known. She disdains repetitive schooling exercises, doing them properly once or twice, then clowning or misbehaving if I ask for more of the same. She reacted as if to insult when I asked her to accept a bitted bridle instead of the rawhide bozal with which I'd begun her training. On that first bridled ride, she threw a snit—and her rider—reacting with wide-eyed surprise at what she'd done. Landing on my feet, I slipped back on without a word, knowing that to scold would give her something to think about repeating. It took weeks, but she learned to work well on a bit.

During my second October at Horsethief, among the trailerload of horses Jack returned to the ranch were two new animals he had been given for free. Jack's reputation as a horseman was such that he sometimes acquired horses this way. One was a short-legged, knobby-headed, roman-nosed little sorrel whom I fondly dubbed Charley (Horse) for his stiff gaits. The other—well, for every Mutt a Jeff. It was almost dark as we backed the horses out of the trailer, but even in the dusk I could see I was in trouble. The tall red thoroughbred whose lead rope I held gazed back at me with a profound aloofness. Not arrogance or meanness, simply an aware, detached distance. "Kicker," Jack told me he was called—but not because he kicked. On the contrary—pastured by his former owner with a flock of sheep who sometimes grazed too close, "Kicker" would lift a hoof and gently but firmly push the sheep away from him.

As I led the long-striding horse to the corrals, I had no thought of owning him, but every thought of making him mine. Next morning, I spent an hour talking softly to him as I groomed him, cleaning his hooves and combing out his long, flame-colored mane and tail. His manners were impeccable; his aloofness remained. Then I saddled him, and we went for a ride that shook me up in more ways than one. The big horse was so fast it was scary, but so manageable I was astonished. Like riding a tractable jack rabbit—but sadly, a lamed one. Part of what seemed to keep the poor horse in control were his tender forelegs. He had run only a few hundred yards when, despite his desire to gallop faster, farther, he slowed to a sore-legged trot. As I turned him toward home, he arched his neck and held his head sideways, teeth bared in his butter-soft mouth, cantering in place, balanced over his center of gravity like a live merry-go-round horse.

By the time we reached the ranch, Kicker had become Moriah, as in "they call the wind..." At the time, I didn't know the spelling or derivation of 'Mariah,' and had thought the wind in that song was masculine. And so 'Moriah' stuck, Moe for short. A week later I phoned his former owner, a woman I knew through Jack, and she told me his story. An abused ex-racehorse, foundered, lamed and broken in wind but not in spirit, he had come into her keeping as an eight-year-old—which meant he must have been in the winnings for six years on the track, where slow horses quickly become dogfood. The woman, who owned several other horses, had re-schooled 'Kicker,' to which he responded beautifully. But after four years, she realized she wasn't using him enough to justify keeping him. Reluctantly she gave him to Jack.

And reluctantly, Jack, who needed sound horses for his adventuresome trail rides, gave him to me. And gradually, Moriah allowed me inside the aloofness that was so deeply a part of his nature, his defense against an abusive world. At night when I checked the horses in the corrals, I spent a long time massaging Moe's legs and talking to him as I warmed my hands under his mane. Too proud to nuzzle me as Aquila or Shasta did, one night he lowered his fine head to my shoulder. As I scratched his forehead, he moved his head to receive the scratching around eyes, ears and jaw. After that, he began to accept mindful petting as a gesture no longer offensive to his professional taste.

Sometimes I think ahimsah, the Buddhist doctrine of "not-harming," is not enough, is too passive. Sometimes the golden rule is better: "*Do unto others...*" There is no sentimentality in kindness: kind ness is simply the deep recognition and respect due any creature's life, which like ours, can't help but include pain. To deny consciousness and intelligence to creatures other than ourselves is to hide behind our humanity, and I am continually stunned, when I read of the cruelties by which we have gained our place in the world, at what animals can forgive.

That is not to say that I believe their intelligence is simply passive, enduring. Quite the contrary. Though I have taught both children and adults, I've never seen higher excitement than that of a dog or a horse who has just learned something new, or performed to the best of its ability. During the summer of turkey-herding, my friend Susan and her sons, Billy and Tom, watched the ranch while I was away. Creator of the pastel drawing over Horsethief's fireplace, Susan is an artist whose skills and sensitivity began with horsemanship. While I was gone, at my invitation Susan worked with Aquila. The basics I had taught the mare had brought us to a plateau beyond which I didn't know how to proceed.

When I returned, Susan and I walked to the corrals while she gave her enthusiastic report. The horses sauntered over to listen, and as we talked, Susan slipped onto Aquila's back. Before any of us realized what was happening, Susan's gestures in describing what Aquila had learned compelled the mare to go through those same motions. Without saddle or bridle, guided only by Susan's legs, hands and balance, Aquila trotted and cantered in tight circles and figure eights, pivoted on her hind legs through fast 180-degree turns, parade-stepped, baby-stepped, and finally reared up on tucked hind legs in a controlled dressage pose.

As many riding events as I'd watched, I'd never seen anything like this—and neither, for all her experience, had Susan. When it was over, we hugged each other and the sweating, blowing mare—a mare whose sense of pride and accomplishment stood out like the veins in her neck.

Yet I shouldn't have been surprised. During an earlier visit Susan had ridden Moriah in the same corral, not teaching so much as discovering the moves he knew. These were a surprise to me—but not to Moe. As if the red horse had craved the opportunity to show himself at his best, he spun through figure eights, rollbacks, sidesteps, the entire repertoire of a well-schooled horse. Even Michael, visiting at the time, expressed amazement: "It's like he can't do enough to please her." "Or himself," I replied. For Moriah, the event marked a turning point—of allowing himself to settle in, to belong. Finally recognized for his abilities, his aloofness relaxed into simple pride, with the honesty and authenticity of any high-minded, whole-hearted creature.

Covenant animals—the good ones at least—want to know what their lives are for. Aquila, Moriah, and above all Koa, are impatient with mere affection and respond with far greater enthusiasm to challenge—whether for Koa it's the excitement of learning a new game, or for Aquila and Moriah the exhiliaration of using horsemind and horsebody in harmony with a rider. I believe that the love of learning is built into protoplasm itself; sadly, we seem to be less concerned with bringing it forth in our own species than with denying it to others.

Since Aquila, Moriah and Shasta remained at the ranch all year instead of traveling on Jack's trail rides like the other horses, they became close friends—by which I mean a mutual devotion equal to that of human friendship. One July afternoon while gardening, I heard one of the horses banging its hoof on a metal hay tank. This was Aquila's habit when alone or hungry—but she had Shasta and Moriah for company, and I knew they had plenty of hay. "Aquila, cut that out!" I yelled toward the corrals. But the banging persisted, so I went to investigate. There was Shasta, lying on her side next to the fence, hooves caught in the wire. No way to tell how long she'd been there, but a dark horse in the hot sun is not a healthy equation. A horse 'cast' on its side or upside down for long can develop serious, even fatal, digestive or circulatory problems.

Aquila and Moriah watched with intense interest as I pulled the fence-wire away, tied a soft rope to Shasta's fore and hind legs, and carefully rolled her over into a position from which she could rise—*if* she could rise. With her two friends nosing her head and neck, and with a little coaxing from me, she finally lunged to her feet and stood there dazed and groggy. Aquila and Moriah nosed her all over, as if trying to determine her condition, and stayed by her side as I led her around to make sure she wasn't lame or otherwise injured. The expression in Aquila's and especially in Moriah's eyes was not mere curiosity, but genuine concern.

I must say that Moriah is flat out the most compassionate animal I've ever known. Maybe this quality is the reverse side of his aloofness; possibly it stems from cruelties he witnessed as a racehorse. In any case I saw enough examples of it to be convinced. One spring day, for instance, while pushing the garden cart to the corrals for some dry manure, I was startled by a worried whinny. On the far side of a wire fence that separated two corrals, Moriah and Aquila stood side by side facing me. As Moe whinnied again, I saw that Aquila's foreleg was caught over the middle wire. I ran to help, but the mare's leg had gone into spasm and I couldn't lift it high enough to free it. Moe kept nosing Aquila's neck as if to reassure her, while I yelled to Michael's niece Sarah and her fiancé, Vitus, who fortunately were visiting.

While I held the weight of Aquila's leg off the wire, Sarah brought the cutting pliers. Moments later, I'd nipped the wire and released Aquila's foot. She wasn't cut, thank heaven, but I could feel the stiffness as I massaged her slightly swollen leg. Sarah was talking to Moe, and when I looked up I saw Moe's head against Sarah's chest, her arms around his neck. Next thing I knew, the big horse stepped all the way around Aquila to where I was kneeling with her foot, and lowered his head to mine. In his breathing I heard the thanks and trust he was trying to convey. It was a moment for which I remain profoundly grateful.

As much as can be learned from the behavior of the horses in the corrals, it's also interesting to watch them on the range. Grazing in a loose herd, they appear no different than a band of born-free wild horses—until you call them by name. After looking up startled, the horses walk toward you, then break into a run, the rumble of hooves becoming a thunder in your bones as they gallop up to you, snorting and milling around. As you greet them one by one, offering each a bite of carrot, the herd hierarchy settles out and you check each horse for cuts, bruises, lameness, eye or nose discharge or difficulty in chewing. You tweak a few cactus spines out of Karamar's rump, untangle sprigs of tumbleweed from manes and tails. You greet old red Snoopy by scratching his long ears, and the white mare Zamar by wiping the tear-crust from her eyes. Eagle allows you to stroke his fine-boned head briefly before charging, teeth bared, at Lazir, a feisty gelding who's too close to Shasta, Eagle's favored mare.

They know you have a bucket of grain in the jeep. While you crawl toward the ranch in granny gear, Shasta follows alongside, Eagle close behind, prancing like a desert unicorn to show that Shasta is *his* mare, not yours or anyone else's. The others trail along in their own order. You reach the corrals ahead of the straggling herd, open gates, hoist a couple of haybales from the stack and place piles of hay around the corrals, spacing them to reduce biting and kicking. One by two, the horses file in, and with little fuss, grab at the piles of hay.

The horses show up often enough of their own volition, without you bringing them in. But this time you need them for a special occasion. As you close the gate behind Snoopy, you think what fun it will be this evening, with a full moon, to treat a group of new friends from the Parks and town to a moonrise ride, pasta supper, and a soak in the hot tub. With no thought of mischief, you review the personalities of your friends and those of the horses in front of you. Who would enjoy whom the most?

One of my pleasures at the ranch was to share the horses with its guests. Few who wanted to ride were expert enough to go galloping over the range, but I enjoyed showing novice riders how to get the best out of their mounts, and introducing children and beginners to the desert on calm horses like Aquila, Shasta and Zamar. There is so much beautiful terrain it's hard to choose where to go, but one ride visitors enjoyed was a three-mile loop up over the mesa to the white rock, and back through dunes and arched rock formations. Guests marvelled at the panorama from the white rock, and the horses were drawn by the bug-free breezes that blew there. Aquila and Shasta liked it so much that several times when ridden by guests, they took their riders there without being guided.

The romance of having a personal wild horse herd came to an abrupt end in January of my third winter, when one of the worst things that could happen, happened. For several weeks I'd been noticing odd behavior from the white mare, Zamar. An 'old maid' who'd never been bred, she began hanging out with the geldings instead of with Eagle and his mares. Then she disappeared altogether. Duce stopped by to say he'd seen her a few days ago among his cows, and that today she was standing alone in the middle of nowhere, staring into space.

Aquila and I rode out to find Zamar where Duce had indicated, circling behind her to herd her home. But not until we came within thirty feet of her did she even sense we were there. I guessed she'd gone blind somehow—but even a blind horse would hear or smell another horse that close. When she startled violently, then neighed and came toward us, I knew something was very wrong. She threw her legs forward in a sort of goose-step, tripping every few paces as if she couldn't feel the ground. But she was eager to follow us, as best she could, back home.

Not until I gave her some grain in a tub on the ground outside the tack shed, did I realize what was wrong. While greedily pushing her nose into the grain, Zamar leaned her head against the wall of the shed. Instead of stepping back so she could lift her head, she panicked, leaning harder and pawing with her front feet at the shed, almost falling down in the process.

She was locoed. Badly. When had this begun? I'd never seen a locoed horse before, but—it was so obvious. Locoweed grew all over the range. Why hadn't I known?

I fed all the horses a good ration of hay and opened the gates between corrals so Zamar could join them, realizing she was so stoned she'd simply lost track of them out on the range. Feeling truly terrible about my failure to recognize what had been happening, I drove to the nearest phone to call Jack and the vet.

Doc Sorenson, the vet, said there was nothing to be done beyond keeping Zamar off the range and feeding her hay. He promised to copy all the information he had on locoweed and locoed horses so I could pick it up next trip to town. When I spoke with Jack, he seemed only mildly disturbed, and said he wouldn't have recognized the symptoms either. He'd be heading out to the ranch in a few days, he said, and we'd see what, if anything, could be done.

When I got back to the ranch, Aquila and I went to look for Bruja, another white mare who'd come in with the horses the day before I found Zamar. Being shy, she'd stayed outside the gate. Now she was missing, and our search led nowhere. Was she locoed too? I felt desperate to find her, desperate to make both horses well.

The next day, Duce came by again to tell me he'd found a white mare up among the junipers on the way to the white rock, dead. "Looks like you've got a problem on your hands, girl," he said with rough sympathy.

Oh, Bruja. I rode Moriah toward the white rock. Bruja was lying with her head against a stone at the end of a swatch of madly churned up sand and brush. She'd fallen, apparently, and pawed her body along for thirty feet trying to get up. Though she could have died of another cause, the fact that she'd gone so far away from the herd wasn't normal, and indicated she'd been as severely locoed as Zamar. I stroked her sandy neck and combed knots out of her long tangled mane with my fingers. The ravens had already taken her eyes.

O you gods. How could I not have known?

I went to town to call Jack again and pick up the information from the vet. By the time I finished errands and got back to Horsethief, it was about 10 p.m. Unloading the jeep, I heard strange noises from the corrals. I went to check, and found—horror of horrors—Zamar upside down in the big oval hay tank. Her neck, head and legs protruded; she had worn her legs bloody thrashing to get out. Still alive, she was trapped in the tank as in a coffin.

The tank with Zamar in it was far too heavy for me to tip over so I could pry it away from her, and her legs were flailing so that I couldn't get close with a knife to put her out of her misery. Calling Koa, I ran to the jeep and raced to Duce's camp—only to find he had neither a gun or any merciful drugs on hand. I sped on to Dead Horse Point, woke Bonnie and Stephen and quickly related the problem. Bonnie was on call and couldn't leave, but offered me her .357 service revolver. Stephen intervened, saying he'd go back with me and take his .22 rifle, insisting it was adequate for such a sad task.

By the time we got there, it didn't matter. Poor Zamar, the sweet, steady, utterly dependable old mare who had brought my nephew David through his fear of horses, was dead. I closed her eyelids with a prayer of thanks for her life and her spirit, kissed her nose, and cried hard, knowing that however locoed, she'd sensed and felt what was happening to her.

In the morning, the metallic smell of terror, blood and death was still nauseating. Aquila and Moriah were very distant toward me, as they had been in the night, when, after turning the other horses out, I'd put them in another corral, away from Zamar'a body. The basis of their logic may have been limited, but their conclusion couldn't be faulted: Zamar had been in agony, and I'd driven off and left her to die.

Duce arrived as Stephen came out of the house. Where did I want to put Zamar's body? I thought about a final resting place, while Duce and Stephen secured a tow chain around Zamar's coffin. Then, with me leading the way on Aquila, and Duce and Stephen following in Duce's truck towing the tank, our little funeral cortege pulled Zamar out the driveway and along a sandy trail to a juniper-shaded ledge a half mile away. My friends pried the steel tank from Zamar's body and hauled it back to the corrals, where I later scrubbed the blood and reek of terror from it. Meantime, I stood with Aquila and wept, repeating my thanks to this good horse's spirit, asking forgiveness for the suffering I'd been too ignorant to prevent.

When Jack arrived, we compared notes on what we'd learned about locoweed: that this insidious member of the legume family is toxic in all its parts—roots, stems, leaves, flowers and seed pods—at all times of year. That it contains alkaloids which are powerfully addictive and cumulatively toxic to the central nervous system of cattle, sheep and goats as well as horses. That well-fed horses seldom eat it, but that a hungry horse who tries it quickly becomes hooked. That once addicted, always addicted.

Jack stayed only long enough to inspect the two dead mares he had bred and raised, trained and treated kindly for twenty years—and to try to relieve me of the terrible responsibility I felt for their deaths. For days afterward, light snow fell from the cloud of fog that covered the desert, and whenever I looked out the window into the flakes, I saw Zamar and Bruja standing patiently at the front gate. The two mares entered my dreams in the same way, until finally I walked out with Koa and sat with Zamar's body in the falling snow, white covering white, until it was too dark to see.

During the next month, I frequently rode Aquila or Moriah out to visit the two bodies, not from morbidity, but in hope that witnessing the natural process of disintegration might help me heal, and perhaps allow my two alienated friends to recognize my sorrow and forgive me. Mercifully, that did happen, but not until spring, when as I've related, Moriah brought my attention to Aquila's plight. Only then was our trust—our covenant—re-established.

Trust. It's such an enormously important quality in any relationship, and so essential to the human/horse covenant. By their nature, most dogs will help create the trust they have in their owner. With most horses, it must be earned. Let me take a few steps *forward*, and introduce Blackie, a wild mustang who taught me much about the nature of trust.

Knowing I would eventually leave the ranch and take Aquila and Moriah with me, I became concerned, during my fourth winter, about what to do so Shasta wouldn't be left alone when Jack took the other horses away for the summer. One day in March, stopping by the BLM office to deliver my precipitation report, I saw a flyer for an "Adopt-A-Wild-Mustang" lottery, to be held in April at the Moab equestrian center. The perfect opportunity, I thought, to provide a companion for Shasta.

With my usual fools-rush-in enthusiasm, I made arrangements—filled out forms, obtained Michael's approval, asked Duce if he'd haul the mustang home in his stock trailer. On lottery morning, I went to town early so I could, along with a crowd of other hopeful adopters, inspect the mustangs—stallions, mares with and without foals, yearlings and two-year-olds—and make a list of preferences to choose from, when and if my name was drawn.

At first I was taken aback by the small size of the horses. But after a BLM ranger assured me they could "carry Santa and his pack with no trouble," I became captivated by these frightened, ultra-wild equines, who milled and darted in their pens like schools of fish. Most were dun and buckskin, along with a few blacks, and all of them had a characteristic head shape that made them appear somehow ancient. From the application brochure, I knew they came from remote desert mountains in western Utah, where they'd belonged to one of the few wild horse herds in North America whose lineage is purely Spanish—as distinguished from other herds descended from cavalry or ranch stock.

The evolution of the horse was something I'd studied since I was old enough to read. Now my mind flashed on the fact that horses had evolved in North America, crossed the Siberian land bridge, continued to evolve on the Asian steppes, and become covenant companions in the tides of human conquest that swept west across Eurasia into the Middle East, and with the Moors across North Africa to Spain. The hairs of my nape rose as I realized that the terrified, weaving horses in front of me were as close as I would likely get to the prehistoric animals who had fascinated me all my life. That I might soon own one was suddenly a thrill beyond belief.

But as the lottery drawing went on and my name wasn't called, anxiety rose. There were, after all, fewer horses than people who wanted them. When the final name was called and a stranger claimed the last mustang, I nearly wept. I almost didn't hear the BLM announcer say that those whose names hadn't been called should stick around, since glitches sometimes happened that would make a horse or two available. But I did hear, and I stuck around talking to a BLM ranger about how they chose which horses to round up, while the mustangs were run through a chute, wrestled into halters and loaded into trailers to be taken to new homes.

Then a Navajo man handed his claim ticket and papers to the BLM ranger I was talking to. "I cannot keep this horse," the man said quietly. "He is too young, too small. I need horse to ride now, for cattle." The ranger reviewed the papers and turned to me. "You're next on the list," he said. "The horse is number 316, if you want him. I think he's a black yearling."

I looked at my own list. Number 316 was on it about halfway down. "Yes, I want him," I said.

As I paid my money and signed papers, I realized I had another problem. No one had mentioned until the lottery was over that all adopted horses had to be taken away immediately or be forfeited. Duce wasn't due until later that afternoon. The ranger suggested I talk to a rancher whose mustang was just then being loaded. "He's a nice guy. His ranch is about a hundred miles north. Maybe if you offered him gas money, he'd take your horse to your place on the way."

And so the arrangement was made, and the rancher waited for the black colt to be haltered and loaded. But the colt had other ideas, like escape, like flying. He was a dozen feet into the chute when he tried to climb over its eight-foot high steel rails, and kept trying, until he had all four legs off the ground and one forefoot over the top. "Jeemus!" the ranger exclaimed, "I never saw a young'un do *that* before. He's like a monkey!" A ranger in the chute was hanging onto the colt's tail, trying to pull him down, while three more rangers ran to help. It took all of them to get the colt to the ground uninjured, and to hold him while they put on the halter I'd brought, with its requisite twenty-foot lead rope. Finally they got him into the trailer, where the rancher's mustang was already loaded, and he calmed down a bit.

What have I gotten myself into? was the obvious question as we caravaned along the route to Horsethief. The rancher's wife backed the trailer up to the corral gate, and we hazed the black colt into a corral without mishap. "We better get that halter off him, afore he hangs himself," the rancher said, picking up the long lead rope and gently shaking it until the colt jerked back and the oversized halter slipped from his head. Spooking at the snaky thing in front of him, the colt wheeled and headed straight for the six-foot high cedar post fence, on the other side of which Moriah, Aquila and Shasta watched intently. Only their presence, I thought later, kept that colt from crashing through the posts and impaling himself.

The rancher and his wife refused to take any money, but did accept a bag of fresh greens from the garden. "It was worth the side-trip just to see this place," said the wife. "You're living on a piece of history."

And now I had another piece of history in the corral. A furious, frightened, shaggy little horse with a string around his neck and a yellow tag that told his name: #316. When I came to the gate, he raced to the other side. If I entered, he pressed against the fenceposts so nervously I feared he might try to go over them. When I left, he returned to his *querencia*, the spot where he felt safest, next to the posts that separated him from the other horses.

I'd never gentled a wild horse, but it didn't take long to see I would get nowhere with the other horses around to create a herd, a support group for the colt's wild instincts. As I turned my three equine friends loose, the colt raced around his corral, stopping only to whinny forlornly after them. "I'm your herd now, little guy. But don't worry, we're going to be friends." I kept talking to him softly from outside the gate as he raced and whinnied. Then I slipped inside and sat quietly in the sand. He stopped and faced me, snorting, then tore back and forth on the far side of the corral, wheeling and bucking. After about ten minutes, I slowly stood up and eased out the gate, put some hay in the tank for him, and left him still whinnying for the other horses.

After two days, I still couldn't get near him. "It's time for some tough love, little guy," I told him. That evening I gave him no hay. Next morning, again I sat in the sand, crooning softly as I'd done several times each day. The colt would take a few steps toward me, then wheel and bolt. Same thing that evening. After two days of no feed, I shook a flake of hay into the hay tank, then sat on the edge of the tank and held out a handful. "If you want to eat, pony, you're going to have to come to me." By that evening, I could sit on one end of the tank and the colt would grab mouthfuls from the other, but wouldn't let me touch him. Something else was called for, and I didn't know what.

The weather was warm, the moon almost full, so I decided to sleep in the corral with him that night. He almost went over the fence again when I carried in a polyfoam pad and put it in *my* spot, on the far side of the corral from his. Around midnight, I unrolled my sleeping bag, tucked my clothes at the bottom and crawled in. I fell asleep with the image of the little mustang standing in his spot, head down like the horse at the end of the trail.

I was wakened at dawn by something nuzzling my toes through the sleeping bag. Don't move, I thought. Don't scare him. For ten minutes or so I pretended to sleep, while the colt nudged my feet. When I moved, he wheeled away. But not *all* the way away. Moving slowly, I dressed, rolled up the bag, and toted it and the pad into the tack shed, thinking, I'll try it again tonight and see what happens. When I turned around, to my amazement the colt was rolling in the sand where the pad had been, as if to get the scent of it on him, as a dog might do.

After breakfast I again sat on the tank and offered the colt hay. This time he grabbed it from my hand, and by evening I could reach out and touch his neck while he ate. He flinched, but didn't bolt. That night I woke to my legs being nuzzled, and come morning the colt again rolled where I'd slept. At the hay tank, he didn't flinch when I stroked his neck. Again the next morning he rolled in my spot, and later let me scratch his back. On the fourth morning I woke to something nibbling my hair, the same something's breath on my face. Ever so slowly, I breathed back. Breathed back his name. *Blackie, pony, Blackie Blackie...*

From then on, progress accelerated. I slept in the corral one more night and woke to Blackie nuzzling my face. Carefully, carefully, I rubbed the hair above his nearest hoof. Wonder of wonders, he stayed put. Later that day, he let me run my hands slowly up and down all four of his legs, rub him all over and scratch around his tail, all of which he seemed to like. The next day he followed me around all three of the connected corrals. I even cut the string and tag from his neck. But I couldn't get near him with a halter.

Blackie had never tasted grain, but it took only one handful for him to relish his morning ration of sweet-feed, which I fed him by sitting on the tack shed step, grain bucket between my knees, halter held open above the grain. I thought it would be fairly easy to get him to put his nose through the halter to reach the grain, whereupon I could buckle the halter while he ate.

It wasn't easy. It took three days before Blackie quit jerking his head up when I tried to buckle the halter. Finally I got the strap through the first part of the buckle, and *almost* had the prong through the hole. One more day, and...

That day a photographer friend, Bill Ellzey, showed up for an overnight. Soft-spoken, a gentle man, Bill had been raised on a Texas cattle ranch, and volunteered to help. While we leaned elbows over the gate catching up on news, I described Blackie's performance in the loading chute. Bill nodded, then asked for the halter and lead rope. "This oughtn't to take long," he drawled as he stepped into the corral. "He's such a little fellow, it might even be easy."

Blackie was wary, but allowed Bill to approach and pet him. When Bill dropped the halter on the sand, Blackie snorted and jumped away. Bill soothed and petted him some more, slowly easing the lead rope around the mustang's neck. Next thing I saw was a flurry and a struggle—then both Blackie and Bill sprawled on the ground with one of Blackie's hooves in the pocket of Bill's canvas jacket. Blackie was up and on the other side of the corral before Bill got to his feet, and when he did, he was holding one hand with the other. "Just a little rope burn," he said dismissively. "Should've worn my gloves." Then added, "That's one tough little horse."

I stepped toward Blackie, but he moved away. "We can try again tomorrow," I said, "but let's get that hand taken care of first."

I'd been so close to getting the halter on and buckled, and didn't want that work undone. I especially didn't want any more injuries, including to anyone's ego. Bill, too, saw that discretion was the better part of valor. As we sipped some wine and barbequed some ribs he'd brought, he told me he'd planned to be on the road early next morning anyway. "Besides," he said wryly, tapping his bandaged palm, "This won't be in shape for haltering much besides Koa."

The next day I spent getting Blackie relaxed again with the halter/grain bucket ruse. The day after, the blacksmith was coming to shoe the three adult horses. Britt, the farrier who'd told me about 'covenant animals,' had moved to Argentina. The farrier I used now, Dan Flower, was a skilled saddlemaker and horse trainer. He was also a good judge of wines—a stranger in a strange land—and I'd invited him and his girlfriend Terri for supper after he'd finished shoeing.

Dan's response to Blackie was much the same as Bill's: "Such a little guy, it shouldn't take but a few minutes to halter him up." Three hours later, after Dan had tried the same method at which Bill had failed and several others, Blackie was still unhaltered and it was getting late. But Dan's lessons had resulted in Blackie developing an obvious respect for Dan. If Blackie chose to run around the corral, for instance, Dan kept him running past the time Blackie wanted to stop. When Dan let him rest, the colt let himself be petted. He even let Dan ease the halter around his neck, but not his head.

"I'm going to have to rope him," Dan said finally, dusk settling around us. "It's going to scare him—he's been roped before when he was brought in from the wild—but at this point it's all I can do." Fashioning a lariat from the twenty-foot soft cotton rope I'd used on lottery day, Dan swung the loop around his head—whereupon Blackie went crazy, racing, bucking, mad for escape. Dan's first toss missed—and sent Blackie crashing through a gap between upright corral posts. Terri and I screamed, sure he'd impaled himself on the post he'd snapped off, but mercifully the colt was instead supported by it, teetering as if on a seesaw.

We eased Blackie off the broken post. Miraculously, he had only minor scratches. Then we roped off the opening he'd made. It was almost dark. While Terri and I guarded likely points of escape, Dan built another loop, swung it and missed again, sending Blackie careening in crazy circles. On the third try, Dan's loop fell around the colt's neck. Setting his boot-heels in the sand, Dan, gloved, held tight as Blackie reared straight up, again and again, pawing and biting at the rope. Then he raced in a circle, from which Dan gradually brought him under control. The last of this Terri and I could see only because the rope was white. When we heard Dan talking to Blackie, we joined them. The dreaded rope was on the ground, the lathered colt was wearing his halter. "Time for a glass of wine, wouldn't you say?" suggested Terri.

Blackie had fought well. Soon he'd understand that he had won, that he was part of a herd of humans as well as of horses, that he would learn much and receive good care. What the BLM ranger had told me rang true: that Blackie and his kin were the very wildest of wild horses, but when one of them bonded with a human, that bond was as unbreakable as the horse's spirit.

One autumn night, when the season's melancholy reinforced a wave of sadness over news I'd received in town, I went out with Koa to the corrals. Shasta and Blackie were nibbling hay, Moriah and Aquila standing together in the moonlight. I sat in the sand at my two horses' feet, stroking the strong legs that stood around me like trees. All of a weary sudden I felt overwhelmed by uncertainty and fear. What would happen to us? Where would we go when we had to leave here? How could I take my horses with me? Worse, how could I leave them behind?

I cried these questions to the desert night, to the equine silhouettes above me. Blackie walked over and all three horses lowered their heads to mine, Moriah breathing his deep, calm breaths, Blackie licking my salt tears, Aquila nuzzling my neck. We stayed that way for many minutes, until sorrow subsided and slowly I stood up, knowing that no human friends could have offered more comfort.

Chapter Eight

A Matter of Life

He arrived at the front gate the day after Christmas of my first year, driving a battered pickup and holding out a map to the ranch. "Hello," he said as I came up to his truck, "I'm Ken. I'm a friend of Michael's. He told me I should come see his ranch. Is this the place?"

"You're here," I said, pulling open the gate. As he drove in, I noted blond, boyish good looks saved from cliché by a strong jaw-line and an odd grid of scars around his left eye and cheekbone. I guessed he was around twenty-five, probably gay in that unobtrusive male way that some of Michael's friends were gay. His green eyes combined awareness and intelligence with a kind of edgy *nolo me tangere*.

My sister Nance and her family were visiting for the holidays, so I apologized for being unable to accommodate him in the main house, and turned on the heater in the bunkhouse. Then we went on a tour of the dry, bare grounds—leafless trees, frosted garden, skeletal orchard, and the corrals, hot tub, and spring. I learned that Ken was a landscape designer, like my sister, and had also studied chemical engineering. His voice, boyish like his face, was interested, informed, articulate. When we reached the house, I introduced Nance, Dave, Malli and David, Jr., who lived in New Mexico, where Ken grew up. As they swapped wherefores, I glimpsed in him a distinct reticence. He was courteous, even friendly, but he held his distance.

During the first days of his visit, Ken kept to himself, exploring the canyons, always bringing back a pickup load of firewood. On New Year's Eve day, he returned from an excursion to town and offered to make dinner for us. "Game hens. It's an old family recipe—you bake them with wine, mushrooms, carrots, and some herbs and spices." What kind? Nance, also an avid cook, wanted the recipe. "Oh, you know," Ken said smiling. "Just herbs and spices." Reticence was beginning to give way to teasing.

And what a meal—the first of many superb feasts prepared by this inscrutable young man. Later, while Dave and the kids played Trivial Pursuit by the living room hearth, Nance and I got into a deep discussion about the tensions and contradictions of our childhood. Our father had been an abusive alcoholic who nonetheless loved and provided for his family and treated us well when he was sober. Ken listened quietly, occasionally adding insights that seemed to come from a quest of his own. At midnight, he said he was going for a walk, and as he left we all exchanged New Year wishes and hugs. Ken's were formal and distant. The reticence was back.

Nance and family left the next morning, and Ken stayed on in the bunkhouse. Winter so far was snowless, continuing the two-year drought. Daily Ken went off exploring, returning at dusk with a load of firewood and stories to tell about where he'd been, what he'd seen, the ruins and artifacts he'd found. Within a week, he knew more about the desert for twenty miles around than I did after months of living here and years of visits. And daily the cordwood stacked by the corrals grew higher—all the more remarkable since the ranch chainsaw had succumbed to the rule of threes, and Ken sawed and split by hand all the wood he brought home.

One morning as I was getting ready to leave for town, Ken asked if I were going to take Koa, "or could he come along with me?" Instead of saying my dog always went where I went, I hesitated only a second before replying that I thought Koa would be much happier riding around in Ken's pickup, hiking and gathering firewood, than he would be going to town. "He can go with me any time," I said, suspecting a touch of lonely in this loner. "Besides, he'll help you rustle up wood. Just tell him to 'get that stick!'"

When I returned from town in the winter dusk, Ken's pickup was parked by the bunkhouse, but was still filled with wood, which he'd always unloaded in the back yard. Koa appeared out of the dark, wagging his tail excitedly in greeting as we walked toward the lamplight glowing from the bunkhouse. Ken was sizzling something on the stove as I knocked, entered, and asked how his day had been. "Well, it was eventful..." He laughed a little.

"Oh? Did you find another white spear point?" I teased, becoming aware of clothing spread over chairs and hung above the propane heater.

"No, it was a little more eventful than that," he replied, eyes turning serious. "In fact, I'm not sure you'll want to hear about it." Of course I did, adamantly. And so, as he made his supper, he told me. "We went down to the riverbottoms. I thought it would be a good place to find some cottonwood logs. We drove upstream to the mouth of Hell Roaring Canyon and found that Denis Julien inscription you told me about. On the way back we stopped at a cottonwood grove next to the river, where there was a lot of deadfall.

"The river's frozen all along its banks, and in some places all the way across. I was dragging a log to the truck when I heard a crash, like ice breaking. Koa was nowhere in sight, so I ran for the river. There he was, paddling hard in a bunch of broken ice, but getting swept downstream toward where it's frozen all the way across—and you know how strong that current is.

"I shouted to him, but he could only swim crossways downstream, not upstream. I jumped out on the rim ice, and it held, but the current was shoving Koa up against the solid ice and pushing him under. Christ, I thought, he's going to drown. So I jumped in.

"I had no idea how deep it was, or how cold. Luckily, it only came up to my chest, so when I got to Koa, I could sort of stand up. I think I grabbed him by his ears and tail, poor guy, but anyhow I threw him up on the ice and yelled at him to go to the truck. Then I used my elbows to break the ice back toward shore where it was shallower and I could climb out."

"Dear God, Ken. You must have been frozen, " I said, trying to take in what had happened.

"I tell you, I was so full of adrenalin I couldn't even feel the cold. I loaded wood for another half hour before I realized I better get back here and put on some dry clothes."

Letting out a long breath, I glanced around the dimly lit room draped with wet clothing— sweater, levis, socks, longjohns, gray Patagonia, tan windbreaker. At Ken standing there in dry longjohns and navy turtleneck, bare feet on the wooden floor, spatula in hand, flipping the omelette he'd been constructing.

"I don't know how to thank you. I owe you a life."

"He's a great dog," Ken said. "Don't be surprised if he's hungry tonight."

As Koa and I walked through the dark over to the main house, I felt stupefied by wonder, overwhelmed by gratitude. Would I have had the courage to save my own dear dog? When I peeled off my gloves to pet Koa, his fur was damp in places. He was still excited, but whether by what he'd been through, or by our reunion after a day apart, was for only him to know. He kept talking playfully in a sort of singsong howl, woo woo woo woo woof, as if he wanted to say something, and he ate all the extra food I gave him.

Neither Ken nor Koa suffered ill consequences from the river, and over the next few days my talks with Ken grew warmer and more open. Occasionally we cooked and ate supper together in the main house, delving into our relationships with parents, our ways of looking at experience. He was candid about his youth in New Mexico, where his closest friend had been Navajo, and where he had participated in tribal initiation rites, including a peyote ceremony. He also told me about his life in Boulder,

Colorado, and the man his own age whom he loved. Honored as I was by his trust, I still sensed pieces missing, chunks held back.

At the end of that week, I had to leave for a few days, so I asked Ken if he would mind looking after things in my absence. He said he'd be glad to; Boulder offered little landscape work in winter, so his time was free. Reassured that the place would be in competent hands, the only question became whether to take Koa with me or leave him with Ken—a question I couldn't believe I was asking myself. "Don't worry, I'll be fine," Ken assured me. "I'm used to being on my own." Almost reluctantly, I took Koa with me.

When I returned, the first snow had fallen, and Ken was itching to move on. "I think I'll go see Las Vegas while I'm this far west. I feel like I'm in kind of a gambling mood," he laughed. "I've never done that before—maybe it's time to see what all the fuss is about." And so he left, saying he'd be back in the spring, "or maybe sooner."

Two weeks later he returned. By then it was February and another friend was visiting, Kirsten Dehner, with whom I shared an interest in both horses and words. We had, in fact, just brought the herd of horses in from the range when Ken drove in at dusk. Declining our invitation to stay in the main house, he toted his pack and sleeping bag into the bunkhouse, saying he'd just be spending the night and leaving for Boulder in the morning.

He accepted our invitation to supper, however, and I watched him relax with Kirsten, whose candid warmth and forthright interest brought out Ken's trust and confidence. As he opened up emotionally, I sensed purpose in his visit, but didn't see what was happening until he related his trip to Las Vegas and his reason for returning to the ranch.

"I came to thank you," he said, turning to me as I stirred soup at the stove. I waited, puzzled. "Yes, I went to Vegas, but I only stayed two days. I even won some money," he added, giggling as if money were irrelevant, instead of the holy grail of Vegas. "But I wasn't comfortable. It was like there was some other kind of chance I was supposed to be taking, something more real and risky. I found myself sitting at a bar in Caesar's Palace one night thinking about what you said to your sister at New Year's, about having to forgive not only our parents, but our parents' parents, and *their* parents, back through all the generations that screwed up their kids."

"I was trying to help Nance understand our father's life," I said, ladling soup into bowls. "The way he was trapped by his Germanic upbringing, by having to find work in the Depression, by starting a family during World War II. He loved us, and he got nasty when he drank. I guess everybody's life requires some forgiveness, but it took me years to reconcile the opposites."

"Forgiveness, understanding—maybe they're the same thing," Ken said, musing. "There was a lot of of abuse in my family, too—physical, emotional, sexual. And witchery," he added, raising an eyebrow, offering a behind-the-mask glimpse into something so ominous I couldn't imagine it. "My mother's beyond talking to—she rationalizes too well. But I thought if I went home, maybe I could talk to my father and get this out where we both could look at it. So that's where I've been. Gambling, in New Mexico," he said with a little shrug.

"And you drove all the way back to Utah to tell me this? That's three hundred miles out of your way," I asked, bewildered.

"Well? Did you win?" Kirsten interjected, keeping things on track.

"I'm not sure. We talked, and he admitted a lot of stuff. But where it will lead is anybody's guess. Maybe we'll get closer, maybe we won't. Right now it's just confusing. For both of us."

"Do you think the abuse in your family has to do with your being gay?" Kirsten pushed.

"Probably not. I knew I was gay when I was five years old. That's not anything you blame anybody for, that's just the way you find out you are. But it may have to do with the years I spent screwing around doing crazy things."

I listened hard as I put bowls of soup on the table. Ken, during his previous stay, had told me about some of those crazy things. I sensed there was something I should know but was blind to, key pieces about to fall into place. And now Kirsten was voicing concern for a friend who had recently discovered he had AIDS, but was in a stage of denial. And then Ken was saying, "It's been six years since I knew I was HIV-positive, and I've gone through a lot of stages, but I still..."

The pieces precipitated. Reticence. Skimpy hugs. Koa about to drown, Ken chest-deep in frigid water, heaving Koa to safety, breaking ice with his elbows. Sheer jeopardy.

Ken returned several times that winter to the ranch, becoming one of its most frequent and welcome visitors. Though he slept in the bunkhouse and spent most of his time exploring alone, we took turns cooking dinner in the main house, each striving to create meals to delight the other. Ken excelled with Thai and Indonesian dishes—rich, exotic, zingy hot. I knew no specific cuisine, but usually managed to put together flavors that worked.

The best ingredient in our meals, though, was conversation. All trace of reticence vanished as Ken sensed that he was accepted without pity, appreciated without condescension, admired without cynicism. Our talks chose their own paths, questions drilling into darkness, leaping from intuition to self-revelation until some long-trapped logic of the heart found utterance and a new comprehension breathed in the room like a visiting angel. Not only was he one of the most lucid and articulate people I'd ever met, he was one of the most whole and healthy—emotionally, intellectually, spiritually, even physically. His self-knowledge on all these fronts was—is—as balanced as it is brilliant, joining the rigor of a scientist with the intuition of a shaman.

I couldn't have chosen a better person from whom to learn about being HIV-positive, or about having AIDS. If my initial ignorance was abysmal, Ken's deep knowledge was more than a match, as was his willingness to educate and his ability to elucidate. I cringe to recall one of my early questions about how the disease is transmitted. My friends Edgar and Elizabeth and their two young sons were coming to visit, and we would all be using the hot tub at various times. I had told them about Ken, including that he was HIV-positive, and I told Ken that I had. He seemed not to mind my giving away secrets that had taken him years to be open about. Nor did he bat an eye when I asked that most naive of questions: How do I assure my friends that they and their kids can use the same hot tub you do without risk?

By the time he'd explained about the virus and its narrow limit of tolerance to temperature and medium, I felt as if I'd stepped from fuzziness into clarity. I recalled what I'd learned in microbiology about the general behavior of viruses. That led to specific questions about the HIV retrovirus and the insidious way it transforms elements of the immune system, primarily CD4+ lymphocytes, into nurseries for the production of more virus. Ken described the process by which the HIV virus tranforms its RNA into DNA, then inserts that DNA into the immune cell's DNA, where it instructs the immune cell to make many copies of the original infective virus—literally turning the body's immune system against itself.

Ken's knowledge was all the more extraordinary for its lack of self-centeredness. He was as interested in others' processes as he was in his own, holding to a balance between objectivity and compassion that seemed innate, yet tuned and disciplined. He used his background in chemistry to evaluate everything that became known about AIDS worldwide, and he shared what he knew with anyone who asked.

Early on, he'd admitted that landscape design was an avocation, and that his main interest, on which he wanted to build, was "importing and distributing pharmaceuticals." In my then-ignorance, I teased him: "Why not come right out and say you deal drugs?" He had the grace to be amused. "It's not the same thing," he said, explaining that from his trips to Thailand and Indonesia he imported antibiotics useful against opportunistic diseases, and in Europe gleaned the latest research on treatment practices and set up imports of HIV drugs not yet approved by the U.S. Food and Drug Administration.

He also imported the drugs themselves, with the FDA's knowledge if not approval. "There's really nothing they can do about it," he said. "Entry inhibitors, peptide-T, whatever researchers come up with, all fall into the category of mercy treatment. The FDA can deem something experimental and hold up its distribution for years until their rigorous criteria are met, but they can't prevent it from being used by people who are dying of an incurable disease."

And so he sold most of what he imported to buyers' clubs, AIDS support groups, and individuals, and provided medications gratis to those who couldn't afford them. When a new drug appeared on the international market, Ken often tested it as part of his own regimen, partly to decide what was best for his own therapy, and partly because one of his major concerns was laboratory quality control. He worked with, and sometimes against, his own medical doctor, who was among the best AIDS specialists in the West. "He thinks I'm not cautious enough, I think he's too conservative. When it's my life, I choose. When it's something I'm acquiring for someone else, I listen to him."

Not only medically, but psychologically, spiritually, and in the deepest meaning of sexually, Ken pursued, explored and participated in himself, layer after layer, with and without guidance. I glimpsed a spirit that soared, keen and relentless, zeroing in whenever he sensed movement in what he called "the shadows." Often I felt my own perspectives reinforced by his, and after several of our talks I wrote down what I remembered. For example:

> When you're learning to deal with your mortality, you have to go in and grasp those shadows and learn them, over and under and inside out. Learn what casts them, how faraway it is, its heat and energy, what direction it's moving in, like you would do with a dream, so you can judge what is the proper size of the shadows and not let them loom, or subside into false and treacherous insignificance.

He seemed unafraid of sadness, or if he was afraid, his fear itself took the form of grief. Several times he came to the ranch to mourn for one friend or another who had died. Upon occasion he grieved for the fact of the disease itself. "It's sad, it's just sad," he said, head in his hands, and I sensed his sorrow for himself as well as for others, a sorrow as devoid of self-pity as it was real and inescapable.

Another time he spoke more philosophically, though somberly, about being gay as "an evolutionary dead end," as he called it, "a sidetrack, like the dinosaurs." I reminded him that dinosaurs were hardly an evolutionary sidetrack, and that homosexuality and the sub-cultures it generated had been around for a long time and were practiced by other species than humans. And that insofar as human civilization was concerned, homosexual culture had during several historical periods greatly influenced the mainstream—"As," I said, "it's doing now.

"I'm not talking only about artists and composers and athletes and designers," I went on as I lit the kitchen propane lamps. "I mean that it forces us to choose who we are, all of us. Not just what form of lovemaking we prefer, but what we'll tolerate as quote unquote civilized. In the evolutionary sense, and politically and culturally too, it gives us the chance to choose tolerance, diversity, individuality, or to reject them in favor of hypocritical moralizing. *That's* what chokes the possibilities of evolution. And makes us more homogenized than a flock of sheep."

My little speech seemed to cheer Ken up, or at least to even his mood, as he often did for me. I began to think of him as a partner, not only in the work of the place, but in the ways he tended to his inner growth, which jump-started my own awareness and forced me into regions I hadn't thought about. Anger, for instance, and the ways it can disrupt both grief and healing, not to mention the capacity for learning and for love. I tended to change passively. Ken did it actively, taking me with him during our conversations, and inadvertently clarifying my thinking.

We talked about many things besides gayness and its consequences, or even our ideas for the ranch. Dream images were important to each of us, and we both had a knack for delving their meaning. We often discussed them over dinner, and if the dreamer couldn't parse the meaning of a dream, the person sitting across the table often could. Ken, whose totem animal is the rattlesnake, once encountered in a dream a monstrous rattler that he chopped into three pieces. Upon waking, he was full of regret for having slaughtered the reptile and wondered if it boded ill for him to have done so. When I suggested he look for three vital forces, or directions, or aspects of his life which maybe were working against each other, the mystery was clear.

Likewise, in one of my dreams a white cow and a white bull were yoked together to a cart so overladen with rocks they couldn't pull it, though in trying they went to their knees. The driver whacked the beasts with, of all things, a large rolled-up scroll. Ken saw in the dream that I was getting bogged down in ranch work at the expense of the writing I'd come here to do.

The positive side of Ken's upbringing had mostly to do with his father's vineyards and orchards, or with his Navajo friend's family and rituals. He had gone through his first peyote ceremony at age fourteen, and later became friends with a medicine man. As he knew it, shamanism was not something to be taken lightly.

"There's as much black magic in it as there is white. You have to be able to enter places of darkness, sickness, evil. You have to be able to surrender your identity in exchange for a transforming vision. You have to be able to vacate your self, find that vision, and come back. You have to be sane enough to go crazy and strong enough to win the deals you make with devils." He paused and shook his head. "I can do it for myself, but not for anybody else."

And yet he had a bent in that direction.

One afternoon in early spring he came home with a load of flat red rock instead of firewood and announced he was going to build a patio around the Russian olive by the bunkhouse. For days he shoveled and leveled, then gathered more truckloads of sandstone slab and wrestled, chiseled, and fitted them into place. When he had tamped red clay into the crevices between his desert flagstones, he asked if there was enough water in the spring to soak the new patio and set the stones more firmly. Though we were still in a serious drought, I told him to go ahead. Surely the gods would see that Ken had just spent a week doing a sort of rain dance, mostly on his hands and knees, and would send a shower to compensate.

That evening he told me his idea of holding a series of retreats at the ranch for some of his friends who were HIV-positive or who had AIDS. "I've written Michael about it, and he says it's up to you. I know how you value your privacy, but we'd stay out of your way—except for one day, when you could give us a project to do for the ranch. Anything but moving the outhouse," he giggled, referring to one of Michael's pet obsessions. "There would only be six of us here at a time," he added, "and you'd be welcome to join us as much as you wanted."

And so it happened in late April that five strangers came to live for a brief while in the rustic bunkhouse. Ken arrived several days early to repair the plumbing, clean up winter's packrat nests, hammer together a sturdy table for the new patio, and generally spiff up the place. Then, while I gardened, he hunkered in the sandy driveway with a trowel, a sheaf of small paper bags, and several dozen boxes of veladoras—stubby white votive candles.

By the time his guests arrived the next evening, Horsethief's entire yard was filled with light. Muted luminarias glowed from the eaves of the house, the limbs of trees, the garden fence, the rim of the hot tub, and the ground itself, where they were spaced so as to create softly lit paths from house to bunkhouse to hot tub to outhouse. A wavering glow illuminated the red-ochre cliffs above the hot tub, apricot leaves flickered in reflection like thousands of green mirrors, and the stone ranch house glimmered like a primeval fortress. The effect was magical.

Ken guided Theo, Paul, Zoe, Jerry, and Kevin on a tour along the luminaria paths, then had everyone sit around the hot tub while he explained what they'd be doing and not doing for four days. They'd hardly had a chance to take it all in before he summoned us to the bunkhouse patio for supper. On top of everything else, my friend of coherent energies had found time to prepare a Thai-style feast. And so we christened the new terrace and its wooden table with a flow of wine and talk quite astonishing for its comraderie and candor. By the time supper was over, we were strangers no more, and it occurred to me that there was such a thing as living of AIDS as well as dying of it.

Perhaps thinking we'd already grown accustomed to the luminarias (I hadn't), Ken suggested we hike to the top of the east rim, directly above the hot tub. While Paul gathered up his camera gear, I fetched flashlights, which Ken nixed. "We'll be blinded by the time we get up there. Let's try doing it by starlight and the feel of the path."

And so we did, stumbling after we left the trail, but helping each other up the steep sections where a slip would mean injury. Talking and joking had ceased, and I sympathized with the uncertainty, the night-fear and height-fear I felt around me. "How much farther is it?" someone asked in a small, childlike voice. And then we were there, at the top, at the edge, swaying with exertion and vertigo, with a skyfull of desert stars above, and constellations of luminarias glowing out of the velvet darkness below.

The next morning Ken marched his friends off on a hike to the edge of Mineral Canyon for the first session of their retreat. Busy with garden work, I hardly saw them that day. But I had offered horseback riding for anyone who wanted, and toward evening Theo took me up on it. While we saddled Aquila and Shasta in the corral, I noted with pleasure that he knew what he was doing, and became curious about this dark-haired, green-eyed man.

As we rode at a walk to warm the horses up, I asked him where and when he'd learned to ride. "I grew up on horseback," he replied. "My wife Joanie and I ride whenever we can get the money and time together. Too bad she isn't here—she'd love this place."

"So you're not gay, then?" Theo had a relaxed, inclusive way about him, a bit different from the others. That he wasn't gay didn't surprise me; that he was married did.

"Call it bisexual. I never could figure out why I was only supposed to make love to half the world. Obviously, it got me in trouble. Now I stick pretty close to Joanie."

"How long have you been married?"

"Three years. She knew I was positive when we met, but she wanted us to be married anyway. And she knows me inside out—we're a lot alike. She's a great lady," he said, adding, "You two would really get along."

Theo was the easiest member of the group to talk to, but the others were interesting, too. Paul, a musician, composer, and stage actor, prepared one of the finest Indian meals I'd ever tasted, with his own blend of curry and a fresh spinach saag from the garden. Kevin, who'd flown in from San Francisco, had a sweet nature spiced with quick humor, and proved hugely helpful. Zoe had come on behalf of her husband, Richard, a hemophiliac who'd contracted AIDS from infected blood—as had ninety percent of all hemophiliacs who received blood during that same year. Freckled, red-haired Jerry, the youngest of the group, was the most skittish, off on his bike whenever the mood struck—though he proved his mettle on Shasta when, at his insistence, we rode out into the most violent winds of the whole spring, our horses spooked and intractable.

The weather quickly became a factor in the group's activities, as a cold front moved in with leaf-tearing, blow-you-over sandstorm winds and predicted freezing temperatures. As if what they'd come here for was to deal with emergencies, Ken mobilized his friends.

My first concern was protecting from frost what I'd so far planted in the garden. Wind was ripping away layers of mulch straw from the newly planted beds, and I watched hours of work blown into the sky like the house of the first little pig. Nothing to be done about that. But all the baby tomatoes, eggplants and peppers soon wore 'hats'—large, clear plastic juice jugs, bottoms cut off so they'd fit over the plants like individual greenhouses. Pressed into the soil, mulch piled around them, the jugs protected the plants and helped keep the mulch in place.

Then the comedy began. The apricot, peach, plum, and nectarine trees had already bloomed and set good quantities of fruit. The predicted hard freeze would destroy the whole crop. Promising everyone a jar of home-made jam if they'd help, I told them my idea. We'd put large plastic trash bags over the smaller dwarf fruit trees, and cut up the rolls of plastic sheeting in the breezeway to cover the bigger ones—some of which were twenty feet tall.

Ken scoffed, saying it was too much trouble with no guarantee of success, and a little while later drove off in his truck. But the others pitched right in. Unfortunately, the trash bags and some of the rolls of plastic were black instead of clear; if the sun came out the trees would bake instead of freeze. But it was late afternoon, the sky clouded and cold, so we decided to risk it.

Fighting the gritty wind, we first hooded the dwarf nectarine and peach trees with trash bags, tucking their branches in carefully as if pulling little kids' arms into winter coats, then tying the wind-whipped bags by their drawstrings to each trunk. Then we cut the rolls of twelve-foot wide plastic into huge 12'x 20' rectangles, binding each corner with balestring for anchorage, and trying to keep what we were doing from blowing away with us all the way to Nebraska. As it turned out, the wind actually helped sail our plastic tents up over the trees, like four-cornered kites, as we gripped the balestrings and hauled the corners down, then secured them to lower limbs and trunks. And as it turned out, Ken hadn't left in a huff—he'd made the quickest ever round-trip to town for another roll of clear plastic.

By dusk, all the fruit trees were wearing hoods or plastic tents like huge babushkas, some of them see-through, some of them black. The visual effect was eerie, and the whapping sound of all that wind-beaten plastic was like an armada of square riggers luffing in a gale. "We should have called in Christo to wrap Horsethief," Kevin quipped.

It froze that night after the wind died, but not hard enough to tell whether our trees tents had worked. In any case, it was a banner year for fruit.

From our talks about the dark side of life—the shadows—I was aware that one of the things Ken wanted to do during the retreat was encourage his friends to probe the darkness of having a fatal disease, and at the same time to see this was *not* their whole identity. For this he took them out to dance on the mesa at midnight. For this he spent hours with each person, in talk, in silence, drawing out fear and terror, bitterness and regret, anger and resentment. For this he'd made the luminarias and taken us to the rim, to look into a pitchy void and find a shining, a way.

From there, perhaps it was possible to think of the darkness shining in and of itself.

I thought about this on the last night of the retreat, while the group was down at the Green River for a farewell supper and a session of dancing around a bonfire. Into the flames went objects each had brought or found, emblems for parts of themselves they had outgrown and could discard, pieces of darkness that fed the light.

When they weren't back by midnight, Mama Hen drove to the overlook above the Green. Peering a thousand feet down into a canyon brimful of night, I saw what I had been thinking about: the darkness luminous with itself, the blackness burning. I stared for a long time, passing in and out of that mesmerized state of seeing. Then, tiny in the deep distance came the headlights of a vehicle. Ken's truck, I was sure. I sensed the glistening of souls.

The second retreat, in May, followed the pattern of the first, but with much better weather. Because one of my cousins was visiting, I didn't get to know this set of Ken's friends as well as I had the first. Still, we dined, laughed, rode, and especially gardened together. The two retreats were my first experience with more than a couple of visitors at a time, or with people who were strangers to the desert. Except for Ken, it was also my first acquaintance with people who either had or were susceptible to AIDS. The intensity of their response to Horsethief and its desert was surprising, though it shouldn't have been. They fell in love with the place and landscape as I had, as nearly everyone did, absorbing the soul-healing, spirit-nourishing qualities of the desert like dry sponges in water. But these people were not "everyone"—they discerned those qualities, and assimilated them, in greater measure than most.

It's hard to leave a place that's been so nurturing, Theo wrote in the logbook. *I go away much more in touch with myself and the natural world, grateful to know Horsethief's desert.*

Even Jerry, the least 'present' member of the group, wrote: *This place will be with me for a long time. It was just what I needed at this point in my life. I am forever grateful.*

Unfortunately, forever wasn't far away for Jerry, whose suicide less than a year later anguished and angered those who knew him. But for two years he was the only one of the group to succumb. I felt privileged to know each of them, grateful for what they taught me about facing disapproval, ostracism, abandonment and above all, mortality. Most of them had learned to receive each day as a gift, but each of them still had to deal daily with the darkness at the end of the tunnel.

Gradually I bagan to see a pattern to Ken's visits. Even more than his friendship with me or Michael, his bond, like mine, was with the ranch and its encompassing landscape. He came to it whenever he went through a period of loss or change. It gave him what he needed: a space to dance beneath the stars, a home that received the gifts through which he built himself and it. More than anyone, including me, he had a vision of what the ranch could become in order to better serve as an oasis of the spirit.

Most of the time Ken arrived alone and unannounced, with a project in mind. Not long after I called him with news that much-needed rains had come, he appeared with the springs of his pickup bed groaning under a load of huge rocks. "I knew one more flash flood down the gully would undermine the driveway there," he said as we walked toward the spot. "What it needs is a dike, a retaining wall about twenty feet long and three feet high. Can the budget pay for a roll of hog-wire?"

The budget could not, at least not without Michael's permission, which was hard to obtain from a sailing yacht on the other side of the globe. So Ken bought the wire out-of-pocket, then wrestled and wrapped it around the bundles of rocks and boulders he amassed and fitted together to form a wall under the gully-edge of the driveway, a wall that only time on an evolutionary scale would ever erode or budge.

These were the kinds of projects he took on, voluntarily, mindfully (Ken called it "obsessively"). He also helped when broken plumbing or machinery was too much for me to deal with, and he often "frittered away" a morning pruning all the grapevines or weed-eating the large weed-choked lawn. Earphones in place, Rikki Lane on tape, reluctant to be disturbed, he went about making Horsethief lovelier, healthier, more orderly and productive.

Meantime, I witnessd his changes. Despite his sense of charity, his pharmaceutical business had grown lucrative, and with it his reputation for integrity, for being on the leading edge, for putting his personal experience of any new product on the line. He was asked to speak at conferences in Germany, France, Italy, and in u.s. cities from New York to Los Angeles, Seattle to Fort Lauderdale. Those trips led to invitations to start or oversee similar businesses in other parts of the world. But instead of riding on these achievements, he expressed, in his clear-minded way, confusion about which way to go.

What he really wanted, he confessed on his next visit, was out. Despite this wave of success, he was tired of being tied to his own business, depressed by watching so many friends and clients die, and above all weary of building his life around his disease. "What I want is to do something normal," he said during one of our discussions. "Like starting a fish farm."

No joke, no mere whim. By his next visit, he had researched the water engineering appropriate to a state of the art trout hatchery, was already looking for rural riverfront property with the water rights necessary for such an operation, and had spoken with several possible partners about financing. Now his talk was not so much of CD4+ cells, retrovirus adaptation and peptide bonding, but of holding ponds, breeding runs, recycled river water. He made another trip to Thailand, where fish farming is an ancient art, and where he sought advice and help from Thai friends and partners. And there things stood when Ken took his parents, who had never been out ot the country, on a personally designed tour of Thailand and Indonesia.

As with most friendships, Ken's and mine has survived its share of misunderstanding, disagreement and distance. I've faced him trembling with outrage at what I viewed as his blatant attempt to control a situation. He's turned a cold shoulder on my nattering and nitpicking about Michael. We disagree about mortality, Ken claiming with an offhand giggle that he came from another planet, where he'll return in death. I, resisting fantasy, wanting him to live, wanting him to want to live as earthbound as he is.

This much at least can be said: that of all the people I know, only Ken and Remo live in such a way that no matter how or when life may be taken from them, their journey through it will have been fulfilled. For now, I'm still learning from my young friend the difference between curing and healing, learning that incurability and wellness are not incompatible, that every cell in our bodies is taking part in earth's unique evolution from stardust to protoplasm, from raw sentience toward a vision of compassionate choice.

Chapter Nine

Too Much and No More

Nature's processes are spun of such subtle logic that often they appear confounding, even magical in their rightness. Here I am currying wads of winter horsehair onto the sand of the corral—and here April's blackbirds arrive, burbling their songs and plucking up the hair to line their nests. Last week the resident bullsnake emerged to gag down a mouse; today waxen shreds of snakeskin dangle in the straw under a rosebush. Rain falls, water evaporates, condenses, falls again. Earth tilts, days lengthen, sun draws sweetness into the hard green nubs of grapes, while eyeless theosophists argue the whereabouts of heaven.

So it is not surprising that Horsethief would have a numen, a perfectly logical magic carpet underlying and creating its oasis—nor that given the nature of desert canyons, such a carpet would be made of stone. Of the two dozen or so layers of sedimentary rock that form the exquisite geology of the Colorado Plateau, Horsethief has only two—but they are crucial. Uppermost is the pocked and porous, creamy rose-ochre Navajo sandstone that forms the walls of the home canyon and much of the exposed slickrock for miles around. Just below it lies the dense, relatively impervious Kayenta formation, a complex of siltstone and shale. This maroon-gray layer acts as a water-collecting pan beneath the sandy floor of the home canyon, and beneath hundreds of acres of surrounding desert that drain into it.

Any significant rain that falls within this huge, horseshoe-shaped drainage sinks into sand and porous slickrock. What is not sucked up by greedy sun or sparse vegetation succumbs to gravity, sinking beneath dune, root and rodent burrow, following the underground slopes of the Kayenta. Some of this slow-moving water collects visibly as Horsethief's spring, where thanks to homesteader Art Murry, it is enclosed in an underground rock-walled tank measuring 6′ x 10′ x 5′ deep. From the bottom of the tank, gravity takes the water through an outtake pipe leading via branch pipelines, to house, bunkhouse, cistern, hot tub, orchard, and garden.

But let's take three steps backward. In a sense, the spring is mere happenstance, an appearance at ground level of what is going on beneath the ground. By an erosional fluke, the Kayenta layer in the canyon is near enough to the surface to make its water accessible, a gift. Were it twenty feet deeper, Horsethief's oasis would not exist. Nor would other seeps and springs in southern Utah that depend on imporous rock layers near the surface. A dramatic example is Zion National Park, where Navajo sandstone is piled into monumental two thousand foot-high domes, at the base of which the Kayenta formation preserves delicate gardens of moisture.

Largesse of both geology and geography, Horsethief's spring is the only year-round source of water for five miles in any direction and the only drinkable water for twenty. If the entire canyon is an oasis, the area around the spring is its core. Shaggy, patriarchal cedars—thirty feet tall, five hundred years old—join with willow, scrub oak, squawbush and desert holly to create sundappled groves and impenetrable thickets. Ferns and equisetum, flowers and poison ivy, reeds and longhaired grasses provide cool greenery in summer, food and cover for small creatures in winter.

Winter or summer, the spring breathes both life and a suspended stillness, blinking in the sun like any creature newly emerged from underground. In wet seasons its overflow forms a small shallow pond around the underground holding tank. Issuing from the earth at a constant year-round temperature of 54° Fahrenheit, the pond is immune to freezing. In winter, bordered and overhung by boughs of snow, flickering with sunlight and bathing chickadees, it glistens with primeval innocence. Filled after spring or summer rains, profligate with duckweed, mosquitos and frogs in every life stage, it retains an aura of pristine fecundity. Even when in drought seasons the pond goes dry, it leaves behind a bed of damp sweet grasses. Stand in them barefoot and you will feel beneath your feet water traveling almost imperceptibly underground. Open your mouth and you will taste the same vapors that caress your skin. Breathe in the humid perfume of desert-cleansed water and all it nourishes, and you will know the healing powers of earth.

If I have spoken of this place primarily in terms of process and geology, I think of it in terms of spirit, of omphalos, entrance and emergence, source and succor, as people of other times and places have thought of their wellsprings. Horsethief's spring tells me stories, it speaks of bounty and forgiveness, of balancing sweetness, salt, bitterness, of the need for thanks, the power of hope and the inevitability of renewal. *How could any ground be other than holy?* it asks in its innocence. *Where in the world is beauty not coming into being?*

But back to process and practicality. Beyond the rich life and spirit it nurtures, a mystery of the spring is the lag time between rainfall and flow. After two years of drought, where does the water, however diminished, keep coming from? Where especially does it keep coming from after a season of guests and gardening? Will it continue to percolate indefinitely despite a lack of precipitation, or is there a point at which it will go dry? These were my questions during year one at the ranch, as I watched virga after virga that never touched earth, never entered the underground part of the cycle, never complied.

By June of that first year, the situation was dire. The water in the spring was just above the outtake pipe. Every time I watered the garden or soaked the orchard trees I chanced draining it completely, with no guarantee it could renew itself. Michael, planning a break from his round-the-world voyage to visit for a month, promised rather mysteriously in a letter from monsoon-swamped Manila that he would "bring rain," but cautioned that "if it doesn't work, we'll have to kill the garden to save the trees."

My poor first garden. I hand watered each row with a hose and doubled the thickness of the mulchstraw that kept the soil moist. Looking up day after day at the same merciless blue, I felt in my throat the plight of millions of people suffering from a far worse, far more extended drought in North Africa. *Water.* I saw that its absence was an absolute, a mighty element of facticity, of torture and slow death. When there was no more, there was *no more.*

With Michael came friends and family. Some brought bottled drinking water or five-gallon jugs—thoughtful and helpful, but it didn't provide the fifteen gallons of water a day needed by each of ten horses, and it didn't do all the dishes or give us baths. To allay my fears, Michael arranged for delivery of a tank-truck load of non-potable river water to fill the five thousand gallon storage cistern near the garden. From that we could water garden and trees for a week or so while the spring replenished itself to the extent it could.

Meantime, with the daily temperature reaching 105 degrees by noon, Michael had taken to rising at dawn. Downing a handful of M&Ms for breakfast, he was out the gate with a mug of coffee and a trenching shovel over his shoulder before the rest of us had cracked an eyelid. When I came to look, he had excavated several yards of a deep narrow trench that began at an abandoned wellsite fifty feet beyond the front gate. Guided by a chalkline, the trench headed straight for the storage cistern. "Rain," was all Michael would say.

Ten days later, with the river water used up, the spring again down to its outtake pipe, and only the thinnest dribble of water available from the kitchen faucet, Michael returned from town with several large cardboard cartons and his trademark grin. By midafternoon two solar panels, framed in two-by-fours, were angled toward the sun, wired to a control box, and thence by buried pipe to a solar pump immersed twenty feet deep in the old well. A flick of the switch caused a faint humming sound to emanate from the well, and—wonder of wonders—when we peered over the rim of the cistern, it was already filling from its intake pipe with... "Rain, see!" Michael said proudly, and indeed, it was cause for marvelling.

But Nature has its own way of solving problems. After a quiet Fourth of July, everyone left the ranch. Next morning, I awoke feeling an odd tingling, an unfamiliar fullness in the air. Walking outside, I saw that the sky was gray. Not clouds, not promises, but *cloud*—a wide blanket of gray had moved in over the desert during the night. By noon, nothing had happened beyond an obscuring of the usual brass-knuckled rays of the sun, a tempering of its heat. Was this just another hope-dissolving tease? I waited, suspending both hope and doubt in favor of thinning young carrots and beets.

The rain that began falling on my bare back that afternoon was so soft it felt like part of my body, like my own perspiration recycling itself. When I checked the corrals at midnight, it was still raining lightly, the best kind of rain, soaking in slowly, blessing every grain of sand for half an inch down. I sank into sleep that night listening to the whisper on the roof, breathing the freshness of a world renewed.

By morning the tempo of the rain had increased, sounding like the word *precipitate, precipitate* repeated over and over, still soaking in. My disbelief had departed for the Sahara, leaving elation in its place. But no sooner had I danced naked in my sneakers through the mud to the bunk-house to see about the leaks in its roof, than the whole sky let loose—a scary, pelting downpour of the kind usually accompanied by deafening cracks of thunder. This storm, like the dog that bites, needed no sound effects. Sheets of waterfall-white rain pounded straight down, obliterating visibility, slashing leaves, spattering sand, smacking rock, roof, metal, glass, in a raucous, skin-stinging cacophony that left no space for breath and threatened to drown me upright.

Uselessly, I put soup pots and saucepans under the trickling leaks in the bunkhouse. As I stumbled rain-blind toward the house, my ears caught beneath the tumult a gurgling, rushing hiss, as of a large serpent behind me. Turning and taking a few steps toward it, I saw to my amazement the west canyon gully behind the bunkhouse frothing with whitecaps—whitecaps reddened by the roiling flood swirling two feet deep down the gully, swift and thick with chocolate mud and cinnamon sand.

I watched, astonishment growing, until it occurred to me to see what was happening on the east side of the canyon, in the shallow depression that ran the length of the back yard to protect that side of the house. But as I sloshed through the deluge, hands shielding my eyes, I saw that the east gully would have to wait. Tongues of water from roof and driveway were flowing into the front yard at an alarming rate and had already created a shallow pool on the patio that was creeping into the kitchen. Grabbing a shovel, I spaded sodden sand into mini-dikes and levees and slashed a rough sluiceway away from the patio toward the garden, until the pool subsided enough to stay out of the kitchen—for the time being.

By then the rain had let up a little, and I could see more than a few feet away. As I splashed toward the back yard, Koa behind me, I recoiled at the sight of a large, frothy, mud-silver *lake* outside the front gate. Its near shore began below the bunkhouse and its body inundated the pumpkin patch, the parking area outside the gate, and the well-site, with several thousand square feet of knee-deep, debris-laden water. I heard the flash flood roaring on down the lower gully beyond, but the lake was still growing by the minute. Koa, ever the waterdog, had waded in and was paddling toward the nearest stick.

Glancing at the solar panels surrounded by water but rising above it like twin black sails, I grew concerned for the pump immersed in the well. But I had switched it off yesterday when cloud cover automatically shut down the solar process, and besides, a more important consideration loomed—was the east side of the house safe? Slogging to the back yard, I was confronted with a second floodstream, also about five feet wide but only six inches deep, running the length of the yard, past house and garden into the newly created Horsethief Lake. The back of the house was safe so far, but to be sure I waded upstream to the orchard. There, waterfalls poured in torrents from the east canyon walls, swelling the stream washing down the path from the spring. I spaded more sand into more dikes and soon had a small holding pond backed up around the plum, pear and cherry trees where it would do some good.

Then, as the rain subsided a bit, I remembered—omigod, the leaks in the house roof. Leaping back downstream, I stepped inside the screen door and heard staccato spatters in several parts of the house—including on the bed in front of me. Grabbing pots and pans, I shoved them under the leaks and mopped up the floors with old towels. Then hauled the sopping towels, quilts, pillows and rugs outside and draped them over the garden fence. What better time to do laundry?

Koa greeted me, happy to be wet and cool. I was squinting at the meniscus in the rain gauge, amazed to see it filled to the 1.2 inch mark, when I heard what sounded like ducks quacking from up by the spring.

Ducks? We had no ducks. Was this a desperate, out-of-season migration due to the rain? As I waded in disbelief up the backyard stream again toward the noise, its rhythm evened out, and I recognized the croaking cadence of—frogs! Canyon tree frogs, to be precise, a species capable of surviving drought by burrowing several feet into the sand and hibernating—for years if need be—until sufficient rainfall triggers the signal to come forth and multiply.

Clearly, sufficient rainfall was what we had. Given that annual rainfall on Horsethief mesa hovers around ten inches, we had received twelve percent of that in one day. Standing at the edge of the overflowing spring pond, I listened to the glad honking of the frogs and thought back through all the dry months, months that could so well have used a fraction of this deluge. *Too much. Waayy too much,* I thought. But the rain continued, and the frogs sounded as if they wouldn't have it any other way.

With nothing more to do to protect the house, I felt the urge to go exploring—to see what the rain had done and might still be doing. Crossing the empty corrals toward the west canyon, I envisioned the horses wet, cool and content out on the range, and envied Koa's nose for a world of fresh scents. Another chorus of frogs garumped as we neared the head of the west canyon, where three small waterfalls poured over ledges into a deep pool. Our presence silenced the frogs, and Koa glided into the pool for another swim. But as soon as he shook himself and we walked away, the mood music resumed.

Sliding down a muddy slope en route to the east canyon, I reached for a ledge to steady myself—only to have it come away in my hand. As I picked up the chunk of ledge, it crumbled like a wet cookie. Licking my fingers, I tasted the faintly salty matrix that held the grains of sand. Navajo rock was indeed porous. Every surface was soft and pasty, like gritty ice cream over the unmelted stone beneath. An eighth-inch of evolution, stone reverting to sand.

Sunset gleamed in a million droplets of water glistening from junipers, brush and grasses as we walked to the little amphitheatre at the end of the east canyon. In this quasi-cavern, curtained by a clear-running waterfall, nodding stems of scarlet gilia grew tall. They'd begun blooming a week ago, while dryness ruled, protected by the overhanging rock. Now their small blossoms flamed intensely red, glowing in the fading light of a rainy day. I bowed in return, then stepped beneath the waterfall. Gritty water poured through my hair as I raised my arms to feel again the ravishing weight of the rain.

In his book *Water and Dreams*, the French philosopher Gaston Bachelard comes to the conclusion that water is feminine and maternal, and calls it "the milk of the earth." Some Native Americans think of springs as earth's tears; others distinguish between hard downpours of male warrior rain, and softly falling female rain. The latter, though not so dramatic, contributes equally to the desert's well-being. *I listen as the rain arrives*, I wrote one cool August dawn, *soft & light as breath, as a mother's fingers on the forehead of a sleeping child, soft as kitten fur, the misting droplets don't so much fall as caress, an infinity of tiny kisses. Through the gentle whisper comes the faraway cry of mourning doves, calling down the long hallways of the rain...*

Rain also revitalizes the desert's colors, intensifying the hue of every rock, juniper, tuft of rice grass, broom of Mormon tea. Opaque, saturated, the reds are richer, ochres purer, greens more vivid, like pigments fresh-squeezed from the objects they color, instead of scintillating motes of dust pressed into service by the light.

One cloudy November day, my once-husband Rob, with whom I had remained friends, visited on his way to do some sailing off the California coast. Ken had recently given me directions to a ruin he'd located down in the canyon of the Green, overlooking the river. I asked Rob if he'd like to help find it, and soon we were crawling along in his jeep down the switchbacks to the river. By the time we reached the bottom, a drizzle had begun, a modest autumn shower.

Parking the jeep near the location Ken had described, we finally spotted the ruin high on a slope of red boulders, under a huge slab of collapsed canyon wall. Protected for centuries by the slab, it was camouflaged by its unusual architecture and afforded guardian views upstream and down. Shaped blocks of red stone formed the walls between ledge floor and slab ceiling. What was rare in this region were the rows of little flat rocks fitted edgewise into the mud matrix between each tier of stones, in the style of the Mimbres people who had lived far to the south. The door frame—sections of cedar limbs polished by the oil of generations of hands—supported a panel of red stone shaped to fit it. Carefully we removed the stone door, and peering into the darkness marvelled at the cobs of colored corn on a rock shelf. With equal care we replaced the door, noting how snugly it fit, how well it blended with the stonework and filled the noticeable hole that otherwise would have drawn human intruders as well as shelter-seeking animals. From the road, the ruin had been almost indistinguishable from the rubble around it. "This isn't a ruin," Rob said. "There's nothing ruined about it. It's still usable, if a person were to need it."

Rain was now falling hard, making us feel less like human intruders and more like shelter-seeking animals. The huge slab protruded out over the ruin, so we weren't tempted to take refuge within. Instead, we sat crouched on stones near the door and shared an apple, staring out over the wide, rain-filled canyon and its river. Flat as a mirror and seemingly motionless, the gray-brown surface of the Green curved before us, prinkled with a billion raindrops. Silver lines of rain sped out of gray cloud, sped past red canyon walls into thickets of vegetation that lined both riverbanks with vibrant subtleties of orange tamarisk, dusky gold chamisa, rusted lacy skeleton-plant, green-yellow willow.

We gazed in silence through the raindrops, mesmerized into a timeless reality. Nothing moved but the rain; I could believe that nothing but the rain had moved for a thousand years. I felt the stone door at my back as one would the heat of a fire, and was warmed by a sensation of continuity, then of identity. I who stared out at the still river, the rain-painted foliage, was the same person who was looking at this scene ten centuries ago. For the while, for the *time being,* we shared the same eyes, the same body, the same time, the same world. It was neither now nor then nor any time in-between. It was always, it was the continuing story.

Some part of eternity later, as we walked back to the jeep, Rob, who lives much of the time in his head and is not given to letting down boundaries, spoke quietly. "Now I know what it feels like," he said. "What what feels like?" I asked, wanting to be sure. "What it feels like to be a person who lived here. Who lives here." I nodded silently and felt myself growing, down through roots and out through branches both. Love is something one leaves behind only at risk of great poverty. I took his arm, and for the time being we walked hand in hand with the rain.

Part of my job was to keep in the logbook a record of all precipitation, rain or snow, and to turn in an annual report of it to the BLM to help them keep track of rainfall patterns on Horsethief's mesa. For my own purposes, I kept track of temporary sources of water as well.

The most ubiquitous of these liquid assets are potholes, water-holding depressions common in less-permeable layers of rock. Filled by rain or melting snow, they liberate wildlife and livestock from permanent sources of water, and allow wildlife populations to expand into new territories by travelling from pothole to pothole. It's no accident that the occasional raccoons, skunks and porcupines who've shown up at the ranch have arrived after periods of rain.

Potholes contain their own wildlife as well, most of it miniscule. Out on Horsethief Point, however, several potholes hold an unsolved mystery. Soon after Michael bought the ranch, he and a friend were exploring this area after a rain, and discovered a number of strange creatures drifting and darting around in a four-inch deep pothole. Dark, translucent, large as a thumb, they resembled a cross between a shrimp and a horseshoe crab. Nearby were other potholes containing the same organisms. Curious, Michael emptied his water jug and scooped a few of the primitive beings into it. One he pickled in a jar of alcohol, where it remains on a shelf in the ranch house. The others he shipped to Utah State University's zoology department.

The report that came back was startled and startling. An invertebrate belonging to the class Eubrachiopoda, order Anostraca, family Apus, the creatures belonged to no living genus or species. In fact, based on fossil evidence, they had been extinct for several million years. Primitive, indeed! How had these ghost 'fairy shrimp,' which predated the dinosaurs, persisted so long in a harsh desert? Did they inhabit other potholes on other mesas, or were they unique to Horsethief Point?

The first question was answered by a textbook reprint on Eubrachiopoda enclosed with the paleozoologist's report. Members of this order typically inhabit pools, ponds or puddles which evaporate during warm dry weather. They survive by producing two types of eggs: thin-shelled "summer eggs," which hatch into larvae almost immediately and mature sexually within days; and thick-shelled "resting" or "winter" eggs, which can withstand extreme heat, deep freezing, prolonged desiccation, and radical fluctuations of alkalinity—and which in fact benefit from such conditions. In addition, either type of egg can be produced with or without a male present. When a male does participate, he usually dies soon after fertilizing the female.

It was fascinating to ride to these potholes after a shower and study their inhabitants. I thought they were dying until I read that they often float or swim upside down. I watched them as they fed, rightside up, on bottom detritus, and snugged into the silt lining their pothole to stir up microscopic food. I spied on pairs as they chugged around clutching each other at odd angles, mating. I observed them in one pothole for two consecutive years. The next year they were gone, but a nearby pothole which had contained none, was now full of them. Everything I learned about these fairy shrimp—including that they have equally ancient cousins known only from a single pool here or a single pond there—led me to believe that the population of Apus surviving on Horsethief Point is unique in all the world.

However temporary or permanent, all water on Horsethief Mesa depends on local rainfall. The Green River, on the other hand, with its headwaters high in Wyoming's Wind River Range, drains more than 45,000 square miles of mostly mountainous terrain in its 730-mile length, and is one of the most powerful river systems in the west. Five miles away and eleven hundred feet lower in elevation, the Green is not a direct source of water for the ranch. But it does allow us to keep horses on several hundred acres of bottomland stretched along four miles of river. It also provides an environment distinct from the exposed mesas, with different layers of rock, different vegetation, and different stories to tell.

One sultry July day, my horseman friend Jack Snobble stopped by, and we decided to ride down to check the horses pastured in the riverbottoms. After crossing the sweltering mesa with its oceanic views, the river canyon beckoned sweetly with an upwelling breeze. Resting our horses at the rim, we gazed into its vertiginous depths at a desert eden: sinuous gray-green river, its surface still as a mirror, curving through groves of green cottonwoods. Sheer red Wingate cliffs enclose the scene like walls of a secret kingdom, above the rubble of Chinle and Moenkopi formations aproning out at their angle of repose. Everything motionless, a diorama.

Reaching the bottom, we found the horses beyond the first bend downstream, all of them looking sleek and healthy as they swished their tails at flies. Not wanting to cause a ruckus by having the herd come running to greet our horses, we turned away and headed upriver. While Jack rode off to explore abandoned uranium mines, Aquila and Koa and I headed to a sandy ramp on a big eddy. Once the near-exclusive playa for Horsethief's visitors, now it was usually crowded with vehicles, piles of gear, and people busily launching or hauling out rafts and other rivercraft. But this was Monday...

No one was there. Granddaddy Cottonwood, gnarled roots exposed like an old man's shins, shaded the empty beach. Koa didn't even wait to see if I was coming. As he paddled around the eddy, I tied Aquila to a sapling and waded in. Rib-deep in the cold river, squinting at its metallic surface, I shivered in snowmelt carried from 13,500-foot peaks to the north. Shivered with the pressure of water pushing, pushing downhill from nine thousand feet above me. Where along its route did this current become relentless? I stood immersed in the flowing force of gravity, the force that would but for Ken have drowned Koa under ice, that drowned kayakers and rafters each year, that could smash me on black rock. Shivering with the sun on my shoulders, toes clutching mud, fishy things bumping at my legs, I studied the towering red walls, feeling against my body the inexorability that had created them.

There was another, much closer part of home whose linearity and direction depended, like the river, on gravity, though it had none of the river's force. Horsethief's underground water system was an engineeering feat of the first order, first envisioned by Michael as the core of a master plan designed to take full advantage of the canyon's potential as an oasis. As soon as he bought the ranch, he spent a year studying the lay of the canyon floor, and perusing gardening books and orchard catalogues. He then made detailed schematic drawings of every tree, vine, shrub, flower patch and garden bed—both the few that already existed and the many he foresaw planting. Next he made equally precise diagrams of the underground drip-irrigation system needed to support this plan.

On paper, it looked great. The problem was that the spring, when full, was only twelve feet above the lowest point in the system—the bunkhouse pumpkin patch some 250 feet away. The lower the spring level, the lower the pressure as well as the amount of water available to the drip-heads that would water every plant. Michael sent copies of his carefully labelled diagrams to a water engineering firm, with a letter requesting their opinion and suggestions. The reply he received politely questioned his seriousness, if not his sanity. So he brought in a consultant from the company from which he planned to purchase the pipe, valves and fittings. This engineer also expressed doubt about the project's success. "You've got no drop, no pressure—at least not enough for so many pipes going off in different directions—and especially not back uphill to that orchard."

I suspect the dust from the engineer's car had barely settled before Michael stuck his trenching shovel into the spot where he wanted the water pipe valve box. He purchased pipe and fittings and rented a ditch-witch from the company who said it couldn't be done, and with help from many friends, in one summer dug the planned network of trenches at a precise drop of 1/4" per foot, and laid in the pipes with their control valves. Side trenches held thin 'spaghetti hose' leading to every tree, vine, and flower-bed site. As long as the spring was at least half full, the whole system worked.

Obviously, water comes from a tap as milk comes from a carton, or comes from the spring as milk comes from a store. Even my U.S. Government pamphlet on 'Rain' designates it "a renewable resource that moves in a cycle with neither beginning nor end"—about as close to metaphysics as government gets. Nevertheless, Michael's 'impossible' water system has functioned pretty much as planned for two decades, providing for the wealth of greenery that fills the canyon today. Every so often a pipe springs a leak underground, requiring major digging to repair. And every now and then a mouse or lizard squeezes under the spring's hatch cover and drowns—not a big deal, since by the time the hapless creature is discovered and removed, it's too late to put back the water one has been drinking meanwhile. The most serious problem is that the main pipe from spring to house, originally put in by Ken Allred, is above the frostline in two places, and during cold winters tends to freeze.

Owlfeathers and polar bear fur, hoarfrost and ice crystals—these are part of the beauty winter makes of water on the desert. One December before I lived at the ranch, I enticed my artist/horsewoman friend Susan and her then four-year-old son Billy into their first trip to Horsethief. The weather was cold, the ground snowless as we ventured in my car down the then-unimproved switchbacks to the Green riverbottoms. I happened to be dog-sitting a friend's Malemute, and we stopped in the shadow of a looming cliff to let Dorje and Koa out to run. In the sand that edged the dirt road, we saw the first crystals. We weren't looking for them, we didn't know they existed—but there they were, delicate, sparkling, some tiny as a tack, some bigger than a silver dollar, hundreds of them. The more we looked, the more there were. *Zillions!* Billy whispered. And then we stepped from the road into the brush.

Unbelievable. At first we just stared, not daring to move. All around us was an ice garden of unreal design. Lacy rime flakes big as saucers clung to sage, saltbrush, every surface. Rocks wore doilies of ice like crystal lichen. Tiers of elegant plates teetered on pads of prickly pear, one atop the next, leaning like stacks of crystal dishes, like the spiny pads they grew from, as if in imitation of their substrate. Long grass stems with no leaves of their own supported rows of sideways ice leaves, turning bare stems into Boston ferns. Icy tiaras capped fishhook cacti like haloes of blossoms. Everywhere we looked, iceferns gleamed, frosty platelets glittered like twinkling mobiles, blooming iceflowers mimicked the real flowers of spring. Every so often, with a faint bell-like clink, one of the sculptures would collapse.

Perhaps a half hour passed before we met on the sunny riverbank, still spellbound. As we stared back into the cliffshadow kingdom, Billy said, "It's really pretty, Mama. Can we take some home?" Susan smiled and without speaking ruffled his hair. I noticed that where the low sun hit, there were no crystals, and speculated that with the sun at its nadir, the cliff might cast its great shadow over the ice-kingdom area for weeks, while river vapor froze on whatever it touched. Day by day crystals would grow in that shade, *zillions of them.*

Guessing at the science of the ice kingdom spoiled none of its magic. We still had no idea why or how ice could mimic the growth patterns of plants and their flowers. It was as mindboggling as it was eyeboggling. We sat on the bank above the river, pondering, watching and listening as thousands of ice islands floated past in the current, chinking and hissing as they nudged each other, water riding water.

Since that extraordinary December, conditions have produced only a few coin-size crystals. But every winter has its speciality. During my second year, bitter temperatures prevailed, and despite leaving the faucets dripping, I returned from town one evening to find the pipes frozen. No water in the bathroom, none in the kitchen. I filled three large soup pots with snow to melt for wash water, but until the cold relaxed its grip, I would have to haul drinking water.

The next day I returned to town with two dinged-up five-gallon water containers. At the hardware store I bought four new ones and on the way out of town filled all six jugs from a permanent roadside spring. Though the horses could eat snow, it wasn't the best way to keep them healthy. So I would keep the battered jugs and three of the new ones to fill the corral tank when the horses came in from the range, as they did once or twice a week. That left five gallons for drinking and cooking, and the hot tub for bathing.

January's deep freeze persisted, but I was in for a surprise. Two weeks after the pipes had frozen, I was awakened one night by a commotion of hooves. Glad as I was to hear the horses, I wasn't about to trek across the icy yard in my bathrobe with heavy water jugs at night. "Stick around, guys. Hay and water in the morning," I promised, and dropped back to sleep. Some time later, I was awakened again—this time by the sudden sound of water splashing into the bathtub. Oh, no—a broken pipe! Then I remembered I'd left the faucets open, just in case.

I got up to see that just in case had happened—but how? As I turned the taps down to a steady trickle, I puzzed over what, other than a drastic temperature rise, could have caused the frozen mainpipe to thaw. A flashlight revealed the outdoor thermometer at ten above zero; I stepped outside to feel biting, windless cold. A low whinny from Aquila as the door squeaked open, the thudding of forty hooves on frozen ground beneath a fat moon... *The horses?* And that was as close as I could come to cause. Had the vibration of all those hooves jarred loose some clot of ice in the nearby pipe? It made no less sense than supposing the moon's gravity could have some tidal effect on a frozen pipe. I went to bed puzzling, and at dawn gave the horses water and extra hay. *Maybe not, but...?*

The following winter wasn't as cold, but the mainpipe froze anyway, and no amount of horse magic worked to release it. I hauled water from the canyon's spring, melted snow, and kept the hot tub warm from mid-January until the ground thawed in late February—which made winter more difficult, but there were compensations. For one thing, I was delighted by the return of the previous winter's desert fog. Just after Christmas, a massive cloud settled over the mesa and stayed put for an almost biblical thirty-three days. Only once during that time did I glimpse the sun, a brief glow in the gray. Occasionally the cloud would snow, but mostly it just breathed a thick fur of hoarfrost over everything. Trees, shrubs, grasses, grapevines, fencewire, horsewhiskers, every surface was blanketed with barbs and spicules of rime. Windowfrost grew three-dimensional at night, subsided to cameos during the day. The longer the air stayed quiet, the larger grew the spines and bristles of frost, fed by the canyon's humidity. Not as spectacular as the ice garden, but beautiful nonetheless.

The fog returned for two weeks the following winter, until a mid-January storm brought a foot of windpacked snow, dense and tough as a coiled rattler. The storm had hardly passed when along came Michael, taking an unannounced break from the sea, slithering in at three a.m. in a rented sedan through the drifts, no jacket, no sleeping bag, no waterbottle, and worse, no cigarettes. Unprepared for his visit, I also wasn't ready for his unreasonable crossness with me—his unfounded complaints about my treatment of his guests, and the additional workload he put on me. Finally I realized it had little to do with anything I'd done or left undone, but with his frustration at being unable to indulge a longtime habit.

Nevertheless, Michael's departure the next afternoon left me feeling vulnerable and wary, and fed my awareness that the work I did and the projects I accomplished were for the sake of the place itself. Though I felt hurt at first, gradually I grew stronger in the knowledge of why I was here and what was at stake. Home, after all, is what you make of it. Even Michael had several times said the ranch belonged to those who cared for it. Though I might now be asked to leave, Horsethief and its desert were where I lived.

What I felt was not possessiveness, not some territorial imperative— quite the opposite. This little canyon with its holy spring and funky rusticity was not 'mine' and would never 'belong' to me—especially since I've never believed land can truly be owned. But I belonged to *it*, and nothing could terminate that. It was the ground of my days, my work, my dreams. It was also the ground on which I welcomed others, for the most part pleased to share the place with visitors who would respect and add to its aura and history.

We humans buy and sell the supposed right to use, abuse, enjoy or destroy pieces of Earth. But those pieces are always part of, and can only be 'owned' by Earth itself. To think otherwise, despite the edifices of corporate government, law and banking we have erected, is a mere game, like Monopoly. Our history as upstarts on the planet is brief, our own lives far briefer, and we haven't created much of a future for ourselves. The worst catastrophe we can produce will leave this blue-green globe spinning in its orbit, enriched or impoverished, with or without us.

That January's foot-deep snowfall seemed to empty the sky. The rest of the winter was cold and sunny, compressing the snow and sculpted its surface in ways I'd never seen. Picture the surface of the desert as a vast rolling whiteness punctuated here and there by patches of rock and juniper. The first thing the sun did was to glaze that surface gleaming silver, especially in the waning afternoon light, purifying the sensuality of every landform, every dip and rise, gully and outcrop. This beauty lasted two weeks or so, while the snowcrust grew thicker and crunchier and the snow beneath more granular and sugary. With the sun still far to the south, gradually the smooth crust roughened into a nap, and the nap crystallized into a texture that resembled nothing so much as the sleeked white fur of a polar bear.

Day by dry cold day, that texture too underwent transformation, the sun deeply undercutting the snow-surface until it no longer resembled fur, but feathers—specifically the downy breast-feathers of a snowy owl. Not since the ice kingdom had I seen anything so astonishingly complex, so achingly fragile and beautiful. For ten days or so, hikes were accompanied by the tiny, faint chink chink of melting feathers.

By then it was March, bare patches of desert showing, and for once spring rains arrived on schedule. Almost sadly, I watched water's form change again, from sublime snowfeathers to soaking puddles and wandering rivulets. Then the feathers were gone, and the only snow left was tucked like sopped cottonballs on the north sides of rocks and shrubs. On our next walk, the clouds that had brought two days of gentle rain were breaking up into a spectacular sunset. In every direction, last rays silvered the wet slickrock, and hundreds of quicksilver potholes gleamed up at the sky like mirrors, like the desert's shining eyes.

Chapter Ten

Eating the Peach

One afternoon in August, while lugging yet another basket of squash from the garden to the sorting table on the patio, my eye was caught by a peculiar quick skitter in the shadows near the patio couch. Zorro, the whiptail lizard who patrolled the general area of patio and kitchen door, had a large something in his mouth and was jerking it about as if trying to subdue it. I set my basket down to take a closer look.

A grasshopper. Zorro had a huge green grasshopper, nearly half as big as the lizard's own body, gripped by the thorax in his mouth. The hopper appeared dull-eyed, beaten, one hind leg askew. As I watched, Zorro relinquished his hold and the grasshopper half-hopped away. Like striped lightning, Zorro pounced and regained his grip. Hopper struggled, hind legs flailing. Zorro whipped his head back and forth, hard, then let go again. Hopper didn't hop. Zorro mouthed hopper head first, like an exploded cigar, lower jaw bulging grotesquely. Then cocked his head as if aware I was watching and skittered behind the patio couch.

Oh, no, I thought—I won't see what happens. But soon the reptile and its mouthful appeared above the couch, climbing the rock wall of the house. Scuttle scuttle stop. Scuttle scuttle stop. Minutes passed between each flurry of movement. I wondered about heartbeat, breath-rate, balance. How could such a light-footed creature manuever its own weight on a vertical surface, never mind that of its ungainly prey? Zorro skittered up under the house beams, reappearing on the metal patio roof. I grabbed a chair and stood on it to watch.

Zorro cocked his head, then took several violent lunges forward, as if regurgitating. Slowly, painfully (to me), hopper's head disappeared into lizard's throat. Its thorax distorted Zorro's mouth dreadfully, its legs still kicked. Long moments, then more forward lunges—but whether to swallow or dislodge the insect was hard to tell. Had Zorro ever eaten anything so big before? Was he being choked, or smothered, by his prey?

What an appalling effort just to eat. No wonder his eyes looked squeezed and glazed. What does it feel like, little guy, all that brittle exoskeleton jammed up against your tiny brainpan?

Gag me with a grasshopper. With a mouth that full, who could answer? For minutes, Zorro was still. Then more lunges, as if forward force alone could enable the lizard to engulf its prey, as if there were no peristaltic muscles in its throat. Finally only the hopper's toes protruded like whiskers from Zorro's mouth. A breeze rustled the apricot leaves above my head. How long would it be before the lizard ate again? Given a chance, he'd likely catch and devour another meal that size, whatever the discomfort. Nature has no regrets, and no Alka-Seltzer.

I pick up my basket, thinking what an apt image Zorro's oversized meal is for the immensity of produce I'm harvesting. So far today I've picked a large wicker tray of tomatoes, a basket each of yellow beans and purple ones, two of green beans, a tray of cucumbers and a large plastic bag of salad greens. Plus the basket of squash I was carrying when I glimpsed Zorro, the three grocery bags of fruit I put in the root cellar this morning, and the peppers, corn, and eggplants still waiting to be picked. And this happpens *every day*. So much for desert sparsity—more like 'add water and stir' and watch Jack's beanstalk grow.

But let's take three steps backward and start with what the desert offered before a garden was ever planted here. Desert vegetation is hardly edenic, but despite its sparsity, it has provided well for ancient and more recent native people. Such staples as meal ground from various combinatins of ricegrass, sunflower seeds, piñon nuts, acorns, currants and squawbush berries were basic. Prickly pear and wild fruit were used fresh or dried. Roots of cattail, salsify and dock were eaten year round. Many plants could be gathered young for greens, and wild onion, mint, peppergrass and juniper provided seasoning. Ephedra—'Mormon tea'—and cota—'Navajo tea'—were boiled into refreshing brews. These and a host of other wild plants were used in medicine, art, and other aspects of daily life. In addition, corn, beans, squash, gourds, peppers, and tomatillos were planted wherever there was dependable moisture.

As they moved west, Europeans loosed a number of plant species on the desert, a few useful, most invasive. My desert friend Jim Fulton taught me to recognize and use several of them, and native plants as well. Russian thistle sprouts (tumbleweed), easy to harvest, make a great steamed vegetable or salad green. The tuberous roots of salsify substitute well for potates. Wild tomatoes, though unpalatable raw, are delicious in stews or stirfries. And the wild carrots Jim pulled for me were so sweet I would have fought Bugs Bunny for a patch of them.

From Remo I learned more, starting with the proper way to brew ephedra and cota. We also peeled and sliced cactus pads and sauteed them with piñon nuts and leaves of wild lettuce. We made delicious salads of young pigweed, dandelion and tumbleweed, laced with fleshy white petals of yucca flowers. We roasted salsify tubers and garnished them with chopped wild onion. One fall we made a trail mix solely of roasted piñon nuts and acorns, lemony squawbush berries, and red currants and serviceberries from Remo's land in the mountains. Tasty, if you don't mind picking seeds out of your teeth for hours afterward.

I also learned firsthand *not* to eat certain plants, but that's a story to be taken up later.

My own history as forager and gardener began in childhood, when I fed my runaway spirit on the bounty of greens, berries, fruits and nuts that grow wild in New England. Much of the lore of wild edibles I learned from my father, who transcended his city upbringing by teaching his three daughters one of the most civilized bodies of knowledge a person can have: the skills of using shovel, hoe, rake, hands, and water to create food. By weekday an accountant for a large corporation, my father preferred to work with his hands. Yes, he often drank too much, and yes, it made him nasty. But the muscles in his arms were tempered hard as iron from building our house, shoveling snow, making toys for handicapped kids, and spading each year's garden.

If have harsh memories of threats and beatings, I also have clear recollections of my father and mother evenings after work, kneeling, putting seeds into the ground or cultivating what grew from them, while we children played in the grass nearby. If I can still feel the back of my father's hand across my face, I can also feel the gentleness of that hand guiding mine as we made rows into which we pressed seeds, covered them with fine soil and patted them snug, my child's hand spread beneath his callused palm. What I don't recall is a time when I *didn't* know how deep or far apart to plant each kind of seed, how much to water the sprouted seedings, and how to tell those seedlings from weeds.

All of which served me well as an adult who has gardened in nearly every place she's lived. Horsethief, with its huge garden of raised beds filled with handmade soil and watered by Michael's intricate drip irrigation system, was a challenge from the beginning. Planted but untended during Chad's last year as caretaker, many of the beds were choked with weeds. The compost pit, intended to replenish the soil in the beds, was a tangle of fruit tree prunings, cornstalks, dried weeds and rotting garbage.

Knowing that Michael planned to visit for a month in June—his first visit since I'd lived here—and would enjoy firing up his gasoline composter and making soil of all that stubble, I ignored the compost pit and instead raked wheelbarrow-loads of winter-cured manure from the corrals. After clearing the beds of mulchstraw and removing each bed's web of plastic pipe, I spread a layer of manure several inches thick over the soil, then double-spaded it in, turning overlapping rows first crosswise then lengthwise, fifteen inches deep. Finally I chopped the soil fine with a hoe, raked it smooth and level, and put the pipes back in place.

Meanwhile I began the chore of ridding the remaining beds of weeds. Some, like pigweed and kochia, gave up easily. But one quadrant of the garden was choked with two of the most tenacious weeds a gardener could encounter: bindweed, a poor relative of morning glory, and saltgrass, a desert cousin of Bermuda grass. Both have extensive root systems, both sprout from stems as well as roots, and both have roots that break easily, leaving more root growing.

Morning after morning I donned gloves and set mind, teeth, and spade to the task. At the end of each day, I'd have created a five-by-five foot square of weedless soil—an area that next year I'd be able to turn over in ten minutes instead of ten hours. Without that hope, and the example of crops already planted, I might have quit. But two weeks later, along with a stiff back, I had weedless beds in which to seed spinach, chard, lettuces, and a big patch of potatoes.

By then the average annual frost-free date of April 29th had passed, and May's weather—I hoped—would be warm enough to put in tomato, egg-plant, pepper and squash seedlings. A thick layer of mulch-straw tucked around each plant and spread over the entire bed helped keep its soil moist, weeds from sprouting, and worms and sowbugs at work breaking down straw into soil. It also helped keep the tender plants from freezing when they were hit by frost.

I felt had an orderly garden under way, one that took advantage of companion-planting certain species together, each of which enhanced the health and productivity of the other. In every bed were insect-repelling herbs and flowers. Aromatic basil fronted the tomatoes, marjoram and sa-vory grew among the beans, horseradish in the potato bed. Onions, garlic, chives and scallions thrived amid squashes, peppers, and eggplants. Giant marigolds, zinnias, and petunias added bright color to every bed.

Meanwhile, during April and May the fruit trees bloomed, scenting the canyon like a Persian garden. Delicate apricot blossoms, weighted with the bumble of wild bees, then deeper pinks of plum and cherry, peach and nectarine bloomed. Apple, pear and almond blossomed white and sweet, and finally the fuzzy yellow flowers of grapevines—each tree and vine with its contingent of murmuring bees. Native squawbushes around the spring and corrals, and the non-native Russian olive by the bunkhouse, offered the heady perfumes of their flowering. Yellow honeysuckle and white bridal wreath outside the bedroom window sweetened my dreams, while the stately iris bordering the front yard, planted for their elegant purple flowers, instead bloomed the rich red-brown of the desert sand from which they grew.

Life at the ranch from early spring on revolved in large part around the garden. Guests almost always wanted to help, to get their hands in the soil, to contribute in some way to the productivity of the place. All of these people left their mark on Horsethief as surely as they felt changed by the experience of being there—including, in mid-May of that first year, my mother.

Most mother-daughter relationships have at least a little touch-and-go to them, and ours was no exception. We could treat each other as adult equals for about three days before things broke down into familial patterns of nag and sass. When Mom told me she wanted to come to the ranch for a week, and spend a second week with her grandkids in Albuquerque, I thought, Well, maybe there's space enough here so it'll work. When she wrote again to say she'd changed her mind and wanted to stay the entire two weeks at Horsethief, with Nance and the kids driving up to visit, I thought, Uh oh. No desert is big enough for that.

Amazingly, things worked out. Except for Mom without asking tossing out all the dried flowers I'd kept in vases to cheer me through the winter, we got along quite well. I drove her around to marvel at the nearby National Parks. She proudly accomplished her wish, at age eighty, of riding a horse for the first time in thirty years. And we spent considerable time in the garden together. She'd even brought her own sunhat.

Watching her one morning as she thinned a row of carrots—the quintessential little old lady in tennis shoes, long-sleeved shirt and cotton pants—I noticed for the first time how long her arms were, how large her hands. Her withered, age-freckled, nurse's hands, so incongruous on her tiny body, as if enlarged by all the years of care they'd given to so many people, including her children. I felt an urge to pick her up in my arms as if she were the child, and tell her how much she meant to my life, how grateful I was for the life she had given me. Instead, I brought her a glass of cold lemonade, thanked her for all the work she was doing in the garden, and told her how glad I was she'd come.

By the time my sister Nance and her children arrived, the lettuces, cress and arugala were ready for salads, and we made the most of them. There's nothing quite like the taste and texture of spring's young greens, that first nibble of tender lettuce leaves pulled straight from the soil. Suddenly winter, with its heavy diet of beans, grains and meat, is far behind. Even if nothing else has sprouted, suddenly one feels liberated from fluorescent aisles of supermarket produce into the cleansing lightness of feeding one's body what it craves and needs.

Though Mother's Day had passed, on the evening Nance arrived we celebrated our mother's day with a dinner of young carrots and peas, a leg of spring lamb, a big salad of baby greens, and a cake decorated with petals of desert flowers. Remo, stopping by on the way to his land, arrived in time for dinner, and later led us in singing old songs from the 1920s, the words to which only he and my mother knew. She and Remo hit it off so well that they were still gabbling after the dinner dishes were done. I bid them goodnight with my hot tub towel over my shoulder. Nance and the kids had gone to the bunkhouse, and as my mother went off to bed, Remo asked if he might join me. "Why not," I said, still thinking of him as a friend in whom I had no romantic interest. After all, he just wasn't my type...

Surprise, surprise. I don't recall how we ended up in each other's arms, but we stayed that way for hours, kissing openmouthed, taking each other's breath away, exploring each other with lips, tongues, fingers, arms, legs, all the skin we could press together, underwater and above, playing, teasing, until we noticed the water had cooled and it was almost dawn. Shriveled like prunes, we went inside, only to begin all over again in bed.

When he left later that morning for his land, a new keen feeling threaded between us.

That first spring, the frosty nights of early June flipped over into weeks of overbearing heat. Friends Mike Moore and Susan Walp arrived from Vermont, joined by a mutual friend from Colorado, George Sibley. Susan, an exquisite and recognized painter, was gone each morning at dawn to sketch and draw. Mike and George, both passionate gardeners, discovered the composter in the breezeway, spent a day repairing it, and were stuffing the noisy monster with stalks from the compost pit when Michael drove in for his first visit since I'd been caretaker.

An awkward half-hour passed while introductions were made and Michael inspected house and grounds and the changes I'd created during the first nine months of my tenure. Not having not seen the place for a year, since the last months of Chad's stay, he seemed vaguely impressed but said nothing. The next thing I knew, he'd added himself and Ken (who'd arrived earlier) to the composting crew. The air was full of noise, dust and bits of plant litter, and the basic element of the garden was being manufactured handful by hopperful—from sand and branches, stalks and husks, garbage and manure—right before my eyes.

Dirt. Dirt until something was planted in it, or until the earthworms went through it. Then it became soil. Great care was given to the proportions, and disagreements flared, barely heard above the composter's thrash and clatter: "More manure!" "No, more sand first!" "Hey, help me get these vines in the hopper." Michael, who with a crew of friends and this machine had made the many tons of soil that filled eighteen garden beds two feet deep, five feet wide and six to twenty feet long, worked with Mike and George until they saw how to produce what was needed. Then he and Ken went off to explore.

When the composter chugged to a halt at lunchtime, silence washed back into the canyon like the walls of the Red Sea. I went to look at the compost pit, running a handful of coarse duff through my fingers and inhaling its raw richness. While I was wetting it down with a hose, Mike, washing up at the sink outside the garden gate, quipped with baritone satisfaction in his voice, "If you can grow good soil, you can grow anything." I made a note to bring back some cartons of earthworms on my next trip to town.

Add water and stir... The stirring part was going along fine now, but I was having trouble adding water. Checking beneath the mulch, I discovered that the dripheads, which were spaced eighteen inches apart on their pipelines and designed to release overlapping circles of moisture along the rows of crops, were in many places making wet circles only three or four inches wide, and in some places none at all. I began hand-watering everything with a hose. Each evening I slow-danced around the garden, aiming the hose so as not to waste a drop, soaking as many rows as I could before dark. Worried that the fruit trees might not be getting water either, I watered each one for thirty minutes or more weekly.

Needless to say, all this took great amounts of water and time. With the spring down to the outtake pipe and my patience at the same level, Michael arranged for a tank truck of river water to be delivered into the cistern. Shortly after that, the solar pump was installed, and between Michael's "rain," the breaking of the drought with summer monsoons, and autumn's cold showers, a whole year passed before I learned the reason the dripheads weren't working. But more of that in good time.

Some of the best gifts are things you don't know you need. We were sitting under the front yard apricot one scorching noon, enjoying a last lunch with Susan, Mike, and George, when a young man wearing dusty clothes and a heavy backpack walked up the driveway and was welcomed by Michael. Ben Johnson, as he was introduced, was on walkabout, aiming to travel on foot from Moab to San Francisco by the straightest possible route crosscountry. Michael, returning from town the day before, had talked Ben into accepting a ride for a few miles, and had invited him to the ranch, which was on Ben's way west. Ben had hiked eighteen rough straight miles that morning from Island in the Sky. He looked ready for lunch.

Meanwhile, Mike and Susan and George had loaded their cars, leaving behind a pit full of well-made soil, a lovely painting over the kitchen window, great conversations, and words in the logbook: *A week under this hot desert sun has been good for the damp New England soul. We'll not forget these canyons, nor the bighorn we encountered, nor the ranch itself and the people we've met...*By the time goodbyes were said, Ben had finished his lunch and was leaning over the table with Michael and Ken, staring at a diagram Michael was making.

Glancing at the drawing while clearing the dishes, I saw plans for what looked like an arbor through the garden's midsection. Fine, I thought, as long as they don't damage what I've already planted. As if reading my mind, Michael explained that they needed me to move the rows of plants bordering the center aisle, but assured me "It'll be worth it. You'll have some shade in the middle of the garden, and a trellis where you can train tomatoes and beans."

If I didn't quite trust Michael's knowledge of hands-on gardening, I couldn't argue with the success of the projects he'd designed to support it—the railroad-tie beds and their soil, the greenhouse he'd had helicoptered in in parts and assembled in situ, the entire irrigation system. I transplanted the squash and pepper plants out of the way.

In the days that followed, Ken, Michael and Ben dug holes, set tall cedar posts in them, then bolted lodgepoles horizontally to form the framework of a sturdy arched 'roof' above the garden's center aisle. Reinforcement wire, stapled over the top and halfway down the sides, left the lower half open so there'd be room to work in the beds. No sooner was this framework complete than Michael and Ben drove to town and returned with a bucket of grapevine cuttings and a potted trumpet vine. As we planted them at the corners of each bed and trained them around the arbor posts, little did I foresee the size and productivity these vines would attain, nor the grace, shade, and vertical growing space the arbor would add to the garden.

Each year's garden was different, not only in what was planted and where, but in the ways various crops responded to that year's rainfall, temperature patterns and insect pests. In many ways, the canyon is an island, biologically isolated from other gardens and their pests—which is why it can be grown organically. It was fun each year to grow something new, like gourds, Turk's turban squashes, strawberrry popcorn, colorful Indian corn. At Michael's insistence I tried peanuts, which worked somewhat, and yams, which didn't work at all. The peanut plants went chlorotic, which is to say they turned yellow from lack of available iron in the soil—an ironic situation, since the canyon's rocks and sand are full of, and colored by, iron. However, most of it is bound up in an insoluble form (ferric oxide) that some garden crops and most non-native vines and fruit trees can't access. To compensate, at least twice a year they must be dosed with a solution of ferrous sulfate.

During Michael's spring visit the following year, he designed an 'apron bed' between garden and driveway, and got Ken and another long-time friend, Edric, to build it. That was the spring I fled to Arizona to escape the crowds of visitors. When I returned, the apron bed was finished, complete with its own drip irrigation hookup. Ken had planted asparagus among the apple trees that already grew there, and another of Michael's friends, a smart jolly woman named Betty, had filled the bed—and thus also lined the driveway—with a brilliance of scarlet petunias.

Edric, Michael's one-time college professor, was a courtly gentleman with a passion for gardening. A resident of Florida, where he held a master gardener's certificate, he visited the ranch each summer with his wife, Beth, and had helped Michael construct the garden early on. Always ultrapolite, Edric would ask me each year if he could plant this or that, and where. Each year I would say "Of course," show him areas of the garden that hadn't been planted, and remind him—*beg* him—to plant whatever he wanted, but *please* to plant it next to drip heads, so I wouldn't have to hand-water his gifts. And each year I would find the oddest flowers scattered here and there through the beds, often replacing what had already been planted, and seldom if ever near a drip head. By 'odd' I mean water-loving, as in lupine, delphinium, even morning glory—cultivated kin of the despised bindweed.

On the other hand, it was Edric who asked, in his courtly manner, if I thought flushing out the garden pipelines and replacing clogged drip heads before planting would help the system function better. *Bingo! Lightbulb!* Something no one had ever mentioned and I had never thought of. *All those hundreds of hours of handwatering, chained to the hose, missing my sunset horseback rides...* It was too late to pull the irrigation lines out from under this year's mulched crops, so I still had to handwater unless it rained. But from then on, spring's first task was to flush pipes and replace drip heads.

As every gardener knows, after planting comes waiting, sometimes days, sometimes weeks, to see what will sprout, what will take hold and grow. Pea-tendrils reach toward rabbit wire, hand-over-hand their way up, blossoming as they go. Spinach, beets, lettuce and chard come from the ground with two tiny leaves spread like dancers' arms, then four, then begin to look like themselves. Tomato plantlings, plain as palm trees, begin branching sideways as well as up, need support, respond to being touched, to being helped into place. Respond with their green scent, their yellow-petalled blossoms, their stems glistening with tiny golden hairs. Baby fruits, hard and green, form behind dropped blooms. Marigolds branch and bud, petunias need pinching off, melon tendrils unfurl, beans put up tri-leaved umbrellas and twirl up the arbor's tightwire, opening blossoms to the bees. Orange mouths of squash flowers open wide, while young corn plants, encountering each other's leaves, whisper like children.

Spring turns to summer the day you pick the first ripe tomato. At Horsethief this happens around the first of July. Meanwhile you've been dining on sweet peas and peapods, mostly in the garden. You've had a dozen meals of fresh spinach and several of chard, and you slice into the second planting of radishes for a radish/purslane/mayonaise sandwich on dark molasses bread. July's garden still has a sense of delicacy. Everything's so young and fresh you hardly bother to cook—you just graze while you're working, or whenever you feel the urge. You make little sushis right in the garden—a sunripe cherry tomato wrapped in a leaf of green or purple basil; a snap pea-pod or baby carrot banded with a feather of dill; crisp yellow or green beans bound with a sprig of savory; a fingerling of summer squash knotted with garlic chives. Every year it's like this. Every year, for a while, you fool yourself into thinking it's going to be easy.

But as the garden's greenery overflows its beds like a river in flood, and everything begins to ripen at once, you start to panic. You're only one person, what do you eat first? A head of broccoli or cauliflower will make three meals. One stirfry will use up two peppers, three summer squash, a fistful of green beans, an onion and a small eggplant—and last another three days. The refrigerator's so jammed with what you picked yesterday you can't find what you picked the day before. Meanwhile, more beans, chard and spinach are waiting, if you made yourself a salad you'd slow the lettuces from bolting, you've hardly touched the spicy arrugala and cress you love, you know when the corn ripens you'll bypass everything else, and right now you're so stuffed with ripe apricots you can't even think about eating.

And this is just the beginning. You've given the top two-thirds of the apricot trees to the birds, and still hundreds of these little globes of orange sugar are smashing on the ground before you can get to them. You split and dry apricots, split and dry cherry tomatoes, slice and dry romas and regular tomatoes, snip and dry herbs, there's never enough room in the drying racks on the roof. You make jam, dozens and dozens of jars to give as winter gifts. You make up shopping bags full of this and that and take them to the food bank, the bookstore, the laundromat to give away. You bring more bags to the Parks for the rangers, or give them to Bonnie to dole out. You stop for the flagman on the highway project and plunk a bag of veggies and a cold beer in his free hand. You dream about finding a section of the garden you haven't touched, you didn't know was there. You find a whole section of the garden you haven't touched, you forgot was there, behind the greenhouse, a tangle of ripe and ripening and over-ripe tomatoes, basketsfull.

In the back of your mind is the compost pile, where nothing ever goes to waste. But this is *food*, food of the highest order, fresh and unpolluted, and everywhere in the world are the eyes of hungry children. Even the zucchinis that hide under their leaves and grow huge, you take by boxfulls to the food bank. As the apricots wane and peaches and nectarines begin to ripen, you realize that if your hands were tied behind your back you could still graze heartily. Michael has suggested planting only half the garden—but which half? Half of each bed? Half of each row? The sunny half, where corn and squashes, peppers and eggplants grow best? Or the shady half, with its greens and root crops and potatoes? Which half of the flowers, which half of the herbs?

It's easier, you decide—every year you decide, because it's there and because you can't help it—to plant the whole thing and just let it go.

And go it does. By August the corn is tall and tasselled, golden pollen collects on silken threads and dusts the green leaves, which rustle and sigh, nudge and shoulder each other like playful lovers. Gone are the orderly rows of spring and early summer, overtaken by chaos. Eggplants peek from beneath the elephant ears of squash plants, tomatillo bushes bear chile peppers, watermelon and canteloupe vines intertwine, writhing like nests of snakes, guerilla armies of gourds are stationed high in the apricot tree, pumpkin vines leap the fence and block the driveway. Tomato, bean, grape and trumpet flower vines enmesh the arbor's wire walls, crisscross the roof, reach three feet into the sky like the tentacles of undersea creatures hungry for light. Each harbors the fruit of the others, grapevines bearing orange trumpet flowers, beans hanging from tomato vines, grapes under the bean leaves, a bewildering synaesthesia of fruits and vegetables you're too busy harvesting to sort out. The only remaining singularity resides in the ten-foot tall sunflowers that tower over everything, heads bowed, leaning with the wind like monks on a journey.

Summer's heat draws fewer guests than spring or fall, but those who come eat heartily while they're here, and go away laden. A friend from California, Hathaway Barry, had written that she would be driving east in August and wanted to bring her ten-year-old daughter, Co, for a few days of horseback riding. No guests were ever more eagerly awaited: *ah, people who can help harvest, help eat!* I felt like a spider about to entrap two damselflies. When they arrived, however, we spent three whole days exploring on horseback. I hardly even thought about the garden except when we'd pick a few things for supper. I was liberated, for the time being, by Co's love of riding and by Hathaway's calm, smiling wisdom. "The Dalai Lama, you know, talks about the kinds of tyranny we place ourselves under. You..." she paused, looking up into the apricot tree we were sitting under, "I think you are under the tyranny of abundance."

The phrase stuck, as did the subtle advice. I continued to try to harvest 'everything,' but my efforts became more detached. I took time to notice what was happening in the garden beyond the baskets of produce I continued to pick. I even sketched in my journal and observed in words several things I'd noted only in passing.

Imagine, among bright red jewels of cherry tomatoes, an oval web about fourteen inches across, not symmetrical, not perfect, but with its radii and spiraling chords in good repair, taut and glistening with morning dew. And in the center, a most handsome spider, bright gold, black flecks on back and sides, ventral parts yellow. Elegant legs banded in tiny rings of black and gold, poised and tapering to fine ebony points. The garden spider, whom I try not to disturb, seems not to move from the center of her web. She is there in the morning as I stand with my mug of tea in one hand, plucking basil seedheads with the other. She hasn't moved when I come to harvest tomatoes during the day, and she's there when I check by flashlight while gathering herbs for a midnight supper. She isn't dead: if I tap her web she turns to face the tapping. I think about the coordination it takes to manage eight legs, and my brain goes feeble. I watch her sidle away from me in two directions at once, one set of legs taking her backwards, the other set sideways. If she has no language or philosophy I can understand, she has her dance.

Not all of the garden's denizens were so attractive, nor fared so well under my scrutiny.

Repulsion and fascination go hand in hand. I could watch for hours the huge green hornworm, translucent in late August light, as it munches its way audibly along a tomato leaf. Its 4 inch long body is chubby with rounded segments, like Alice's hookah-smoking caterpillar, but more colorful, with its large eye-like spots—black dots ringed with white and yellow. Even more interesting is that what appears to be the hind end, unmarked and smooth as a baby's bottom, is actually the head. The end that looks like a head, with its half-inch pointed 'horns,' prominent eyespots, and suckerlike 'mouth,' is a decoy. Any bird hungry enough to jab at that formidable 'face' would be spearing a beakful of 'tail.'

Like Alice's caterpillar, the hornworm has a voice. When I disturb it with the trowel I am going to use to kill it, it clicks a loud protest: tsk tsk tsk tsk tsk. Lewis Carroll, stoned, might have read words into this reproach. So do I. Clinging heavily with its stubby proto-feet to a denuded leaf stem, the creature is difficult to dislodge. So I break the stem off, placing it and its cargo on the garden path. I cover it with a large sunflower leaf before whacking it hard with the trowel—to avoid being spattered by the leaf-jelly it has digested, and also so I don't have to see the murder I'm committing—the green, gooey, skinless mess I make out of such an intricate, cleverly formed trick of nature.

By the end of August each year I'd become so intimate with the garden that by day it seemed part of me. The garden at night, however, withdrew from intimacy and took on a powerful presence. Though I knew it as well as I knew my hands, I hesitated sometimes to enter, fearing to disturb the living, breathing being darkness made of this jungle. Sunflowers no longer monks, but hanged men silhouetted against the sky. Rustlings caused not by wind or lizards but by the breathing of plants as they sensed my presence. Spooky. Before stepping through the gate, I tried to breathe in resonance with the breathing around me. In one way, it was like going into something benevolently monstrous. But in another, what I felt was simply logical: plants undergoing cellular respiration at night, completing the cycle of photosynthesis they were bound to by day. I thought of the story told me by a favorite poet, W. S. Merwin, about Fiji islanders who worship ficus trees as gods, and who, when the ficus trees grow so huge as to threaten their homes and streets, gather in ceremony and feasting to prune their gods.

As September's sun slants toward fall and its heat subsides, a sense of mild urgency arises in the canyon. By this time the lettuces have bolted, and the peas have spent themselves in the heat. The early corn has turned to stalk, to linen, though if I've planted smartly I may have fresh corn until mid-month. Late peaches and early apples overlap, and in the upper orchard blackberries are beginning to ripen. Most of the garden is still producing prolifically, and most of my days are still spent harvesting, often by stepladder.

A year and a half after she visited in the spring, my mother came for a week in September. I wanted her to see what her spring labors could produce, and share with her some of the bounty. Above all, I wanted her to see that she deserved, and should accept and enjoy, some reward for her labors. Often I had stood before my canning shelves in Horsethief's root cellar, remembering my mother's shelves, stocked each season with hundreds of jars of canned tomatoes and tomato sauces, green beans and peas, cut corn and creamed corn, carrots and beets, peach halves and pear halves, pickles and relishes, fruit butters and a dozen kinds of jam. Not blessed with her stamina, I was awed to think of the labor she put into preserving so much, especially while working full time as a nurse, sewing our clothes, packing lunches, preparing meals, and all the care she gave to us.

This visit, she brought with her curtains she had sewn for the windows, burnt-orange burlap lined with off-white monk's cloth—appropriately rustic and sturdy—that would help keep the house warm in winter. As always, she refused to relax. She mended window and door screens, the fireplace screen, the screen sieves for hot tub and cistern, the drying rack screens between uses. She helped harvest and dry tomatoes and herbs, dig potatoes, pick berries, make peach and nectarine jams. She mended all my clothes that could be salvaged. And complained there wasn't enough for her to do.

Not until I took her to hear my ranger friend Bonnie's campfire talk at Dead Horse Point, did I realize my mother's age and fragility. As I helped her from the car, at an altitude eight hundred feet higher than Horsethief, she complained of shortness of breath. She balked at looking out over the canyon rim at the view, saying the wind would blow her away. And then she balked altogether, insisting that she had to go back to the ranch, *now*, that the wind was taking her breath away. By the time we reached the ranch she felt better, but was adamant about not going to that altitude again. Two days later, as I drove her the hundred fifty miles to the airport for her flight home, I foresaw that this would be her last trip to Horsethief. I did not envision it would be her last trip in an airplane, her last visit west, her last visit anywhere outside her home town. I grieved for her aging. Even more, I grieved at that being her life's reward.

Returning to Horsethief, I listened to the voices of the corn, now all gone to linen, now scraping and scratching, hitching and coughing in the voices of old men, old women. I listened. I needed to understand what they were saying. But the wind took their words away.

I consoled myself with munching translucent clusters of sun-ripened grapes, and with eating the season's last peach, so heavy with juice it had to be sipped from its skin on the tree. I wished I'd been able to slice it into a bowl for my mother. Wished she was still here to enjoy the plums and pears now at their peak, the dark sweetness of thumb-sized blackberries. The garden just wouldn't quit, and I thought of my runaway life through my mother's eyes. *I keep waiting,* I wrote, *for this wild growth to slow of its own accord, to be halted by the sheer weight of leaf and stem, flower and fruit it has put out, to relax its reach, consolidate its gains, squeeze its strength into what is already ripening. But I have not lived my life that way, either.*

October days strung themselves out like gems on a necklace, windless and radiant, perfected by the kindly angle of the sun. Pumpkin vines continued to insinuate themselves among the potatoes, loop over the grapes, and roof the arbor, orange globes dangling like Chinese lanterns. It was easy to be fooled, then, to think fall would last forever. But the crickets, my chirping prophets, began sounding more subdued.

Then one day the lizards would be gone. The air would tighten, the wind begin to blow, or a cold rain start to fall, and the twinge in my bones warned of killing frost on its way. Did I back off in relief, bow to the inevitable, thank the season for its bounty, and retreat? Did I feel what Robert Frost expressed in "After Apple Picking"— *For I have had too much / Of apple-picking: I am overtired / Of the great harvest I myself desired...?*

I did not. I grabbed every basket, box, paper bag and plastic trash sack on hand and raced out to pre-empt the frost. I picked every tomato that stood a chance of ripening, and then I picked the green ones. I picked beans and more beans, cucumbers, peppers, eggplants and squashes of all sizes—anything beyond the blossom stage would do. I picked every melon that might ripen. I pulled up all the herbs and hung them in paper bags upside down in the root cellar. I did this as the air froze or rain or snow fell, freezing my hands until I had to use gloves, freezing my wet-gloved hands until I could pick only with opposable thumbs or knuckles pressed together. I did this under gray sky, or at night by headlamp, working until I could no longer see or feel anything, or until everything that could be frost-killed was safely stored. Only then did I go inside, thaw my fingers until I could unbutton my clothes, and sleep.

In the morning, I went out to face a garden of black rags. Bean and tomato leaves frozen olive drab. Potato plants flattened and charred. Marigolds burnt ochre, umber. After living with and from the garden for half a year, I was always surprised to feel so little sense of loss. But there were still potatoes to dig, and the hardy greens like spinach, chard, and sorrel would last until harsher cold throttled them, too. Meanwhile, I still had some of the best fruit to look forward to: tangy garnet-red winesaps and jade granny smiths, sweet blue-purple plums, dark musk-sweet blackberries.

I soaked each fruit tree once more before draining the pipes, then argued in my mind about whether to strip the garden of its spent stalks and vines, rake the debris from each bed and feed it to the compost pit, and leave the beds ready for spring, bare and stark as rows of coffins. Or whether to leave the garden as it died, to provide food and shelter for winter birds, color and texture for me, a polyphonic orchestra for the wind.

Usually I compromised, clearing some of the beds, smoothing them flat for the white sheets of snow that would soon cover them. The rest—the lacework of dry pea vines along the fence, the lattices of bean and tomato plants woven into the arbor, the sunflower and pumpkin leaves furled like black umbrellas, the burnt lacy marigolds going to seed, and especially the bleached linen cornstalks—these I left for winter to deal with.

As night after night of frost went deeper into the ground and the earthworms retreated downward, I went about downloading fruit into yet more cardboard cartons and winterizing the rest of the ranch. Gradually the sap in the trees sank into the roots; tarnished leaves gilded the yard. Sitting on the edge of an empty garden bed, I thought about the fruit and produce stored in the root cellar, the tomatoes that would ripen for Thanksgiving. I thought about the snapshots I'd taken of the outdoor table laden with a colorful array of produce, my mother standing next to it, arms raised in invitation. I thought about the soil under my hand, resting around its billions of inhabitants. And I thought about how the first snowfall would look, making visual music of the garden, while the pale, skeletal cornstalks whispered like ghosts.

Chapter Eleven

Work and Play

Holding Koa's stick in my gloved hand, I licked red sand from my lips and teeth and spat it out. Then winged the stick over a slickrock outcrop, hoping it might take Koa long enough to retrieve it so I could haul the log at my feet to the truck. No sooner had I heaved it into the bed atop the other logs, than Koa was back, chomping the stick and asking me to throw it again, not at all bothered by the red sand in *his* mouth.

Remo was coming! We were gathering hot tub wood in a juniper woodland several miles from the ranch. For once we'd found a good source—lots of clean, solid logs and branches that hadn't rotted into the sand. Seldom was woodgathering this easy. Mostly it was like pulling teeth—decayed ones at that: yanking sand-impregnated limbs from under trunks too heavy to move, tugging logs out from under cowpies. Some spots would yield hardly a stick to throw for Koa. But today, in less than an hour I'd dragged to the truck more than half a pickup load. Half still to go, since it was October, time to stock in enough to last the winter. My eagerness to fire up the hot tub for Remo's visit was no excuse for skimping.

Even when gathering was easy, it was second only to tar-patching the roof as the dirtiest job on the ranch. My shoes and gloves were full of sand, bark and twigs. Sand in my ears, nose, and eyebrows. Bark in my hair, shirt and jeans ripped by spiky branches, I might have appeared, had anyone happened by, like some wild cross between Ophelia and Lear. But tonight my lover was coming—anticipation made me feel I was wearing black lace and gathering armfuls of roses.

Since there was only Koa and me, we could ignore appearances and make a game of it. For Koa, sticks were the only game, fetching them the only rule. But he could be coaxed into a variation: wrestling useful-size logs to the truck while growling fiercely and wagging his tail. For me, the game was in becoming familiar with a new area of desert woodland. My pleasure came from noting the health of its vegetation, the condition of its cryptobiotic soil, and signs like animal tracks, owl pellets, the quantity of juniper berries and piñon cones.

Another hour's playful labor and we were jouncing home, overloaded with wood. While Koa kept an eye out for rabbits, I mused on my attraction to the eccentric man who would be visiting me tonight, and with whom I'd soon be going on a ten-day camping trip. Twelve years my senior, trimmed beard and wavy hair gone silver gray, olive-skinned with dark eyes, a large nose, and a Brooklyn accent, Remo was attractive in a Mediterranean sort of way. But I'd never been romantically drawn to anyone like him, and kept telling myself he wasn't my type.

Nonetheless, I could find a number of reasons for wanting to spend time with him. Foremost was his passion for and extensive knowledge of the desert. For thirty years, he and selected friends had made lengthy camping trips into almost every nook of southern Utah's canyon country. Eventually he'd bought fifty acres of gladed woodland in the foothills of the Abajo Mountains, where he spent several solitary weeks camping every spring and fall. Perhaps because my appetite for solitude and privacy rivaled his own, I'd become one of the handful of people allowed to visit him at 'Marmo,' as he called his land. This fall we would spend some days there, then a week camping in what Remo promised would be "a special place."

We had already taken one camping trip together, and I'd stayed at Marmo a few times. I had also been permitted to stay at his cabin in Aspen, another breach of Remo's legendary privacy. Even his longtime best friends were disinvited to drop by, making it notable that I was even invited in. That, and his oft-declared refusal to commit to any relationship, perversely made him more attractive. Content with my life at Horsethief, I needed no 'commitment.' But the notion of opening such a closed, resistant creature of habit was intriguing.

On the other side of the personality coin, I was finding him to be one of the more upbeat, witty, talented, and intelligent men I'd spent time with. He spontaneously whistled, hummed, or sang everything from antique glee club airs to jazz tunes to classical pieces like Prokoviev's 'Love for Three Oranges.' He told poignant stories from his childhood growing up in a condemned Brooklyn tenement, where his immigrant parents ran a candy store and he and his three brothers became Americanized. "I knew we didn't have any money," he said, "but I never knew we were poor. My mother wouldn't use that word."

The spirited mother, Antonia, and the quiet father, Stephano, raised the boys Catholic. More important, raised them with a sense of fairness and responsibility. "I had a happy childhood," Remo claimed. "Until I was in high school, I thought everybody did." High school brought out his considerable artistic talents, and a brother in the military sent him through Pratt Institute of Design. College years at Pratt became a major turning point. Extracurricular design jobs allowed him to move into his own apartment, much to his mother's dismay. Far worse from her point of view was his decision to reject Catholicism. After a dream in which he pushed over and smashed a glass cabinet laden with statues of the Virgin and other saints, there was no turning back. After two "boring" years as a designer on Madison Avenue, he packed his belongings in a trailer and headed west, celebrating his freedom by stopping along the way to indulge his fondness for fishing, and taking eight months to reach Denver.

From there it seemed inevitable that his design mastery would combine with his love of fishing to take him to Aspen, and that the momentum of westering would lead him to the canyonlands of southern Utah. He did enough design work to eventually purchase the Aspen cabin he'd rented by the river. Much of the rest went toward camping trips with various friends.

He told compelling stories about those, too. About getting his friends lost without water; about the bloody sheep they found hanging from a bridge, being butchered by two Outward Bound runaways; about winching a jeep out of a canyon for Bates Wilson and a group of dignitaries who were working to create Canyonlands National Park; about camping their way through empty canyons for days, only to come upon a biblical baptism scene of epic proportions—dozens of white-robed extras milling around waiting to be filmed with John the Baptist for a movie on the life of Jesus. Never one to spare himself, Remo would break into laughter as he related his first trip through Glen Canyon, soon after moving to Aspen. Exploring a grassy riverbank, he reached down to pick up what looked like a saucer of coiled clay, only to have the 'Anazazi ashtray' begin buzzing the rattles of its tail.

Backing the truck up the narrow laneway between garden and cistern and parking it next to the hot tub, I let go the stories, let go the musing as I unloaded and stacked wood. After all, love is not reasonable, and to be honest I'd have to admit that high on the list of attractions were our times in the hot tub together. They'd been the beginning of many surprises.

Before going out for wood, I had drained and scrubbed the tank, tightened the bolts on the two benches and rinsed it all down with a hose. Now, vowing not to overheat our aqueous love nest, I screwed the drain-cap closed, opened the intake valve, and waited for a few inches of water to pour in before lighting the kindling I'd laid inside the furnace door beneath the tub. Next, sticks and small logs from my new stash, then bigger logs and chunks of piñon, until the fire was roaring. It would take an hour to fill the tub, and at least three to heat its chill spring water to a comfortable, non-scalding soak of 100 degrees.

Meanwhile, I prepared supper. That I had no idea what time Remo might arrive, or whether he might be delayed for days, as had happened before, didn't lessen my anticipation. I stuffed a free-range hen with a rolled lemon, crushed garlic and fresh rosemary, tucked it in the oven. Then built a fire in the living room fireplace. I scrubbed the sand and debris from skin and hair in the indoor tub and soaked in lightly scented bubbles, breathing deeply to invoke the spirit of Hokoji, the eighth century monk and teacher whose words I'd read recently: "How wonderously strange and miraculous—I draw water, I carrry wood." His life perhaps was simple, mine complex. But oh yes, how wondrous...

Curled in the armchair in front of the fireplace with a book in my lap, I relaxed, musing further about this undousable attraction. Perhaps love was something like light, shapeshifting, luminous, streaming in from outer darkness and hurtling its particle waves smack through our bodies. After all, didn't I fall in love at least once a week, whenever I went to town? With a little darkhaired boy trying to ride his bike and eat a popsicle at the same time. With an elderly ranch wife, wispy white hair, wrinkles like canyons seen from the sky, easing herself blue boots first out of a pickup. With an Indian man in the supermarket for his expression of incised awareness, his quiet readiness to count coup. All my life I'd been tumbling into love like that.

And now? Through all this musing didn't I have both ears tuned to the growl of Remo's Bronco coming in the driveway? Two years into the relationship, part time though it was, was I still merely infatuated, or—where were we going? Just camping pals, with an occasional movie date when I came to Aspen? I shook my head, poked up the fire, put another log in place, went outside to do the same for the hot tub. Love, I was thinking as I came back in, love has stamina. Takes risks. Enjoys play, but doesn't shirk hard times, hard work. Where were we going?

Several times I had come close to calling the whole thing off, tired of thinking the relationship could grow, only to have Remo lay down another rule: "No commitment." "No monogamy." "No expectations." In frustration I'd written our mutual friend Bruce Berger a while ago, *He's playing games. It's not a woman he wants, but a lifestyle hedged by emotional rules. He's froth, not wave, spume, not substance. Why should my heart be held hostage by someone who doesn't want it anyway?*

Just then Koa woofed, then barked. I heard the throb of a car engine and stepped out into the midnight dark in slippers and silk robe to open the front gate. Koa whined excitedly as Remo drove in, and I swung the gate closed. I reached the Bronco as he was getting out, and was enfolded in familiar arms, kissed by a mouth I couldn't get enough of. "Sorry to be so late," he apologized in Brooklynese. "I had a doctor's appointment and couldn't get away, and then—"

"No worries. I'm just glad you're here safely. Have you eaten? Come on in. What can I carry?" I flitted in place like a bird in the wind, taking the small duffel bag he handed me, hearing a soft rattle like a rainstick within, and remembering: the pills, the heart condition, the triple-bypass surgery a few years ago, the heart attack. "How are you feeling?" I asked casually as we walked to the house.

"Well, I'm tired. But I'm glad to be here. I don't think I should eat anything this late..." Then, as we entered the aromatic kitchen, removing his hat, eyes smiling, "Well, maybe a few bites." Another bearhug, another long kiss. "Come on," I said, pulling away for air. "Food first."

"How's the hot tub?" was the first thing he asked as he devoured the small plate of roast chicken, couscous and salad I set before him. "It felt just about right when I checked it a half-hour ago." I replied. "There were still hot coals in the firepit, so it should stay that way for a while." We chatted lightly about things that had happened since our last time together, two months ago, when I had driven to Aspen to hear the final performances of the summer music festival. An appreciation of good music was another thing we shared, and I was pleased when Remo took from his duffel three tapes he'd had made for me of concerts I'd been unable to hear: the Emerson Quartet on two tapes, performing Bartok's six string quartets; and a Glinka-Tchaikovsky-Corigliano concert featuring Sarah Chang, which I put in the tape player. It was still playing as we walked out the back door with our hot tub towels, Koa trailing along.

Our dance, Remo called it. With other lovers, finding artful ways of reaching orgasm had always been the point. Our hot tub loveplay was more a dance, floating, standing, sitting, entwined, apart, water rocking with the motion of our bodies, exquisite caress of fingers, wrists, mouths, tongues, ache of near-climax sustained by water's friction, never quite happening, never quite not-happening.

And our dance had only gotten better. On last spring's visit, the second night we were in the hot tub Remo took my hands to stop me from touching him, held me close, and said he had something to tell me. Immediately I grew wary. "You know, I have these friends I told you about, Lon and Cindy. You haven't met them yet, but we go out for dinner together sometimes. They keep trying to get me to join their circle of friends, but it's not my thing," he fumbled, obviously diverting himself from whatever he was going to say. "Anyway, I've told them about you, and the ranch, and, well —" he blurted it out, "Cindy says I'm in love with you."

Heartbeats went by while I waited for him to add something confirmatory, like "And I guess I am." But that didn't happen. I began to realize that this man who could be blunt to the point of rudeness also had a timid side, and that his unwillingness to commit to a relationship was no measure of his involvement in it. I hugged him and held on, waiting a few more beats before whispering in his wet ear, "Nobody's told me, but I think I'm in love with you, too."

And now, tonight, water temperature perfect, vapor rising into cool October night, star reflections bouncing in the ripples, there seemed no need to say anything. We found each other's mouths underwater, surfaced breathing each other's breath, Remo's tongue taking my breath away, drawing my body inside out, nipples tingling, genitals imploding, friction of water under our fingertips creating unrelieveable arousal as we touched the thinnest, most intimate membranes of each other's bodies, lightly, less lightly, until breathless, laughing in wonder, we pulled apart and stood side by side in the water, staring at the studded sky, hearing the flutter of cottonwood leaves in the tree nearby. Here was the world with us, participating in our joy.

Remo was perhaps the most playful adult I'd ever met. His tendency to make a game out of almost anything he did—or at least to enjoy it—was the attractive side of the grump who laid down rules. While I questioned whether this lilting man was capable of a serious relationship, I couldn't help but be caught up in his good humor. He loved to give gifts, some but not all of them products of his addiction to garage sales. And whatever the gift—a jar of wild mushroom powder from his rambles in the mountains, a lovely heishi necklace from his collection, a kitchen utensil he noticed I needed, a set of elegant bath oils—it was always thoughtful, usually surprising and often wrapped in a hand-fashioned box made for just that gift.

He also loved to cook—and what a gift that was! His breadsticks and focaccia—*figassa* in his family dialect—were legendary among friends. But breads weren't the only food he'd learned from his mother. *Turta*—squares of rice, parmesan, bread crumbs, egg and spinach—become a staple of our camping trips. *Erveu battieu,* 'beaten egg,' a hot concoction of coffee brewed in milk, sweetened slightly, thickened with a beaten egg and sipped from a bowl, made a full breakfast. Another treat was *puding di maioti,* 'pudding of the sick,' a luscious custard flan his mother had fed him when he was ill. Recovering, he'd been given *gnocchi verdi im brodo di pollo*—spinach noodles in chicken broth. Remo also took pleasure in serving ranch guests *pasta achuita*, capellini with steamed potatoes, green beans, mushrooms, fresh pesto and parmesan.

"Peasant food," Remo called these dishes. "It's what I ate growing up. It's all we had. Now you can get focaccia or gnocchi verdi in any Italian restaurant." He added that he could only spell phonetically the names of what he made, since his parents came from an area north of Genoa where the spoken dialect was ancient but unwritten. In any case, Remo's meals, as much as Ken's or mine, had inspired the phrase "dinner at the Horsethief Restaurant."

Another of Remo's qualities, one which complemented his love of cooking, was his meticulous attention to detail. Sometimes this took the form of a preoccupation with minutiae, as when he was packing for a camping trip and had to have everything in its proper place, down to the spare tentpins. On the other hand, during a stay at Horsethief he spent four days at the grimy, chaotic breezeway workbench, sorting and organizing every nail and screw, nut and washer, plumbing part and hand tool—a laborious expression of play for which Michael, when he learned of it, sent him a thank you from the other side of the world.

Remo's ability to make play out of work did much to shift my attitude in that direction. While I was far from fox-trotting through every chore, I'd begun to see that most work, even tasks like weedpulling, could be performed as meditation, if not play. Even dreaded repairs like plumbing breaks and roof leaks could be handled without bitching if I lowered my resistance and took them one breath at a time. The problem came when an emergency arose just when I had other deadlines to meet. Or when facing multiple projects that had to be done at once. Hard to keep one's playful cool when the horses went AWOL the day before the farrier was due—the same day the orchard pipeline sprang a serious leak and the oven door fell off. Too often such *complexities du jour* married the Rule of Threes to Murphy's Law, with panic as offspring.

The saving grace was that often guests showed up, or Ken arrived, or Bonnie and Stephen dropped by, and suddenly I had unexpected help. Guests, of course, came to relax and enjoy the ranch, the desert. But something about Horsethief also invoked a desire to work: to plant or prune, repair the chainsaw, saw up an armload of firewood, pull a forest of weeds from around the bunkhouse. Especially I appreciated organizations that used the ranch for staff retreats, board meetings or reunions, since they often scheduled a work session to help the ranch in exchange for using it. From each according to ability, to Horsethief, which was ever in need.

By letter one winter I convinced Michael that Horsethief needed new gates, that it was time to replace the massive, makeshift corral gates that needed turnbuckles and cables tightened frequently to keep them off the ground. The same for the snag-your-shirt, rip-your-hand, trip-your-horse barbwire gates that had to be dragged open and closed, and fastened with wire loops and lots of elbow grease. I counted: we needed twelve steel-rail gates of various widths, which the Moab hardware store would sell for a discount on a purchase of ten or more. At first Michael balked. Then amazingly he agreed not only to pay for them, but to set up a fund for such special projects as long as they didn't exceed $1000 a year.

Major breakthrough! Chad, the former caretaker, Gil, the one before Chad, and myself had each struggled mightily to keep the ranch going on a strict budget of $100 per month, which had to cover everything from nails and roofing tar to hay, horseshoes, repairs and emergencies. Chad had admitted spending most of his savings on the ranch in the three years he was there, and I was spending too much of mine. Relieved, I hauled the twelve new gates home and stored them in an out-of-the-way place until—

Until what? Gates required stout, deep-sunken posts for support, of which there were only a few already in place. They required digging deep holes in the ground, setting new posts plumb and solid, drilling horizontal holes in each post for the hinge-pins that held the gate, screwing the hingepins into the holes so they both stuck out the same length, and finally setting the gate on its pins. I felt hope draining into a sinkhole as I thought about all the spare time I didn't have. Not for one gate, never mind twelve.

But again, guests to the rescue. The first new gate, the main one into the front yard, was installed by Michael's daughter Katie and her then-boyfriend, Kirk. Recently graduated from high school and headed for pre-med on full scholarship, Katie was a lovely young woman who had avoided spending time at her father's ranch on grounds it was "too rough, too macho, too full of animals skulls and rattlesnake skins." For Kirk, a city-bred academic, it was a first visit. I winced inwardly when they offered to set the front gate.

But they did it. They did it in two days, and they did it right. I was amazed and elated. And they, deservedly, were full of proud satisfaction. After all, it was something Katie would be able to point out to her grandchildren—not an idle thought, from the look in Kirk's eyes.

Mostly, guests made my life easier, but not always. One journal entry tells as much as need be told of those stories:

Arrived home tonight after Megan [Michael's younger daughter] &
four friends were here, leaving house tidy & clean. But outside, found

huge gouge in firewood stack by living rtoom door. Then found 2nd huge hole in stack by corrals. A half-cord gone? Just for fireplace? Two nights & two days? Checked hot tub, water still very warm 2 days after everyone left—& omigod—wood in hot tub pit half-gone, after I stacked it full before leaving. Pool covers warped crisp—fried like giant blue potato chips.

How could so much wood have been burnt in so short a time? Many fireplace logs must have gone to heat hot tub. Plus the hot tub wood, which alone is enough to have boiled half the missionaries in Africa. Must have had continuous bonfire in fireplace too—but still can't imagine so much wood used up in so short a time: the physics of it just doesn't compute.

How very little is needed! But they don't know that, just as I didn't before living here, just as most people in this country don't know: how little is needed. There seems so much available, so of course one uses all one can—isn't that our patriotic duty? No one was here to say "Wait, this is hard to come by, and you only need a little. Here, try this much. Then you'll actually be able to get in the tub and enjoy it..."

To be fair, like her sister Katie, Megan at that time had rarely visited the ranch. After she learned better, she made an art of always firing the tub to a perfect temperature. A wise and lovely young woman, she became an enormous help to the ranch and to me.

Ken, of course, was Horsethief's single biggest benefactor. Next for 'helpful hero' honors was my neighbor, Stephen Haan, who proposed to Ranger Bonnie in the hot tub, and whom she married the following July. Like Ken, Stephen seemed to arrive just when I needed rescue from some jam-up of urgent projects. In addition to making the desert's best strawberry pie, Stephen repainted the hot tub's rusty interior one summer, drained and painted the cistern that fall, flushed the garden irrigation system and replacing its clogged drip heads in spring, and with Bonnie and me, sealed the ranchhouse roof with new tar-and-grit roofing paper.

On another occasion Stephen saved my face, if not my life, when the pilot light on the water heater went out and refused to re-light. Stephen stood by holding a flashlight while I lay on the bathroom floor twisting the stiff control button with one hand and trying to locate the pilot port with a lighted match in the other. Suddenly everything huffed in my face and I smelled burning hair, at the same time I felt Stephen's hands clapping fast and hard around my head. After we got the pilot lit, he offered to give me a haircut—one of the best I've ever had.

A fine horseman and graceful rider, he also kept the horses' hooves trimmed between farrier visits. He had developed a design for what he called "hush-ponies," tough rubber pads that adhered to the bottom of a horse's hooves and, unlike metal shoes, protected the hooves while allowing them to expand and contract in a healthy, natural way. Stephen had experimented for years to formulate the rubber for the pad and the glue that held it on. Then, working with a small laboratory in the Pacific Northwest where he was raised, he'd produced a prototype set of hush-ponies. These he guarded with ultra-secrecy—not even Bonnie knew where he kept them, nor did he make any effort to market them or any other of his inventions.

And that was the unfortunate side of Stephen. Affable and witty, intelligent and inventive, competent and generous, he always came up against the wall of his bipolar split personality. Only a few months into their marriage, harmony was being eroded by Stephen's irrational jealousy and defiant inertia. At one point he'd taken Bonnie's service revolver and driven off in the red bus, threatening to kill himself and blaming Bonnie for "making him do it." His dark side took a sad toll on Bonnie. Genuinely sweet, thoughtful and giving, she blamed herself and tried harder to please, not realizing the futility of her efforts.

I had no idea this was going on until one evening when I'd invited them for dinner and only Bonnie showed up. She told me Stephen had gone off in his bus and she hadn't seen him for five days, but didn't mention the gun or threats of suicide. As we sat outside talking about it, Stephen drove up in the red bus, parked it outside the gate, and tried to greet me warmly while ignoring Bonnie. I wasn't playing that game, and when he turned to her and addressed her sarcastically as "Ranger Benson," I stepped in and suggested they talk out their problem while I finished making dinner. They disappeared into the bus, and when they hadn't emerged two hours later, I took a tray with plates of food and two glasses of wine to the bus. By then things seemed fine between them. But I had seen Stephen swallowed by his darkness, and from then on could offer Bonnie some of the support she needed to deal with it. Neither of us knew how serious the situation was, mostly because Stephen's bright side surfaced as often as its opposite, and there seemed no ground within him where dark and light recognized each other.

Stephen continued being helpful to the ranch, and I made a conscious effort to accept both sides of him without questioning, without trying to 'fix' him, in the hope that acceptance might strengthen his rational side—and in the awareness that it might not.

During the January after their July marriage, before the Green River froze over, Stephen volunteered to ride with me down the switchbacks and bring back the horses pastured on the riverbottoms. That morning I woke to three inches of new snow on the ground, more falling. Stephen was due at nine. Meantime I dressed in warm layers, packed two lunches and fed Aquila and Shasta, whom I'd brought in the day before from the herd on the upper range. By then the snow had stopped, and cloud cover kept the temperature above freezing. Stephen drove in as I was saddling the two mares, and we set out, Koa yipping after a jackrabbit.

Cloud cover remained thick and the air still as we headed west. Under the gray, colors were intense. Red rock, gold grasses, orange weeds above the snow, our faint blue shadows moving over it. Then other blue shadows loping along, as we were joined by the small herd I'd taken Aquila and Shasta from. All of them squealing and pawing in greeting, no way to shoo them off.

After the horses settled down, we rode amid the sounds of snow-muffled hooves. I thought of something Mark Twain had written: that work is something a body is obliged to do, while play is something a body is not obliged to do. I disagreed. First, I was obliged to bring the horses up before the river froze, so they'd have water. Second—I trotted Aquila up to Shasta and asked Stephen, "Have you ever had anything to do with horses that you could really call *work?*"

He caught my point, thought a moment, and replied, "No... only when I had to bury the horse I grew up with. Even then it wasn't work. It was grief." I thought sadly of locoed Zamar and Bruja, their bones now scattered. I nodded, and we eased into a lope, the loose horses bucking and farting, whirling and kicking. All in play, of course.

When we reached the rim and opened the barbwire gate, we decided to let the loose horses follow us down the switchbacks. Best the two herds have their reunion away from any entangling fences. At the bottom, around the second bend, six shaggy horses lifted their heads and snorted loudly. One, the white Arab stallion Eagle, high-stepped away from his herd and circled toward us. At the same time, our four-horse herd started toward the others, and in moments they were all caught up in a melee of squealing and pawing, rearing and ducking through swirling snow. Our two mounts rocked against their bits, beside themselves with impatience to join the others. I gestured to Stephen that we should head toward the switchbacks and see if the herd would follow. As I rode off, Stephen on Shasta circled the milling herd at a lope, yipping like a coyote to start them after me. Soon Aquila and I were headed up-trail among a raft of equines who seemed to know where they were going and be eager to get there. At the rim, we yipped the horses through the gate and closed it, while the whole herd went into another paroxysm of horseplay and headed for home without us.

After securing Shasta and Aquila to a juniper, Stephen and I swiped the snow off a boulder and ate our lunch. I asked him questions about his childhood, and he answered amiably enough that his father had died when he was young, that he hadn't gotten along with his stepfather, but that he had been close to his mother, who had passed away a few months before Stephen took to the road in his bus. He'd had a live-in girl friend for two years, "but she left me when my mother died," he said in a tone that edged on self-pity. Rather than encourage that, I suggested we tighten our saddle girths and take the high route back to the ranch.

Up on the rolling back of the mesa, where we could see the shapes of buttes and canyons for dozens of miles in every direction, Stephen turned Shasta toward a rock formation some ways off, saying he'd catch up later. Relieved to be alone, I dismounted and studied my great white rock, two miles east and flattened by distance—until Aquila shoved me with her nose and and sent me flying. Ears pricked forward, eyes wide with innocence, she snorted as I dusted snow off my jeans. I shook my head laughing as I swung onto her back. "You must get tired of watching me watch things, girl. I suppose *you* want to go with Shasta, but *I* want to go home."

As we wove around blackbrush and cactus, I mused on her playfulness, which surfaced rarely, and that of other animals I knew—none of which approached Koa's. If the capacity for play is a measure of intelligence, I wondered, what about the so-called lower animals? The lizards, which I secretly believe chase each other in play as well as in defense of territory. The wad of baby garter snakes in the greenhouse, writhing in and out of the tight ball of themselves apparently for no reason than the pleasure of each other's company on a hot summer day. Who could think that schools of fish don't play with each other and with currents in the water, just as ravens, raptors and other birds do in the air?

Aquila's shoes on slickrock aroused me from these thoughts as we neared the home canyon, and I patted her neck. But then I got thinking of the baby kit foxes outside their den at Needle Rock, doing backflips and somersaults over each other. "Learning their survival skills," a behavioralist would say. Fine, but the youngsters haven't entered teleology school yet, so why make play a form of work? Besides, what about adults, who've already learned their survival skills and still love to play? What about the corraled horses after a gully-washer, who chase each other back and forth across the stream that temporarily flows through their corral, leaping it with oodles of room to spare and immediately wheeling around to do it again? I thought about lines from a poem by a man who had lived near Moab, Donovan Roberts, now deceased:

Work and Play

...Can it be that the
World is but the great word that
Speaks the meaning of Joy?

*

Now it was October, and Remo, Koa and I were camped at Marmo. How I relished Remo's happiness here. And how I relished this home away from home. Late morning sun slanted through scented evergreens, gold leaves trickled through the air. Koa slept in the shade. Remo worked on a project somewhere in the trees. Now and then came the steep sliding laughter of a canyon wren. Remo chose well when he put a claim on the peace of this place. I could become a connoisseuse of wind here, listening to the orchestra it made of the huge rocks and trees. Low notes from boulders and ponderosa, tenors of many tones in piñon and juniper, alto rustlings of dry leaves, soprano riffs of wind high along the cliff-band. Even the woodland grasses whispering the cadence, the pitch.

This morning while we ate toast and eggs at the picnic table, a shrill *screee, sc-reee* had spiked the air above the cliffs. A golden eagle flew low along the rim, every wingbeat audible. Grateful for the gifts of morning, I wanted to sing with delight at such a master brushstroke: eagle's flight above eagle-colored cliffs, across blue sunshine that kindled life in the earth at my feet. There, the soil glittered with tiny diamonds of mica, and a single gold leaf the size of a demitasse spoon lay curled into the shape of a musical staff. An amber flake of worm-tracked bark made me want to thread it around my neck as a rune, while nearby, a pink stone capped with a green powderpuff of moss had me imagining I could dust my cheeks with its dew.

After Remo washed the breakfast dishes, we luxuriated over second cups of tea, something unheard of at Horsethief. We talked quietly until something one of us said, some image we'd conjured, had us laughing so hard tears ran down our cheeks. Then another volley of rifle-fire stopped the laughter and made us listen. It was hunting season, and we'd been hearing that sound since dawn. As another shot reverberated, Remo turned serious, then recalled a story of fishing at this time of year with his friend Felix and finding, on the way down a steep bank to the river, a deer on its knees, its side shot open and covered with flies. A deer on its last legs, who leaped up when Felix tried mercifully to brain it with a rock, leaped up and fled to the river, fell into the current and vanished floating upside down.

More tears ran down my face as I wept for the deer, for the terror and pain in the world, for the portion of it I have caused. I stumbled to a huge boulder and pressed against it, face, breasts, hips, legs and tears. And yes, rocks don't press back, but yes, the sheer presence of everything we recognize presses back into us. Only Remo's arms around my shoulders could separate me from the boulder and from my sadness.

"I want you to be well," I mumbled, turning to him, putting my hand over his heart, thinking of the long history of his battles with his body.

"I'm okay," he said, kissing my forehead. "It's just at night when I'm lying down and I'm afraid I won't be able to breathe. I'm fine now. Don't worry. This is a place for us to relax..."

I nodded, and he wiped my tears with his artist's fingertips. Then, in a lighter tone he said, "You know, I've been thinking. I found a good price on airline tickets to Virginia for the holidays, and I'd like to take you with me. We'd have to fly by December 20th, if you can find someone to fill in at the ranch..." My brain swung round, and I barely heard the rest of what he said. I knew Remo spent the Christmas holidays with two of his brothers' families in Virginia, and wintered with the third brother in Florida. I also knew from Bruce that Remo had at different times brought two former girlfriends to Virginia for an Italian-style Christmas. Still, I felt something special about his invitation. "I think I'd enjoy that, Remo," I said more calmly than I felt. "I'm sure I can find someone who'd like spend the holidays at Horsethief."

A near-full moon kept me awake that night as I lay beside Remo in the camper, replaying scenes of our time together to see what this invitation might mean. The pleasures of the hot tub versus the cool, distancing 'rules.' The delight we found in each other's company limited by "Too much of a good thing will spoil it." I had no desire to be married again, but I did want to feel consistently *wanted*, no matter how infrequently we got together.

Beyond that, I sensed I was straddling increasingly separate segments of my life. The often joyous independence and satisfaction of my life at the ranch was basic, was home, was my place—but I would have to leave it some day. Threading out of the past was the deep love I still had for my ex-husband Rob. Though I couldn't foresee living with him again, he was, and I hoped always would be, part of my life.

And the future? What would that bring, and would it have anything to do with Remo? Did I even want it to? Beyond his often poker-faced approach to our love, there was his age, his health, his frequent insistence that "If I were to drop dead today, I'd have lived a full and happy life with no regrets." Which was wonderful and I admired him for it, but where did it leave me?

As a cloud passed the moon, I eased out of my sleeping bag, pulled on jeans and down jacket, put on Remo's slippers, stepped from the camper with journal and headlamp and walked on moonlight across the glade to the picnic table. All those questions in such a small space had given me claustrophobia. I needed the night, the moon and its shadows, the cliff and boulders and trees, needed nothing but to turn on my headlamp, focus it on a blank page, and write.

Chapter Twelve

Cowboy Maintenance

One October afternoon while working at my computer, I smelled something sharp and unpleasant. Ammonia. Even as I rose from my chair, the odor became stronger. Sneezing, I pulled my shirt collar over my face. The caustic reek was coming from the kitchen. Oh, no—it's the fridge! I shut down the computer, grabbed a jacket, shooed Koa out the back door and followed him, eyes tearing. Then, tugging turtleneck over my nose and yanking workshirt over head and eyes, I made several breath-holding forays back inside, shutting off the propane valve to the massive Servel fridge, opening windows and grabbing sleeping bag and journal.

It was a weekend, with guests staying in the bunkhouse. I had no idea how long the fridge would continue to spew toxic ammonia fumes into the house, but obviousy it wouldn't be healthy to spend time there until they were gone. I rapped on the bunkhouse door and explained the situation to Michael's two Icelandic friends, Thora and Oly. "No problem," Thora said graciously, "come in, come in. You can have the bunk right here in the kitchen, near the heater. We're very comfortable in the bedroom. And you know we have to leave in the morning."

I thanked them and arranged my sleeping bag on the bunk. Oly, an architect, asked if there was anything he could do. "I don't think so," I replied. "It's Saturday, I can't reach the propane man until Monday, and meanwhile I don't think anybody should be breathing those fumes. Apparently it's time for that old mammoth to give up the ghost." Wrapping a towel around my face, I returned to the house to fetch my toothbrush and Koa's food dish and kibble. Overpowering fumes had spread through the house, so I held my breath and hurried to gather what I needed.

When I got back to the bunkhouse, Thora was slicing carrots and sauteeing garlic and onions for a lamb barley stew. I took a deep, grateful breath. We enjoyed a hearty supper and an interesting conversation about Iceland, but in my mind was the question of what to do about the fridge. Thora and Oly departed the next morning, leaving me to wonder if it could be repaired and what that might take. On Monday morning, with the house still full of fumes, I drove to town to find Bill Parmenter, the propane man. A Mormon gentleman with graying hair, Bill drove the tank truck that delivered propane to outlying ranches, and had a reputation as the most knowledgeable person in the business. He usually came only twice a year, when I notified him that the gauges on the two tanks were low. When he delivered propane, he checked the pressure valves from tanks to house and bunkhouse, cleaned the heater pilots and answered my questions. He also took time for coffee and conversation, and we had some interesting talks about our respective beliefs.

Bill said he'd drive out in a couple of days, and meanwhile would see if there was any way to repair the fridge. When he showed up, the ammonia reek had subsided and we could enter the kitchen. As he inspected the Servel's innards, he told me he'd been unable to locate anyone, anywhere, who rebuilt elderly gas appliances. "It would have to be re-cored, re-coiled, re-primed and filled with ammonia or freon, and I can't find anybody who does that. I can get a crew out here to load it up and cart it to the dump, but that's all I can do. I've called around from Idaho to Arizona to find you another Servel, but nobody who has one wants to let go of it."

Bill looked as unhappy as I felt about the prospect of having to junk such a piece of history, almost as if we had before us an incurably sick elephant that had to be shot. He promised to continue searching for a replacement, and to come back on the weekend with help. As he drove away, I began the sad task of emptying the Servel of its contents and transfering them to the pint-size bunkhouse fridge. Later, by phone in town, I sent word to Michael, at sea on the other side of the world, via his secretary, Irene.

On Saturday, Bill came with two strong pallbearers who efficiently maneuvered the Servel onto a dolly and eased it out the door, across the yard and into Bill's pickup, leaving an large gap in the kitchen that would depress me for months. Next trip to town, I stopped at Bill's office to learn any news of a replacement. It had become a serious inconvenience to walk over to the bunkhouse every time I needed something from its refrigerator. Bill's secretary handed me a slip of paper with the name and phone number of someone in California who dealt in 'antique' Servel appliances. The search was on...

I called the California number and spoke with an old man who sounded like an antique himself. Yes, he said, he had two 1950s Servel refrigerators in working order. The price of either was $500 plus shipping. As I started to respond, he added that the doors of both were hinged on the left. Dang! I thought, knowing I'd have to redesign the kitchen and drill a new gas-line hole through its two-foot thick stone wall to accommodate that configuration. I asked the old man to call me if he found one that hinged on the right, and I'd send a check that day.

Two weeks went by and I heard nothing. But Bill Parmenter, extremely apologetic, told me he'd learned of a company in San Diego that rebuilt old Servels. Meantime I'd received an urgent message from Michael, ordering me not to junk the old fridge. "No way to retrieve it from the dump," Bill said. "It's a goner." I knew I was in trouble—I should have known better than to let the fridge go. I called the old dealer again, only to have a woman who said she was his daughter inform me that her father had died the week before. After offering condolences, I rudely asked if he had taken in any Servel refrigerators during the last weeks of his life. "Not that I know of," she said. "He did ship one out, but..."

In desperation, I went to Bill's office and talked to his partner, Ray, who handled sales of new propane appliances. Paging through the catalogs on Ray's desk, I found nothing anywhere near the capacity of the old Servel—and capacity was crucial, especially during the harvest season and when there were guests. The only refrigerator that might be large enough was in a solar appliance catalog, and cost around three thousand dollars. Michael, I knew, would wring that amount from my neck before he would spend it.

Feeling I'd really screwed up by not storing the Servel somewhere until all possibilities for repairing it were exhausted, I sent a heartfelt, bended-knee apology to Michael. But because the bunkhouse fridge was so obviously inadequate, I asked him to okay the purchase of the largest refrigerator in Ray's catalog, which was the same size as the one in the bunkhouse. With great reluctance, Michael gave his permission, and Bill delivered the thing. Size-wise, it only half solved the problem, which meant the problem remained.

Why am I telling this story? Partly because it was the most unpleasant, miscompleted, drawn out task I'd faced at the ranch, and partly as an example of the supposition that in 'the New West,' ranch work has as much to do with machinery, vehicles, tools, even appliances, as it does with horses or even sometimes cattle. Horsethief isn't a working stock ranch or even a dude ranch. It's more like a 'working retreat.' Nonetheless, my job description in many ways paralleled that of a contemporary ranch hand.

I was responsible for maintaining and repairing vehicles, tools and mechanized equipment, house and bunkhouse from roof to root cellar, plumbing and irrigation systems, corrals and fencing. It was my duty to keep the place clean and ready for guests and to clean up after them when they left. I had to stock fireplace and hot tub wood, note propane pressures and keep track of the level and condition of the spring and storage cistern. I made daily logbook entries, communicated as necessary with Michael via his secretary Irene, and kept records for the BLM. It was my choice, for the most part, to plant and harvest a large garden and tend the orchard trees and vines, and it was my pleasure to care for the horses. Note that the above are overall categories. Daily realities had more ramifications than a five-hundred-year-old juniper.

Though it was not something I often thought about, it was intriguing to note how performing these tasks brought forth both female and male aspects of myself. I was aware that among many tribal people, including Polynesians and some Native Americans, a person who embodies a balance between the two sexes is to be admired. My model for this was a Polynesian sculpture I'd brought to the ranch. Carved of gray basalt a foot high, two stylized, almost-identical figures squat back-to-back, hands resting on bulbous bellies. Huge almond-shaped eyes stare blankly, wide lips closed. One figure has breasts, the other a penis. Daylight shows between their spines, but the backs of their heads are joined like Siamese twins. For me these figures, each facing outward into the world but united in mind, speak volumes about the complementary relationship of the sexes and their balance within oneself.

Years before he bought Horsethief, Michael had salvaged a huge cast-iron bell from a church in Iowa where he grew up. Later, he had two employees truck it to the ranch. Judging from their efforts to unload it, the bell must weigh nearly a ton. And so it sat on the ground for a couple of years. One Fourth of July, visiting friends of Michael's—Hal and Betty and their friend Tom—decided it was an appropriate time to tackle the project of mounting the bell in its original wooden frame, parked in the sand next to the bell. The frame included a handle by which the bell could be swung back and forth so it would clang. Betty and I chose to stay out of the way, cook up some supper, and bake a couple of pies.

After a day of jacking, levering, and balancing, the bell was securely mounted in its frame and slow, brassy *BONG...BONG...BONGS* resounded through the canyon and out over the rim. When we came outside, Hal and Tom were jumping around swapping gimme fives, laughing and cussing. Turning to Betty and me, Tom said teasingly, "See, men do biiig things. Women make pies..." I laughed, thinking of some of the biiig, if less dramatic, projects I'd tackled since I'd been here. Tom might claim that only a man could understand the shuck-and-jive elation that comes with accomplishing something big and tricky. But I understood it, too; the male in me savvies the 'big,' the female in me values the pies. Even

Tom seemed to catch an inkling of this as he later forked the last chunk of crust and said to Betty, "Lady, you build a damn good pie."

The first dim sign that I had a male streak in me came when I was seven and my father, by day a nine-to-five accountant, began teaching me how to use his hand tools. Ever since I could remember, I'd watched with interest as he made useful things of wood: our house, garden cold-frames, toys and enabling equipment for crippled children, whatever was needed, whatever he could invent. My father had inherited his tools, and perhaps his love of using them, from his father, a master tool and die maker who had learned his trade from 19th century German craftsmen. So those were the tools I learned with: hammer, screwdriver, pliers, wrench, chisel, drill, plane, saw, tapemeasure, level, square, vise. The wooden handles and grips of these tools were coated with a grimy patina of use and smelled of metal and sweat. I grew fond of them.

My first project was a Trojan horse, influenced no doubt by the Greek myths I was reading, and by the rocking horses my father made and gave away. It was a long-term endeavor which I worked on after school, before my father returned from work. One evening he came home early, while I was nailing a leg to the horse's body. Intent on pounding the nail straight, I didn't know he was standing behind me watching until he put a hand on my shoulder and said, "I always wanted a son, but you'll do just fine."

I never knew, and still don't, how to take that statement. My father wasn't given to such comments and I didn't dare ask him to explain. What I do know is that my early enjoyment of hand tools became ingrained, spawning respect for larger tools—axe, scythe, cat's-paw, sledge, machete and so on—and appreciation for the clean click of precision designed into, say, a fine camera or shotgun. Most tools you use to get the job done, but a few seduce you into using them for the pleasure of how they feel in the hand, *how* they do what they do.

Mechanized tools are another matter, however. Beyond noise and smell, there's nothing intrinsically unpleasant about a lawnmower, chainsaw, weedwhacker or composter—they're time-saving, efficient, and I couldn't do what I do for the ranch without them. But too often either I'm a jinx or they're fickle. No sooner do I fire up the chainsaw than the chain spins off a sprocket. The composter I tuned up chugs into action, then sputters and dies. I go to use the Makita to drill a hole and listen to its bit whirr and gyre to a halt as the batteries give out. To offer a more feminine ex- ample, I had always sewn my own clothes until I came to Horsethief and my trusty old Bernina began jamming when I used it. When I took it for repair, I was told there was nothing wrong with it. So that mysterious machine sits in a closet for now. Except for the lawnmower, with which I've so far enjoyed a peaceful working relationship, I've spent almost as much time fixing as I have using whichever rusty, sand-clogged, gummy-oiled machine I needed. The situation slowly improved as Michael allowed me to acquire new equipment, and there's been satisfaction in helping Horsethief evolve out of the duct-tape/tie-wire/balestring era into a stage where, mostly, things work.

The Bernina certainly would be a boon to my wardrobe, had I been able to get it repaired. I think of all the torn workshirts and ripped garden pants I could have mended with it, instead of painstakingly stitching them by hand or stuffing them in the ragbag. 'Wardrobe,' of course, is a euphemism on a ranch, but there are ways in which the term applies.

At Horsethief, the first item of wardrobe for any activity or travel, in any season, is a waterbottle. I keep several liter bottles and gallon jugs filled with spring water behind the kitchen door, ready to go, year round. During the warm months there are gallon jugfuls in the jeep and my car, and a five gallon jug secured in the bed of the pickup. If a radiator blows, I can at least get a few miles farther down the road. I've been laughed at, as was Ed Abbey, for my seriousness about carrying water on the desert, but I've seen what the lack of it can do.

In August of my first summer at Horsethief, several weeks after the pourover that broke the drought, I went away for a week to participate in a writers' event. I left the ranch and a set of typewritten instructions and phone numbers in what I thought were the capable hands of a young woman named Chris, a part-time Park Ranger who had stopped by one day and offered to ranch-sit if I ever needed a substitute.

Figuring that her position as ranger implied a certain level of responsibility, I didn't worry about the place until, on the way back, the rear differential of my car blew out and I was forced to spend an extra day waiting for it to be repaired. At dusk that evening, I arrived in the driveway to be greeted by a pair of panicked, hysterical wraiths. Aquila and Shasta, the only horses at the ranch then, ran up to the car screaming for help. In the headlights the two mares appeared gaunt as greyhounds, deep shadows between their ribs. Greatly alarmed, I got out of the car at the front gate, only to be nudged almost to the ground by the desperate animals.

No lamps were lit in the house. On a fast hunch, I ran to check the gully gate that should have been left open so the horses could get to the water tank in the corrals. Dear sweet Jesus, it was closed, chain hitched around the post.

I raced to the corrals. The water tank with its automatic tap was full—no problem there—but if I let the horses drink in the state they were in, they'd be dead most painfully within the hour. I shut the gate to the water tank corral and ran to open the gully gate. The mares galloped up the arroyo and into the first corral, neighing piteously.

Meantime I rushed to the tackroom, grabbed two halters and leadropes, and put them on the mares. Then tied Shasta to a post so she wouldn't push through the gate while I led Aquila to the tank. One at a time, I gave each horse five seconds for their first crazed slurps, then tugged them away from water back to the other corral. After offering them hay—which neither would touch—and waiting fifteen minutes, I again led them one at a time to the tank for another five-second sip, then tugged them back. Fifteen minutes later I allowed them a seven second drink. And so on, slowly increasing their drinking time but still waiting fifteen minutes between drinks, until almost dawn, when their craving for water seemed more normal.

In between, I went to the house, lit a lamp and found a note from Chris on the kitchen table, on top of my page of instructions. *Sorry to have to leave early, but my boyfriend's father has to have eye surgery. Thank you for this opportunity...* and dated five days earlier. I let the note float to the floor, pressed hands to face and sent a long deep breath of thanks to the universe. Horses require twelve to fifteen gallons of water a day in hot weather, and like humans, can die from going more than three days without it. Aquila and Shasta had somehow survived, though not without consequence. I guessed that after a certain period without water, they'd have become unable to eat, and that their skeletal condition was a combination of dehydration and starvation. Shasta seemed okay the next morning, but later in the day Aquila showed signs of lameness. Stephen happened to stop by, so I stood Aquila's front feet in two buckets of cool water in the shade and handed him the halter rope, while I drove to the nearest phone to summon the vet. "A mild case of founder," Doc Sorenson stated after he'd checked both horses. Handing me the bill, he added in his no-nonsense manner, "You're lucky she's alive."

I kept the mares in the corrals and offered them as much hay as they would eat. In a week they were almost back to normal. But months later that harsh lesson was in my mind when I happened to be riding Aquila out the driveway, and met a low-slung sedan coming in. A woman, perhaps in her thirties, was driving, and the car was crammed with at least a half-dozen kids. "Excuse me," she said, tilting her face out the window, "Is this the way to Moab?"

"No," I replied, and while the kids oohed and aahed and punched each other about the horse, I gave her directions to town.

"That's funny," she said, "I think I went that way, but I didn't come to any paved road."

"Where are you coming from?" I asked, the *uh-oh-lost-tourist* alarm buzzing in my mind.

"We're from Denver," one of the kids piped up.

"Well, I think we were at the state park, uh, Dead Horse Point," she replied vaguely.

Totally unable to imagine how she'd gotten ten miles west to Horsethief on a dirt road, when the highway from the Parks to Moab was plain as day and paved, I told her to follow me back to the house. While the kids ran around yelling outside, I drew her a clear, user-friendly map to Moab. Then explained equally clearly in words how she should get there, all the while thinking I should just lead her back to the highway in the jeep.

"Do you have water in the car?" I asked, handing her the map.

"Water? No... We had a six-pack of sodas, but the kids drank them all before we..."

"Here," I said sternly, reaching behind the kitchen door, "take these jugs with you. It's good spring water and it'll last until you get to Moab." I handed her a bag of apples, walked her to the car, and placed the two gallon jugs on the passenger-side floor. "Don't let the kids spill these," I said, making sure she took a head-count as they all climbed in. Eyes rolling, I watched her car disappear down the driveway, hoping I wasn't going to be responsible for a ditzy woman and six kids ending up at the bottom of a roadless canyon.

Perhaps the second most important item in a ranch wardrobe is comfortable footgear. Sandals are okay for gardening, but good shoes count when hiking, riding, or driving; and warm boots are a necessity in winter. I avoid cowboy boots—uncomfortable for walking if one gets stranded—even if Duce laughs at me. I love the feeling of digging bare feet into silky sand, but the sand around the ranch is infested with cactus spines, tumbleweed stickers and the needle-sharp prongs of goatheads—tough enough to puncture a tire, viable enough to last for years.

A pair of gloves—leather work-gloves or cotton garden gloves—are another wardrobe necessity. Dry air creates splintery wood, and even with gloves, slivers are common. I keep a basket in the kitchen filled with several matched pairs of more or less intact work-gloves for guests who want to help. The life span of a work-glove is short but often interesting. As Duce said once, "You know your gloves are broken in when you take one off and it looks like your hand is still in it."

Perverse as it is, I seldom wear a hat or sunglasses. Many of the women who have drawn my attention over the years have been farm or ranch wives, or Native American mothers and grandmothers, women with faces crinkled as the canyons. As a teenager I'd think, *Gee, she looks like she's lived an interesting life. Bet she knows things I'd like to know.* Adulthood cured me of such naivete, but I'd still prefer to age with laugh-lines and crows-feet intact. I love being a woman. I love my life and don't mind if it shows.

For trips to town I simply put on whatever shirt and jeans are clean and free of rips and stains—which leaves few choices. Once I wore a skirt to meet a friend for lunch, but it made me feel like somebody else. And one fall day, when I had to drive directly to the airport for a flight to New York, I walked out of the house in a tan pigskin suit, red silk shirt and red suede boots. Before I reached the car, the ravens were shrieking with laughter.

Given the spectrum of Horsethief's activities, I'm not sure there's such a thing as a 'typical' trip to town. Most trips involve multiple needs and reasons for going there. Spring through fall, when there are lots of projects to keep up with, that could be as often as three times a week. In winter, when the ranch is battened down and I had time to read and write, I interrupted that luxury as infrequently as possible—once every ten days or two weeks.

Whatever the season and whatever else I had to do, several stops were obligatory. I collected the mail from the post office box, shopped for groceries, and checked and returned phone messages at the home of a generous couple who'd been my neighbors in Aspen before we each moved to Utah, and who invited me to keep phone and answering machine in their guest room. Maria and Fritz were thrifty folk who grew appalled, I fear, at how much time I spent sprawled on the carpet making and answering long-distance calls. But I did this on average only once a week, fitting in all the personal and business calls most people make daily.

The phone was one way Remo and I kept in touch during our long periods apart. We also sent each other letters, postcards, news clippings, film and book reviews, cartoons, and gifts. There was no agreement to do this, of course; it was simply a long distance way of sharing observations and enthusiasms, and even settling misunderstandings. On the few occasions there was nothing from Remo in the post office box, I'd allow myself a quick snit before going on to Fritz and Maria's. Usually Remo had left a message, and had lots to tell when I called.

Inevitably, there were other errands—laundromat, dump, recycle center, feed and hardware stores, bank and bookstore, sometimes the state liquor store for a bottle of wine. Occasionally I'd meet a friend for lunch or dinner. On the way back to Horsethief, I'd check the coffee-can mailbox for messages, now and then finding an invitation to supper at Bonnie and Stephen's. And rarely, I'd find a note from Duce that he'd be moving cows and did I want to come along—an offer I couldn't resist. After all, it meant some real riding, an opportunity even the most mechanically-inclined ranch hand would jump for.

Two things are needed for playing cowgirl: a horse and some cows. I'd grown up on horseback, mostly riding bareback and knowing no greater pleasure than sitting my yellow horse in perfect balance at a full gallop the length of a grassy valley, horse and I moving in absolute trust and harmony. I taught myself to rope, to shoot arrows accurately from my little bow crosswise under my horse's neck at a run, and to fall at a gallop and roll—perhaps the main reason I've never been injured when I've fallen or been bucked off. I rode in horse show classes but found them stuffy. Rather, I dreamed of the West, knowing I would live there one day, knowing west meant home. And nevermind that my husband Rob and I had lived for a year in California and a year in Hawai'i, Horsethief was as far into the 'old west' as I'd been.

Horsethief, however, offered few chances to participate in the working west of stock ranching. Instead, I rode out alone as often as possible for the pleasure of exploring of every area of the mesa. For me, a horse's back offers the ideal scale and pace by which to travel cross-country. You can cover a lot of ground, but you can also see the ground you're covering. I've found arrowheads and other artifacts while riding, followed a pair of hunting coyotes for miles, and studied deer and bighorn sheep that, afoot or especially on a bike or in a jeep, I'd never have seen.

But there was another kind of riding I craved. It took a while to figure out that the very thing that made pleasure riding so pleasureable was the same thing I sometimes felt was missing: an aim, a goal, a purpose for the ride—or maybe just the chance to exercise a different set of skills. Whatever it was, it was satisfied by riding after cows with Duce.

While I hadn't grown up on a farm, each spring a farmer brought his pregnant cows to graze in the huge woodland pasture that was my playground. It was my self-appointed job to know these bovines, to follow them when they were going to calve and to notify the farmer when they did. For every calf I reported, I received a quarter from the farmer. When I came west to study veterinary medicine at Colorado State University in Fort Collins, I arrived a month early and hung around the vet barns. For some reason, I was allowed to make the round of local ranches with the vets and senior students who treated ranchers' ill and injured stock as part of the teaching program. As a female, an Easterner and a first-year student, I had three strikes against me. But I earned the respect of this crew by being the only one among them who could rope a cow.

Before I moved to Horsethief, Michael had given me money to find and purchase two horses for the ranch. A few days after Shasta and her sister Annie were delivered, Michael and I rode them out with Duce to gather and push a herd of cows into an adjacent grazing allotment. As it happened, I didn't see Duce again until I lived at Horsethief. After several get-togethers that involved herding cows from place to place, we found we could withstand each other's teasing, and became friends. Sometimes I'd stop by his camp on the way home from town, and we'd swap news and stories. He'd met Remo a few times and always asked "How's Sancho doing?" Often his wisecracks had me almost on the floor. Of a tourist who invaded his camp to take pictures, he said, "Got as much sense as two dead ants." A local politician, full of promises, was "all hat and no cattle." And once when I was estimating the distance between two buttes, he simplified the matter: "Looks like about four cigarettes on a slow horse."

Moving pregnant cows in fall or winter was generally uneventful. The cows mostly knew where they were headed and didn't mind going there. But in spring, gathering and moving mamas with their calves could be a hassle. One breezy April, a visit from my sister Nance and her family coincided with Duce's date for moving 136 cows-calf pairs off the Horsethief range onto the pastures east. Niece Malli, then twelve, was a good enough rider that I invited her along. Shy and gentle yet smart and gutsy, she saddled Shasta while I readied Aquila, and we headed west along the Horsethief Trail.

The two of us circled out across the range, gathering scattered cows and their calves. But around noon, a strong wind came up, and soon turned into a shrieking sandblaster. Malli and I were a few hundred yards apart, each pushing a group of cows east, to leeward, and circling out to bring in others. Pulling my hat down tight, I swivelled windward in my saddle and spotted Duce moving the main herd along the Horsethief Trail. At the same moment, I glimpsed Shasta rearing straight up in the air, Malli clinging to her neck, then Shasta dropping to the ground and rolling as Malli stepped off and somersaulted to her feet. Yelling a git-git-git toward my cows to keep them going, I spun Aquila and headed fast toward Shasta, who was still acting up even though Malli, afoot, had managed to hang on to the reins.

Praising Malli for her gymnastics, I took Shasta's reins and held her next to Aquila, as Duce galloped up. Malli said her leg felt bruised, but insisted on getting back on. But Shasta, totally wind-spooked, refused to settle down. I'd never seen her behave like that, and told Malli it would be best if I kept hold of Shasta's reins. Tying her hat back on, she nodded agreement. Aquila was holding steady, and I knew that despite the strain of leading Shasta, both mares were better off together.

We pushed Malli's group of cows along to catch up with mine, git-git-gitted both groups over to Duce's herd, and circled out to gather more cows and calves. Tugged along beside Aquila, Shasta behaved, but the wind wasn't giving in and I knew Shasta wouldn't either if I left her in Malli's hands. As we headed toward Duce's herd with another bunch, I shouted above the wind that when we reached Horsethief's driveway, she could take Shasta and lead her home. But Malli shook her head, shouting back "I'd rather go with you."

We kept circling out to gather cows until we reached the driveway. There, the whole herd started to spook, and it was all Duce and his cowdog Zeke could do to keep them from stampeding. Malli and I on our horses blocked the driveway as cows milled around bawling for their calves and calves skittered about maaa-ing for their mothers, churning sand and dust into the flying air. Then a big yellow one-horned mama charged Duce's roan. As it went to its knees I urged Aquila forward to shoulder the cow away while Duce's horse righted itself—but Duce yelled, "Stay clear of her—she'll take you!" With most of the cows past the driveway, we brought up the rear and kept one side of the herd from scattering while Duce and Zeke whipped through brush and gullies, flushing AWOLs back onto the road.

Finally, wind still screaming, we got everybody moving again. It was only a mile to the cattleguard, but seemed like five. When we neared the gate through which we'd have to funnel the spooky herd, I led Shasta off a ways and tied her to a juniper, asking Malli please to sit tight with the reins. Then Aquila and I pushed the lagging cows along while Duce, flashing his lariat, got the first cows through the gate. From then on we could almost relax, as the herd flowed through the opening and spread out over the piñon pasture, rumps to the wind.

While Duce closed the gate, I rode over and released Shasta, taking back her reins. Malli and I squinted at each other through the wind, grinning, rings of sand around our lips and nostrils, unable to utter a word. We rode over to where Duce was loading his lathered roan into the trailer, and I yelled an invitation. "Come to the ranch for supper—my sister's making chili!"

But Duce shouted back, "Nope, thanks, got to bring a load of water to that herd." Then he added, "But you girls can ride with me anytime."

The friendship between Duce and me was prime evidence for my theory that in the West, friendships were often formed not only despite distance, but because of it. When I told Duce I was starting into my last year at the ranch, he asked why I was leaving. "I can't afford to take out a bank loan to go on working here," I told him. "I'm going to have to find a real job and—"

"Whoa, girl," he cut in, "You need money, you come to me. I can loan you enough to get by on, and you can pay me back when you publish those books of yours. Hell, you might as well use it, if it'll help you stay."

I was honored, and thanked him. "Let's just see what happens," I said.

Not long after that, Stephen went to work for Duce, driving the water truck and helping out on horseback when the need arose. It arose one day when the two of them stopped by to let me know they'd located a missing cow about two miles west of the ranch. But they had no horses with them and couldn't round her up. "She's probably got a calf," Duce said. "We'll come by in the morning with horses to bring her in and take her over east with the herd."

I thought I might surprise them. Shasta was with the horses out on the range, Aquila was in the corrals with a stone-bruised hoof. That left Moriah, who covered ground quickly, but was hardly a cowpony. At least we could go out and find the cow, maybe even bring her back. Next morning, I put myself into think-like-a-cow mode and Moriah into his long-striding walk, followed a couple of hunches and found nothing. Followed one more—and there in the gully below us, half-hidden under a thick piñon, was mama nursing her calf.

The first step was to get in behind her and move her out of the gully. That meant asking Moriah for an acrobatic stunt I wasn't sure he could do—tuck his hind legs under him and slide down the steep thirty-foot embankment. I spoke softly to him, stroked his neck, and gently pressed him toward the bank, trusting that if he didn't think he could do it, he'd let me know. To my surprise, he slid down tucked and smooth as any cowhorse.

The cow was already moving out of the gully, waggle-tail calf behind her. I asked Moe to wait until she was out in the open so we could get behind her. The big thoroughbred was excited and wanted to run, but did as I asked. The hardest part was getting him to slow-walk so he didn't crowd the cow and make her run. Reining him side to side and turning him in circles kept his mind from getting in front of the cow, where he thought he belonged, and soon we were nearing the ranch.

As we topped the last rise, I was surprised—and frustrated—to see Duce's truck and stock-trailer heading slowly out the driveway. They were leaving! Reining Moe away from the cow, I shouted, waved, spun Moe in circles to catch their attention. But they kept going. Trying to think what to do, I put Moe behind the cow again and trotted her down the slope toward the water tanks. Maybe she was thirsty, maybe she'd stay there...

I gathered the reins, and Moe was off like a jackrabbit down the hill, over breakneck ledges, across shallow gullies and up a rockscrabble bank, erupting on the driveway in front of Duce's truck. Duce braked to a halt and leaned out the window as I caught my breath, pointed back toward the tanks and said, "There she is. All you have to do is load her up."

While Duce and Stephen unloaded their saddled horses, Moe and I went back down the rocky bank and wide around the water tanks and cow, into a position on the grassy slope between the cow and where she'd come from, to discourage her from trying to return there. Meantime, Duce and Stephen rode toward the cow, easing her away from the water tanks toward the ranch, where she could be corralled. The cow went along without fuss, but suddenly her calf seemed to freak at the horses and took off running west, tail in the air.

In the ensuing pandemonium, Duce held the bellowing cow where she was while Stephen and I raced after the calf—who doubled back between us. As we turned our horses, Stephen's saddle slipped sideways and put him on the ground. While he cinched it back on tight, the calf reversed direction again, hightailing it west toward me. I urged Moe forward to turn the calf, but it sped right past our noses. Stephen and I zigged and zagged our horses after the calf, who was always headed someplace we weren't. Moe at a run had the turning radius of a freight train, or a race track, and the calf zipped by us several times before heading over the hill west, Stephen in hot pursuit.

As I drew Moriah in to a rocking canter-in-place, I noticed two things: mama cow trotting in the direction her calf had taken, and Duce leisurely sitting his horse halfway up the nearby slope, watching the circus. Realizing the game was over, and the cows had won two to nothing, I walked Moriah up the hill to Duce, who was laughing in his beard. "That Stephen," he chuckled. "Reminds me of the time I roped a cow and my saddle came off with me in it. Some sleigh ride that was." He shook his head, still grinning. "Now you know. It doesn't do any good to chase those danged critters. Best to let them go 'til they pair up again, then start over. She'll find her calf out there, and then you can go bring them in. You just let me know when you've got them corralled, and I'll bring the trailer and pick them up."

At first I thought I was being teased again. But as Duce rode off toward his truck, I realized I'd been given a trust. One it would be a pleasure to meet.

Chapter 13

Equally Near, Equally Distant

Most of my days at Horsethief were spent in non-human company, but the human visitors with whom I shared the ranch at various times were also interesting. Most guests returned whenever they could. A handful, however, passed through but once. Among these was a young Brit, Tom Harrison, whom I met at Island In The Sky ranger station while I was researching rattlesnakes. It was a cold, windy March day, threatening snow. As I walked to my car, a young man bicycled to a halt next to me. Green-eyed, dark-haired, very handsome, he asked politely in a strong accent, "I say, you wouldn't by chance be driving through the Park, would you?"

"I hadn't planned on it," I replied, but as disappointment flitted across his face, I added "But I could..."

Explaining that he'd already cycled up the Shafer Trail that morning and pedalled through Dead Horse Point State Park, he nodded toward the heavy clouds blowing at us from the northwest. "I'd like to tour this Park as well, but the weather doesn't look favourable for doing it on my bicycle. If you were going sightseeing, perhaps you wouldn't mind a passenger?"

I hadn't seen Island In The Sky since its roads had been paved, so this seemed a good time to reacquaint myself. As we cruised the Park, stopping at viewpoints, Tom told me that he leased a cheap government flat in London's east end, where he designed and built contemporary furniture. "You must live in Moab, then?" he asked as I parked the car and we started up the trail to Upheaval Dome.

"No," I said, "I live on a ranch, and in a few minutes I'll show you where it is."

When we reached a high point where we could look north across Taylor Canyon to the rangeland beyond, I stopped and squinted. "You can't see the ranch, it's hidden in a side canyon right over *there*." I pointed. "But if we had binoculars, I bet we could see our herd of horses."

"It sounds like the Westerns I used to watch on the telly," he said with cautious enthusiasm. "And you really live there?"

"It's nothing so grand as in the movies," I replied, "but I do live there. In fact," I blurted, "if you'd like, you're welcome to stay there tonight instead of going back to Moab." Tom looked as startled as if I'd begun removing my clothes. "No, no," I assured him, "I'm not trying to seduce you, and I don't mean to offend you by offering a bit of Western hospitality. But the ranch is a little piece of history, and I thought perhaps you might like to see it."

"Well, ah, yes, I'd like that very much, if you're sure it's not, ah, an inconvenience," he stuttered. "I'd have to bicycle back down the Shafer Trail, and find my way to your ranch in my rental car, if that's not a problem."

"Not at all," I promised. "I've a map in my car that will get you there in time for supper."

On the way back to the ranger station, Tom made sure I understood that he had a live-in girlfriend, Mary, a dancer, very pretty, who was taking care of his cat, etcetera. As soon as I'd explained the map and Tom was out of the car, I laughed at myself. "Probably he won't even try to find the place. Good thing I didn't tell him about the hot tub."

Despite my doubts—and his—Tom spent three nights and two days at Horsethief. One day he bicycled the switchbacks to the river, the next he rode horseback with me to look back across Taylor Canyon at Upheaval Dome. He'd brought groceries with him, and on the second evening prepared a scrumptious Indian dinner, with curried chicken, spinach saag and a chutney I accused him of flying in from London, if not Delhi.

"I did bring it in my pack from London," he admitted, laughing. "I thought I'd never get to use it. But this is just the right place for it—what with the Purcell and the Britten," he indicated the tapes we'd been playing, "and especially the Shankar and Bhatt."

On his last evening, I slung a thick towel over Tom's shoulder, put a flashlight in his hand, and pushed him out the back door into bright moonlight toward the hot tub I'd carefully heated. "Try it. You'll like it," I said as I returned to the kitchen to clean up the dishes. And he did. In the morning we exchanged addresses, and later corresponded for a few years. Before he left, he wrote an appreciation in the logbook:

What an idyllic place. So many of my ideas about the dream home I would like to build are embodied here. The timbers in the house, the hot tub and cistern, the space, quiet, animals, the potential of the garden, the spring up behind. I really find it hard to imagine a more beautiful place to live. And on top of it all, my first hot tub— and at full moon. I only wish I could stay longer. I find my hands twitching to work in the garden... Thank you for a wonderful visit.
—Tom Harrison, London, England

Among Horsethief's other 'foreign' visitors was the French author Pierre Furlan, whom I met through poet friends in Aspen. Pierre, educated in California, was researching a fourth novel, to be set partly in the western United States. It seemed only natural to invite him to Horsethief, and I was glad I did. Skilled chef, able horseman, efficient weed-puller, Pierre was delightfully French during our dinner coversations, as we sipped a good red wine under the apricot each evening. Right away, he recognized that Horsethief was no idyll, at least not for me. "You are not seeking a utopia," he stated during one conversation. "You are seeking to communicate. Like many writers, you do this best out of solitude. And solitude itself is a communing."

I nodded, bowing my head. No oracle could have said it better. I thought of the timeless times I'd sat on a rock, on a horse's back, on the ledge with my juniper, meditating, emptying my mind, making room for others. Reaching out with imagination toward friends far away, seeing into their lives. Watching them converse, cook dinner, bathe children and read them to sleep, plan, worry, remember, dream. Reaching into Remo puttering in his kitchen. Rob on his sailboat studying sea charts. Friends Kirsten in New York and Bonnie nearby. My mother in the ache of her aging. Susan helping sons Billy and Tom with homework, her next painting forming in her mind. Bruce at his computer, measuring words. Ken with his gentle Thai friends, their feet in the froth of the sea. Edgar checking his film camera in preparation for an ascent of Amadablam, while at home his wife Elizabeth chats on the phone, sons Weston and Morgan fingerpainting at her feet. And so many others, including now Pierre. What a treasury of distant friends right here within me.

"No utopia without responsibility," Pierre said before he left. "That is why God's Eden failed; he put the blame on Eve and Adam instead of accepting it Himself. That is why most utopias fail. But the catch 22 is that taking responsibilty cancels the idyll. As you know."

Yes, Pierre. And as I watched you drive away to your next destination, I thought of your two daughters whom you spoke of, and how fortunate they were to have you as teacher as well as father. And I thanked you for what you wrote in the log, even as I translated it:

Unexpected oasis, the most interesting place of all on this trip to the United States, thanks to Karen's hospitality and her understanding of animals and plants. Even the heat carries the place to an almost unreal layer of existence. Thank you, and long live the Horsethief Ranch.
—Pierre Furlan, Paris, France

I admired and appreciated Pierre for many reasons, among them that he had unknowingly erased the bad taste in my mind left two months earlier by another visiting Frenchman—or French Swiss, to be precise. One April afternoon, Koa's bark called me from a bunkhouse plumbing mess. Crawling from under the pipes, I heard a car horn blaring somewhere out the driveway. Plumbing wrench in hand, I went to investigate. As Koa and I rounded the corner by the cowbone skeleton and 'Turn Around Here' sign, we came upon four young men, two of them black, standing by a small blue sedan. Interesting, I thought, calling out "May I help you?"

"I am friend—of Michael's," called back the taller of the two white guys, in a thick but oddly timid French accent. "Your—dog...?" he asked, meaning, I guessed from all the hands still clutching door handles, does he bite?

"Yes, he's my dog," I nodded, not about to tell any truths. At that, the friend of Michael's stepped forward with a hand-drawn map and a scribbled note in Michael's handwriting.

"Je m'appelle Olivier. I meet Michael on ze beach in Thailand, and he says me I should vizeet his ranch," Olivier explained, introducing the three men who had driven him from Los Angeles to Horsethief on their way to Denver. Dave, an African American, and Hans, a young Dutchman touring the States, asked if they could see the place. So I gave them the tour, fed them lunch, made sure they had water, and waved the three of them on their way. Dave and his buddy Jeff would stop back in a week to pick up Olivier.

So began one of the strangest Horsethief sagas ever.

Olivier opted to stay in the livingroom/bedroom of the main house instead of in the bunkhouse, and since I needed parts from town anyway to repair its plumbing leak, I abandoned that project and turned to gardening. I had pounded in a stake to suppport the first tomato plant, when Olivier appeared and asked if he could help. "Sure," I said, and told him where to find a pair of work gloves in the kitchen.

Minutes later he reappeared, wearing nothing but the gloves and a fairly large hard-on. He bounced through the garden gate and asked what he should do, adding an offhand apology for his nudity. "I hope zees okay I wear no cloze. Ze air feel so nice on ze skin."

"Fine with me," I said, indicating the stakes and fencepost pounder, "I do it all the time."

I started to show him where I wanted the stakes put when he asked, "Zo why not now? Why not you take off ze cloze too?"

Feeling a warning itch of irritation, I patted the cutting pliers in the cargo pocket of my shorts and replied, as if speaking to a child, "Because I'm comfortable this way. I can carry what I need, and I don't have to go look for where I put it." That seemed to satisfy him, and he busied himself pounding in the stakes, hard-on bobbing up-down-and-sideways.

I went to the greenhouse to fetch the tomato plants, returning with them to find the stakes in place and Olivier nowhere in sight. Fine. I troweled a hole for the first transplant, removed it from its pot, and was pressing soil around it when an odd motion caught the corner of my eye. There was Olivier just outside the garden gate, watching me and jacking off. Aww, yuck, I thought, turning around. "You can just take that act somewhere else," I said sharply.

With a little pout he responded, "Ah, I am zorry. You do not like ze sex?"

Exasperation rising, I growled, "I like sex just fine. But not that kind. Now go find something else to do."

If he didn't understand the words, he heard the attitude, and I didn't see him again until after dark when I came in to make supper. Spring evenings being chilly, at least he had clothes on when he walked into the kitchen and asked me about the hot tub. "I'll show you how to heat it tomorrow morning, before I go to town," I said. "Would you like something to eat?" I indicated the skillet of stir-fry veggies on the stove. "Plates are in that cupboard, knives and forks in that drawer. Help yourself," I said, focused on a journal article I was reading. But Olivier had other things—or an other thing—on his mind. As he sat down with his plate, he asked, as if it were the most normal topic of conversation in the world, "What kind of sex you like?" Before I could tell him it was none of his business, he went on, "You like sucking? You like—"

"Olivier," I cut in, aiming my annoyance straight at him, "Ecoutez-moi bien. Whatever kind of sex I like, it is not available to you. I am not the wench who comes with the place."

"Wenj? What is wenj?" he asked as if bewildered.

"Whore. Prostitute. That is what I am *not*." I said, returning to the article.

"Ah," he said enthusiastically, "I have many frienz whores. Zey teach me many zings. I have girlfrien', too. I teach her. I teach you, too?" he asked, tilting his head toward the bedroom. "You be my deziert girlfrien'?"

"No, Olivier," I said with an exasperated sigh. "I have a boyfriend. I don't need another one. Especially not you."

"But he eez non here," he persisted. "I am here. Why you non want sex wiz me?"

"Olivier," I said sharply, rising from the table and switching off the propane lamp, "I am going to bed now. Alone. I will *zee* you in the morning."

Next morning I showed him how to heat the hot tub, hoping that would keep him busy. But *non*, he wanted to go to town with me. Reluctantly I said okay, then mentally kicked myself and added, "But I don't want to hear any more about sex. Talk to me about something else, or keep quiet." And, except for taking my hand from the gear-shift once and attempting to put it on his apparently perpetual hard-on, he behaved. I got the mail and purchased plumbing supplies at the hardware store. In the supermarket I turned a corner with my cart—and almost ran into my friend Dick Dorworth, with his cart.

"Hey," he said, opening his arms for a hug, "I'm just stocking up to come out and see you for a few days, if it's okay. I came to do a little climbing, and—" Unable to believe my good fortune, I kept hugging while I said in his ear, "Of course it's okay. It's wonderful! In fact," I whispered, "I need your help rather urgently." Dick, trained to stay cool in any situation, asked no questions and politely acknowledged Olivier when I introduced him. Then we parted, to meet later at the ranch. "That," I told Olivier in the car, "is my boyfriend." A lie, but maybe it would keep him away from me.

That evening, after I'd explained things to Dick, the three of us ate supper together, and Olivier managed to mind his mouth. He talked about life on the beach at Phuket, Thailand, where he had met Michael, and his mini-business of renting surfboards, until Dick and I went out to the hot tub together and soaked and chatted for a hour or so. Then Dick, an early riser, went off to bed in the caretaker's room, while I wrote at the computer in the middle room. Sure enough, out of the dark like a moray eel came Olivier, naked and erect, *pssst*ing me to join him. "Go back to bed, Olivier," I said quietly. "I'm busy."

Later, after I'd shut down the computer and curled up in the narrow bed in the middle room with my journal, he tried again, upset that I would sleep by myself. "He eez non you boyfriend," he hissed petulantly, indicating Dick's room. "Why you non sleep wiz heem if he you lover?"

"That's *our* business, Olivier," I retorted with muffled anger. "Now leave me alone!" And to make sure he did, I switched off the lamp, took my journal and slipped into the wide bed in the caretaker's room without waking Dick.

Next morning, Dick was off early to rock-climb. He promised to be back by dark. "I think I can manage until then," I said, shaking my head wryly. I knew I wasn't in any danger from Olivier; he was a sex addict, not a rapist. As long as I kept telling him No, he'd leave me alone. But I was tired of telling him, tired of having him around.

More garden work that day. Without Olivier in the shadows, it was almost peaceful—until I saw him up at the corrals with Shasta and Aquila. Fool that I was, I asked if he wanted to ride. "I am zinking," he said without answering my question, "I am zinking how beeg box to make me high like horse."

At first I didn't understand what he was saying. Then I recoiled with shock and fury—"You get anywhere near those mares with that sausage of yours and I will personally remove your—Aghh! Just get away from here!"

Still later he had the chutzpa to ask me *why* he couldn't misuse the mares. I couldn't believe I stooped to answer him, but trying to stay calm I said, "Because it is abuse. Because they are horses. Because they have no choice. Because it would be rape. You understand? If I catch you near the corrals, we'll both of us take a little drive to Aspen and see Michael. In fact," I said, "maybe we'll do that anyway, since Michael needs his jeep."

"Okay," Olivier responded. "I like zee Michael, stay zome days, come back here for time my frienz zey pick up me."

That evening, Dick agreed to spend two more nights at the ranch to keep an eye on things. In the morning, I opened gates so the mares could come and go for water, packed a few items for Koa and myself into the jeep, and showed Olivier how to drive my car. When we reached the highway, I stopped at phone to tell Michael we were coming. He'd said he wanted to use his jeep during his break from sailing, but not until we got there did I tell him why I'd brought it to him. Michael, visibly upset, kept saying, "I had no idea, no idea he was like that." But by then all I wanted was to be with Remo in his cabin across town by the river, and plan our spring camping trip to some clean, remote desert canyon.

When I told Remo about Olivier, he understood I was in no danger, and thought the whole thing almost amusing. And maybe, except for the horses, it was. But I didn't want to think about it. I still had to drive Olivier back to the ranch. Next morning, I bought some flats of Iceland poppies, shasta daisies and blackeyed susans, and made a rock garden of perennials around the doorway of Remo's cabin, which pleased both of us. That evening we dined with friends, then went to a movie. By the next day, I felt distanced enough from Olivier to make the return drive with him. I put tapes in the tape player, and we drove without talking all the way to the ranch. Dave and Jeff drove in at noon the next day, and with utter relief I watched Olivier leave. Later, hands in the soil, I mused with a tiny shred of leniency at how harmless he'd been. Obnoxious, yes, sick with addiction, but compared with the child abusers, the gang rapists, the snuff filmmakers, those who prey violently on others, Olivier was merely a repulsive tomcat.

I befriended Susan Obermeyer during the year I worked for her father's skiwear company in Aspen. Though she was half my age, we shared a sense of adventure that made our friendship stick. When I took her to Horsethief—the winter of the ice crystal garden—Susan enjoyed it so much that I introduced her to Michael so he could give permission for her to go there on her own. Little did I suspect she'd already been back to the ranch and had developed an intimate relationship with Chad, who was then the caretaker. Soon after, Susan returned to college to complete an art degree, and I didn't hear from her until the following November, when she called me at my Aspen condo and said she had something to show me.

It was a cold rainy day, and the infant in the stroller was all bundled up, but nothing could hide the blue eyes, rosebud mouth and white-blond hair he had inherited from his father, Chad. Susan, who had divorced her older son Billy's father when he became abusive, had no desire to marry again. But she felt Chad had a right to know his son, whom Susan had named Tom. So began a time of upheaval in both their lives. Chad wanted marriage, and it tore him apart when Susan refused. But later, during Tom's second spring, they lived together at Horsethief with both boys for some months so Chad and Tom could form a bond.

Just as I saw in Susan's spirit a reflection of my own at her age, I also saw parallels between Susan and Ken. I told each about the other, and when they met at Horsethief it was as if they'd been born brother and sister. Susan's best friend, a dancer named Annie Murphy, was there, and all that afternoon, with Susan beside her, had been lying on the grass in the upper orchard, sick with dry heaves, trying to come to terms with the sexual abuse she had suffered as a child.

Ken, having barely met her, knew nothing of this, but that night he dreamed that Annie had been abused by her father. It was the nature of Horsethief, somehow, that people sometimes ended up dreaming each other's dreams. I had experienced it when Susan and I related the same or similar dreams, and other guests had told me about it happening to them. It was as if, just as desert water moves underground, people's dreams are freed by desert air to go visiting.

Susan became the second most frequent visitor after Ken, coming with Annie and the boys when I needed a substitute caretaker, and on many other occasions. One of her log entries gives a glimpse into her special way of loving the desert:

By now many wonders compile into awe. A moonlight ride along the Green with Annie & boys, searching for bones I found a few days earlier, bats falling out of darkness, silver river snaking past moon-bronze cliffs, hooves in soft sand ready to return home. Midnight clouds and lightning on the way up the switch-backs, with gusts of warm, wind-carried sprinkles. The rest of the ride filled with old songs and stories, horses' feet clopping on clay road, Tom curled into

Annie's rebozo, dreaming to the rhythm of Aquila's walk, Billy asleep in my arms, swaying with Moriah's stride, until everything slept but the moon.

Most visitors came by land, but there were exceptions. One spring morning, while several guests and I were enjoying a leisurely outdoor breakfast, we were buzzed by a convoy of planes—friends Edgar Boyles, Paul Ryan, and Bob Fulton in their Cessna 180s. One by one they swooped low to drop airbags of gifts: a bag of croissants from an Aspen bakery, a book of poems from friends Lito and Linde, music tapes from ex-husband Rob, card and scarf from Paul, teas & spices from Edgar and family. A startling surprise for everyone, including me. We stood with our hands raised, waving as the three planes faded into the blue.

My Cessna pilot friends, each award-winning cinematographers, were on that occasion headed to work—Paul as second unit photographer on the film "A River Runs Through It," Edgar to shoot aerial photographs for a major book on the disastrous effects of clearcutting, Fulton to take spectacular aerial shots for his own film on the Colorado Plateau. Edgar had made several airdrops to me at the ranch, including a Christmas card addressed "Air Mail—Special Delivery."

Fulton had also overflown the ranch previously, circling the house three times according to agreed-upon protocol before landing on the Horsethief Trail. Three circles was my signal to meet a plane at the driveway intersection, where large rocks served as tie-downs. The first time, Fulton had stayed only long enough for a tour and a glass of lemonade. On his second visit, when I met him with the jeep he was standing next to the plane playing tunes on the saxaphone that flew everywhere with him, belted in as co-pilot. After many minutes he put down the sax to greet me. He'd run into bad weather while filming in the Four Corners area, he explained. Could he spend the night so he could make another try at dawn? Of course, I said, and after a supper of roasted garden veggies we lounged in and around the tepid hot tub—it being July, and too hot to bother firing it up—talking about Tibetan Buddhism, Tantric practices and Hindu deities. I knew little about such matters, but Fulton had studied deeply while making films in Ladakh and Tibet. Fascinated, I listened and asked questions.

Later the same year, Fulton's third visit was part of an annual gathering of a national organization called Great Old Broads for Wilderness, a response to the good ol' boys who so often oppose anything wild. I had offered to host the weekend event, and was pleased when two dozen over-fifty outdoors folks showed up with tents, food and water and set up their camps in unobtrusive spots in and around the canyon. The youngest was a man who had just turned fifty; three of the liveliest were women in their eighties. All were inveterate hikers and campers who pooh-poohed the notion that 'wilderness is only for the elite.' For three days they hiked, horsebacked, hot tubbed, shared meals and discussed how they could bring more attention to the necessity of preserving as much wilderness as possible.

The first night went down in Horsethief history, as we sat outside under the apricot tree viewing Fulton's Colorado Plateau film on a TV monitor powered via extension cord to my solar outlet in the house. Without a glitch, we watched thirty minutes of breathtaking, ground-skimming aerial images that left us hungry for more. Next morning, while everyone was setting out on hikes, I asked Fulton how he went about filming from the air. "If you want to go up with me, I'll show you," he responded. "There are some landscapes down around the Green River I want to look at." I'd always loved flying in small planes, and as we drove out the driveway I asked how long he'd been a pilot. "My father taught me when I was about eleven," he said. "I began soloing in my teens." When we reached the Cessna, I unhitched the tie-down cables while Fulton performed the checkout on his plane. Then he showed me his custom 16mm film camera mounted under the left wing, so sleekly designed it was almost invisible.

Then we were in the plane, seatbelts fastened, saxaphone strapped in the rear seat, motor revving, taxiing west along the Horsethief Trail, into the wind, rangeland passing faster and faster until the moment the wheels left the clay and we were airborne. We gained attitude only slightly as we neared the deep canyon of the Green, and as we swooped out over the rim it dropped away so suddenly my stomach fell with it. I peered down, scanning the bottomlands where I'd glimpsed wild horses a few times from the river, but didn't see any. Then we arced over Horseshoe Canyon and do-si-do'd around some low buttes.

Thrilled as I was to see this landscape from the air, I wasn't ready for Fulton's next move. Slowing the plane almost to a stall, he dropped down into a wide part of the Green River canyon and switched on his camera. We followed the river downstream, skimming along a dozen yards above the water, banking with each bend of the red walls as they deepened and narrowed until the wings seemed about to scrape the cliffs. As Fulton pulled up the plane to where the canyon was wider, we passed what I recognized as the mouth of Hell Roaring Canyon, then eased down for a landing on the deserted sand strip of Horsethief International Airport. Fulton cut the camera and the engine and we climbed out, Fulton with his saxaphone. September's cicadas chirped loud rhythms, and for a quarter of an hour Fulton counterpointed them on alto sax, while I listened in awe to an impromptu orchestra that would be heard only that once.

Another environmental organization to bring a group to Horsethief was the Southern Utah Wilderness Alliance, known to its many supporters as SUWA. Boldly effective, SUWA had invited six key U.S. Congress-people and their families on a raft trip down the Green, in hopes of convincing them first-hand of the value of desert wilderness. Susan Tixier, SUWA's then vice-president, had contacted me to ask if their rafting guests could use the ranch as a last stop on their journey, to clean up and have lunch before catching planes back to Washington. As a longtime SUWA member I welcomed the opportunity to speak for wilderness by showing that humans could live comfortably and compatibly with wild places.

So it was that on a sunny September day, Senator Wayne Owens of Utah arrived with Congressman Bruce Vento of Minnesota—Chair of the House Subcommittee on Parks and Public Lands—and Representatives Beverly Byron of Maryland, Sam Gejdenson of Connecticut, and Doug Bereuter and Peter Hoagland, both of Nebraska. Plus family members, SUWA staff and raft crews. Congress-people who had plane connections to make were given first dibs at the hot tub, the bunkhouse shower and the bathtub in the house, to wash off days of river silt and change from shorts and tee-shirts into traveling clothes. A mad scramble ensued, soap bars, shampoo jugs and bath towels flying every which way while I answered questions and set out lunch on wooden tables under the front yard apricot.

Others helped, of course, and soon pots of steaming corn ears, platters of sliced ripe tomatoes, sweet peppers and cucumbers, bowls of herb-dressed salad greens—all from the garden—vied for space on the tables with baskets of homemade bread, trays of cheeses and deli meats, pitchers of iced Mormon tea and a palette of ripe orchard fruits. The pink sunburned bodies I'd glimpsed splashing in the hot tub filed past in city clothes, filling their plates and cups. Astonishing, how fast it was all devoured! Goodbyes were being exchanged among the first wave of bathers while the second wave was still drying off. I didn't get to speak my support for wilderness, but the setting expressed it far better than I could have. Senator Owens was one of the group who signed in:

> *I brought five congressmen to see Horsethief Ranch and wash up after a spectacular three days in Labyrinth Canyon, where we focused on my proposal to designate 5.4 million acres of wilderness... It was an unprecedented success. Horsethief Ranch is a welcome oasis—the hot tub and the garden vegetables and fruits... topped off our trip.*
> *—With gratitude, Wayne Owens*

Every now and then I was asked if everyone who came to the ranch responded to it positively. Other than Olivier, whose response was limited to one part of his anatomy, I knew of only one person who refused to enjoy it. One July afternoon, Harry, a longtime friend of my ex-husband Rob, stopped by with his wife Marcie and another couple. Harry had visited before, and at first I was pleased to see him and Marcie and to meet their friends. The woman's name was Cindy, the man was Harlow, whom Harry had spoken about for years. How tough he was, how cynical, as if those qualities were, or hid, something admirable.

The four of them wanted to soak in the tepid hot tub, and despite my protest, downed several bottles of wine while they did. Harry, Marcie and Cindy sat on the tub's underwater benches while Harlow stood exposed and regaled them with tales of places he'd lived that were "much more exotic than this." When he repeated "If you think this is far out, you've seen nothing," Marcie rose up out of the tub in disgust, pulled her clothes on and took the car keys from Harry's pocket. As she marched unsteadily to their vehicle, Harlow shouted, "Good riddance, y'old hag!" Grinding gears and just missing the gatepost, Marcie swerved out the driveway. Harry's reaction was "Don't worry, she won't go far," but he accepted my stern invitation to use my car to follow her. Upon their return, Harlow yelled, "Why didn't you get lost, bitch," whereupon I told them it was time to leave. Bathos, I growled later, picking up wet towels. So much for Harlow. His great white hunter act was stale forty years ago. Sure there are other unique places on the planet, but this *is* one of them.

Sunset that evening found me sitting with my juniper, fingers entwined with its twigs, breathing mind into desert, desert into mind. After a timeless while, I felt as emptied of the day as was the darkening sky. The first stars were visible, and looking up at them I thought of the gifts that had come to me here. The big ones, like gratitude and friendship, beauty and solitude, infused my very being. Primary as material blessings were good water and food, followed by cherished gifts like the rainstick Betty had given me during the drought. The farm cheeses and salsas my sister Nance always brought. Music and books from Rob. A magnificent red blooming amaryllis from a friend of Ken's. Duce's lariat. Susan Walp's painting. Remo's always-thoughtful packages. The list of gifts was endless, but it began with the givers. Every person who came through the front gate was a gift. Even Harlow, even Olivier, widened the bell curve of diversity, sort of like scorpions and goatheads, but they taught me things I didn't want to know, and that was a gift for growth.

Thanksgiving was and is my favorite holiday, the only one I insisted on spending at the ranch. The first Thanksgiving, with a cousin and her family, and the second, with sister Nance and hers, were landmarks, like buttes on a horizon. The third began a tradition of Remo, me, and our friend Bruce Berger gathering with others for the holiday meal. A week prior to that date, I'd met Bonnie and Stephen for the first time—and they had just met each other. Since they were my neighbors, it seemed natural to invite them, and Duce, to join us for a dinner with wild turkey as its centerpiece. But Duce had a prior invitation, and Bonnie had been scheduled for Park ranger duty. When Bruce and Remo arrived on Tuesday and I told them we were our only company, we decided to spend the days hiking instead of preparing mounds of food.

Recently I'd been told by Moab bookstore owner Jose Knighton about a canyon not far from the ranch, in which could be found a cavern, a rock 'playground,' some powerful pictographs, and in a thumb-like side canyon, the remains of a livestock trail made of logs anchored to its steep wall. On Wednesday morning, after poring over a topo map of the canyon, we decided to try to find the hidden route into it that Jose had described. After a chilly day of hiking and searching the rim, we finally spotted the obscure ledges and three-sided tunnel zig-zagging into the depths. But by then it was dusk. Now that we knew where to start, though, we could return tomorrow to make the descent and explore the bottom.

Thanksgiving morning dawned gray and portentous. I tucked the covers around Remo, brewed tea and coffee, and finished making the apple, herb, dried blackberry and piñon-nut dressing I hoped would honor the first of the two wild turkeys I had sacrificed. By that time Remo was up, and held the bird while I stuffed and trussed it. Bruce appeared, and over Remo's hearty pancakes we speculated on the hike we were about to take. By the time chores were finished and we were ready to leave, it was almost noon. I put the bird in the Wedgewood's blackened oven and set it at 275 degrees, figuring we'd be back by dark and the fifteen-pound turkey would be roasted and ready.

After we found the route that led to the ledges, lifting an eager but arthritic Koa down the exposed cliff-bands was the only difficulty. At the bottom, we opted to save the cavern at the canyon's head for another hike, and view the playground and pictographs en route to the thumb canyon. There we hoped to hike out by way of the cliffside log trail and complete a circle back to the car. Soon we were walking downcanyon on a slickrock streambed, noting tracks and bird calls while Koa pursued Thanksgiving rabbits. The playground was indeed that: a small area of zanily eroded boulders forming caves, tunnels and a shrine-like alcove upon which we posed Koa and each other for pictures.

Hiking on, we located the pictographs at the base of an enormous overhanging cliff. Prominent among the painted shapes was a lifesize figure with head, hands and feet emerging from a quadrangular brick-red body. I stepped back to study this figure, noting the upturned palms, the tilted head and mournful yet indifferent stare of the eyes. In awe, I returned the stare, then noticed the subtle ochre lines that sprouted like hair from the top of the figure's head and fell full-length down both sides of its body. Its aura? Its power? Its spirit overflowing? No way to know.

To the right of this figure, a comet shape floated near the upturned palm, arcing above what appeared to be a medicine bundle. On its left were two vertical, streamlined fish shapes, one with two ghostly eyes, the other with no eyes at all. While Remo and Bruce investigated other pictographs, I steeped myself in the humanesque form in front of me. For some reason I felt I should do this; that if I allowed myself to succumb to that hypnotic stare, I would comprehend the meaning it was imbued with. But soon Remo was calling me to catch up, reminding me it was mid-afternoon on a short day and we had unknown miles to go before we reached the car.

Though we walked fast, the sun had almost set by the time we reached the canyon's thumb, and dusk was gathering when we finally found the trail we anxiously hoped would lead us to the rim. I was worried about Remo, who, rightly convinced I didn't exactly know where we were going, had earlier hiked up a steep, rocky slope to see if he could locate the trail. His face was flushed and his breathing fast and shallow, but he said he was okay and urged us on.

We had hiked upward only about two hundred yards when suddenly from above came the dull clack of falling rock. In a flash we hit the ground, at the same time looking up toward the noise. Above us, silhouetted against the sky's last light, a deer, antlered head held high, forelegs in dive position shifting to find ground, plunged with elegant poise through three hundred feet of air and landed with a heavy thud, as we screamed NO NO O GOD NOOO...

Sick with shock, we stared at the motionless body of the buck a hundred yards away across a deep gully. Then stared at each other, speechless. Long minutes passed, me crying, then Remo said quietly, "There's nothing we can do for the deer. We'd better try to make the rim before dark." Slowly, still stunned, we turned from the crumpled buck and went on up the trail.

Fortunately, the path was marked by low walls of stone and brush intended to keep sheep or cattle moving along it single file, minimizing the chance of accidents caused by animals bunching up in precarious places. And fortunately, the log ramp spiked to the cliff face, though badly dry-rotted, was intact enough to bear, one by one, our weights. I crossed it clutching Koa's ruff so he couldn't fall. As we reached the rim and stood catching our breaths, Bruce said into the darkness, "I guess even nature makes mistakes."

The night was moonless, but we had flashlights in our packs. Remo and Bruce used theirs; I was more comfortable following the rim by starlight. After what seemed hours, Koa and I reached the car and waited for the flickering flashlights to arrive. Driving toward the ranch, Bruce speculated about what had caused the deer's demise. Were we in some way to blame? Had it stepped on unstable rock in an attempt to satisfy its curiosity about us? Was it chased by a human? A cougar? A pack of coyotes? Had it been wounded during the recent hunting season and become suicidal? Many questions, no answers. Oscillating between stunned disbelief in my mind, and grief for the deer in my heart, I thought of the painted figure I had met that day. As I would do many times in years to come, I crawled into its mind and stared out with its mournfully impassive gaze, trying to accept and encompass what had happened.

Turning onto the Horsethief Trail, we were signalled by the blinking headlights of an oncoming vehicle. When it stopped and Bonnie and Stephen got out, there were some moments of readjustment as I returned to the holiday world. A fellow ranger had offered to take Bonnie's place so she and Stephen could enjoy their first Thanksgiving together. They'd already been to the ranch, found the house dark and empty, and were worried about us. We started to blurt out the event that was still happening in our minds, but I suggested we go back to the ranch to tell the sad mystery, so Remo and I could finish preparing dinner. I was thinking of the bird that had been so long in the oven, anxious that it still be edible. Not only to make the centerpiece of our meal, but because I couldn't bear that another wild life be wasted.

Bonnie and Stephen had bought cheeses and nuts, wine and spiced rum, and pumpkin pie for dessert. Stephen poured drinks, Remo sliced yams and potatoes into a broiler pan, Bonnie created a salad of store-bought greens and windowsill-ripened garden tomatoes. I retrieved from the bunkhouse fridge the cranberry-orange relish and beet-parsnip-carrot mousse I'd made days earlier. The wild tom turkey, slow-roasted in its own juices for seven hours, was fall-apart tender and succulent—far and away, we agreed, the most delicious turkey any of us had ever tasted. While everyone filled their plates, I lit the candles on the table and around the kitchen, then doused the propane lamps. In the flickering glow, we took our places round the table. Stephen offered a blessing:

"We gather here in friendship and love, to share and give thanks for this special nourishment of body and spirit. We are grateful for the beauty and bounty of the universe, and for its mysteries as well. May the days bring peace."

Chapter Fourteen

Visions and Ancestors

On my first trips to Horsethief, in the years before I became its caretaker, I hiked all over, exploring the mesa and its rims. One day while following a shallow slickrock gully back toward the ranch, I stopped to check my bearings, and felt my eyes drawn to the ground at my feet. I looked down. There, on a fragile pedestal of sand, was an arrowhead of red-brown jasper.

It was the first such artifact I had ever found. I stared, then knelt down to see it better. But something stopped my hand as it was about to touch the stone. I felt I should ask permission, or at least pay homage to the ancient person who made such a thing, before disturbing it.

Still hunkered over the arrowhead, I looked around. Out of the corner of my eye I thought I saw something move behind a piñon tree about thirty feet back up the gully where I'd come from. As I stood up and stared, a boy stepped from behind the tree and stared back, wide-eyed. His black hair was tangled and windblown, his dusky skin bare from the waist up. He wore buckskin leggings and moccasins, and a small leather pouch on a thong around his neck. His right hand clutched a bow, and he may have had a quiver slung over his left shoulder, which was partly hidden by piñon needles. He looked about twelve or thirteen years old.

Apprehension and curiosity filled his roundish, highboned face as, poised to flee, he struggled to take me in. Equally startled, I became aware of my khaki shirt and pants, and dark disheveled hair. For a moment's crazy hope, I wanted not to appear alien to him. But then I saw that his gaze was fixed, with a mixture of incredulity and envy, on my feet. I glanced down at the nylon and leather running shoes I was wearing, with their bright magenta trim, silver mirror patches on sides and heels, and fat, flared, air-cushioned soles. Moonwalk shoes, magic moccasins that might allow me to outrun him.

When I looked up, he was gone.

Intent with wonder, I walked up the gully to the piñon tree where he had stood. There were no tracks or scuff-marks, not the slightest sign. Nape-hairs on end, watching my periphery, I walked back to the arrowhead, taking shallow wary breaths. A breeze rose up, but except for the air, all was silent. I felt spooked. The boy was not there, yet I had seen him there. Who was he? What was he? Where had he gone?

Trying to think through my wonderment, I reviewed the details of what I had seen. His features were so distinct I could draw them, could trace in my mind the shape of the eyebrows, the earlobes beneath the blowing hair. As I did, the notion took hold that perhaps my request to pick up the stone had in some way been granted. I bent down to study the jasper point resting on its island of sand, as if it had been waiting there for centuries to draw notice to itself. Had it belonged to the boy? Had he made it? Had he come to retrieve it? Had he given it to me?

Divided by these questions, I couldn't decide whether to leave the point in the gully and return in a few days to see if it was still there—or to take it with me as a reassurance that, no matter what realm of reality it had come from, I had seen what I had seen. Tracing its outline with my forefinger, I soberly thanked the powers around me for what I had experienced. Then I picked up the arrowhead, pressing it between my fingers, fitting it into the heartline of my palm, feeling its finely chipped edges, the indentations of its tang. It felt comfortable in my hand, but as I caressed its perfect shape, I had the sensation that it was held not in my own palm, but the boy's—or rather, that my hand and the boy's were one.

I placed the point back on its island of sand.

My father's known lineage goes back to a Swedish mercenary who settled in Germany after the wars of the Reformation and produced a clan of burghers and merchants. My mother's people were middleclass manufacturers from the north of England. Although I have tried to imagine and even to identify with their lives, nothing resonates. For all the consanguinity I feel with these people, my blood could be oil and theirs water.

I feel the same lack of attraction to the European greenscapes in which my ancestors dwelt, and even to the familiar prettiness of New England where I grew up. Though landscape is lovely and precious wherever it has been left alone or carefully tended, since childhood I'd been drawn to the scale and color, the sere and magnificent shapeliness, of the American West. And to those who lived with that land in some basic way: to traditional farmers and ranchers, to native tribal people, to the early hunter-gatherer-cultivators from whom we all, at various times and places, evolved. It was as if, unable to find roots in the industrial civility of my blood ancestors, I must leap further back in time to recognize a fostering heritage.

Another dimension of ancestry popped out during a visit from the Chickasaw poet and writer, Linda Hogan, who had been teaching at the Desert Writers Workshop, a conference held annually near Moab. I was honored that Linda had accepted my invitation to visit Horsethief and rest before returning home to Colorado. But her fatigue went deeper than what she had given her students. Weary of watching the world spin more and more out of control, Linda spoke of returning to live among her people. "It's time," she said. "Before the white man's insanity takes over completely. Before there's no one left to go back to, no one left to learn from."

I thought about her words and felt a twinge of sadness that bordered on envy. I could not pretend to be Indian and had no desire to usurp a legacy that wasn't mine. But I suddenly felt the loneliness of an orphan or an only child, as if I were the only container of my blood, a unique combination of genetic material and inclination of spirit. "The only heritage I can turn to is childhood," I said, feeling foolish. "I read everything I found then about Indian ways, and practiced as many of them as I could without being part of a tribe. I still do," I went on lamely. "This *place* is kind of my tribe..."

"From what you say, that might be enough," Linda said gently. "Maybe that's part of what you're doing here—reconnecting with that heritage." I was silent for long moments before I thanked her for her insight. Then, by way of thanking her for her writing also, I asked if she would care to drive out to find the horses, in particular Moriah, who seemed to fit the image of the red horse in her first novel, *Mean Spirit.* But search as we did, the horses seemed to have vanished—just as the red horse in *Mean Spirit* kept doing.

Childhood aside, ever since I first came to the desert it had grown increasingly valid to think in terms of a lineage of landscape and climate, a kinship of place. The relatedness of different generations and civilizations who worked and worshipped and withstood the same environmental conditions became for me a stronger bond than was a genealogy of name, bloodline, or genepool. Especially after moving here, I felt I had considerably more in common with those who dwelt in the same searing heat and cold, drought and drenching rain, immense beauty and serenity that I lived with, than I did with the chill-blooded folk to whom such a landscape would be meaningless, or cause for names like Hell's this or Satan's that.

At first this sense of kinship was passive, innate. I had no more desire to seek out ruins or search for artifacts than I had to peer in my neighbor's windows or go around picking up his tools. But the encounter—call it hallucination or vision or visitation—with the Anazazi boy was a revelation in many ways. It opened me to the rich heritage of inhabitance, past and present, all through the West, and deepened the affinity I'd felt with tribal people ever since I could recall.

One night in late November, as I was driving back from town along the Horsethief Trail, I stopped the car with a gasp and got out to look. All across the northern horizon, high into the sky, were shimmering curtains of red—shifting, wavering, quivering, without pattern or form. I had never seen the aurora borealis, and was totally awed—keeping my eyes on the luminous display while I reached into the car for a down jacket. Mesmerized, I stood watching for a long time, trying to take in such a marvel. I thought of the fourth grade social studies book I'd taken such pleasure in, reading about Mongolian and Saharan nomads, Congo rainforest people, and the Eskimo people of the north who call themselves Inuit. There had been a photograph of the aurora in the book, and I remembered wondering how the people who lived with the northern lights ever did anything but watch.

That those people—those ancestors, those teachers—and their lifeways are for the most part gone—slaughtered, assimilated, or forced aside in the name of that euphemism for ignorant greed we call 'progress'—is and always will be a knot of sorrow in my heart. So many ways of knowing and embracing life and death, eliminated forever from the awareness of future generations, and replaced with the gewgaws and trinkets of consumerhood. So many dances, so many songs, so many stories, so much spirit, so much connection. Gone.

As I walked backwards to the car, still watching the aurora, I recalled a story told by a man of good spirit, who had lived with the Yupik people of St. Lawrence Island, in the Bering Strait between Alaska and Siberia. The Yupik are whaling people, and the storyteller had been invited to accompany one group of hunters in their umiack. When a pod of sperm whales was sighted far off across an open stretch of sea, all the men began chanting in prayer, thanking the whales for showing themselves. They kept chanting as the whales closed together in a sort of huddle, and they sang their prayers yet more strongly as one whale left its kin and swam toward the hunters to be killed.

Shouldn't we, too, sing our thanks to what sustains us?

At Horsethief, my personal door into the realm of those-who-came-before has taken the form of a woman who, when I first began visiting the ranch, planted herself in my imagination and refused to leave. At the time I had a friend, a Spanish filmmaker, a civilized bear of a Basque Madrileño, who called me "Tia Cojonuda," which translates as "old aunt with balls." Somehow that name and epithet have been claimed, wrong language and all, by the figure of an Anazazi woman who has grown on me and in me, a kind of alter ego.

She is not the witch of southwestern mythology, La Llorona, the Wailing One, the sad Medea who steals children to replace her own that she has killed; but they know of each other. Tia Cojonuda, spirited crone, wears her shaman's wits about her like unbound hair. Observant, keenly lucid, she stalks the desert of my aging, implacably female and monkishly sensual behind soot-creased skin, cracked-lip smile, jet-flint eyes. She is counselor and mediator, medicine woman, mixer of pigments, fine artist of her people. Numberless infants have taken their first breath in her arms, their first cry, and she has watched the well of death rise up and overflow, has escorted many into its waters. She has hungered for love and fed on broken taboos, has feared until fear has become her, become simply the grasses she strokes, almost absently, in the arthritic vigor of her stride.

Children run from her, then to her. She tells them stories, fools them in ways they love, does not lie or dissemble. She helps around the cookfire, but not placidly. She gossips and jokes and sings and then she is gone, and no one has seen her go. She has gone to study the stars, or to grind her pigments, or to paint the delicate, magical figures that are her people's stories.

I think of this Tia as someone who lived here and still lives here on the mesa, sometimes wandering its shallow gullies, sleeping in sand under sky or with the ant lions under ledges. I doubt I would be much surprised to look up from a hike and see her sitting in the shade of a juniper, a wrinkled rag of iron gray hair and laughter. The laughter hearty, not haunted, aroused by some small thing, lizard-antic laughter, the sound of falling rock, the sound of ravens in playful flight. I do not think she would run from me. I think her black eyes would glint, but she would take no other notice of my presence. We would sit apart in mutual solitude, politely not looking at each other, and commune in silence, or with the bellows of our breath.

What would I learn from her?

Perhaps that I am part of a community in time as well as space. Perhaps a stronger way of knowing that I am contiguous with my surroundings. That whatever I see, hear, smell, touch, taste, is part of me, as I am of it. That black pinocate beetle is me, is other. Same with that clump of cactus. Tia's presence might help me absorb this eternally paradoxical state of things with more of the innocence of childhood. Perhaps I could sit there and quit contriving, stop the self-consciousness, the posing and sirening, the sway between enthusiasm and cynicism, the need always to give something in return. Could quit justifying. Could receive.

Or perhaps her presence would answer certain riddles. Who was the boy in my vision? Did you yourself ever live, or are you a composite of women who did? How did you get into my imagination? Most vital, how do I find my way in the terrain of spirit?

One day, hauling home a load of hay along the winding road between the massive, shapely walls of the Colorado River canyon east of Moab, I was thinking about the ancient Greeks. How certain places like springs, caves or clifftops, were once abodes for gods and demigods, and later for oracles and interpreters. Studying the mud-silver river, the varnished red walls above it, the brushy vegetation between, I tried to distinguish a likely locus for such a 'spirit of the river canyon,' or even a spot that could be dedicated to 'the spirit of this *part* of the canyon.' But nothing stuck. It was like fishing, when the river keeps flowing past and nothing takes your hook. Just as the the canyon's beauty is continuous, so its spirit must be. River, cliffs, vegetation, shimmering air—all spirit, confined only by the matter that reveals it.

But the question remains: where does Tia Cojonuda fit into these musings? The truth is, I don't know and she isn't telling. Maybe one possibility is that, since matter and energy are interchangeable and in constant flux, spirit must inhabit both. If energized spirit were to seek matter by which to be manifested, a being such as Tia or the Anazazi boy might come forth. And, imagination being a form of energy, it seems solipsistic to deny that they could possess reality beyond my mind. If on any level they do, then we exist for each other as doors in time, cancelling its linearity and creating holes in eternity itself.

Can our visions, our dreams, in a sense be ancestors that we grow from?

Ever since I'd been old enough to think about it, the Sunday School notion of an almighty, omniscient, yet jealous and patriarchal god had seemed the most transparent—even treacherous—of myths. Far more appealing was what we learned in high school about pantheism and transcendentalism: godhead embodied in every iota of the evolving world, spirit manifested in every detail of the universe. To me this seemed empirically obvious—certainly more reasonable than anything else I'd been subjected to—and I couldn't see why, even in school, it was given such short shrift.

I had similar problems with the idea of dichotomy. Experience—my father loves us/my father beats us, my father is a cruel man/my father is a good man—had taught me the validity of paradox—the idea that two opposite things can be true simultaneously. From there, I found it much more realistic, not to mention liberating, to think in terms of a spectrum or field of possibilities, rather than accepting simplistic either/or's. Especially I resisted the Cartesian attempt to hack subject from object, body from spirit. Instead, I found resonance in the study of Buddhist logic, where synthesis derives from multiple theses, rather than the narrow duality of thesis and antithesis. From reading Jean Paul Sartre and the French existentialists, I evolved my own idea of freedom, in which choice is paired with responsibility. With Buddhists I believe that all life is sacred; with native Americans that all life is equal. Ultimately, it seems the Chinese dictum "No right thought, only right action," is of the essence. One simply tries to be a good person, to take only what one needs, to help others have their share.

*

It was May, and I had been working even harder than usual to put the ranch in shape before I left. Michael's friends Ana and Jim Egnew, both forest rangers, would be ranch-sitting while Remo, Koa and I went on what Remo had said would be our last camping trip, at least a while. Instead, the time we spent together would be devoted to finding a new place to call home.

"After forty years, I have to sell my place," Remo had told me by phone. "Remember the real estate signs in front of the woods across the street? Last week they cut those trees down and broke ground for *three* monster mansions surrounding the cabin—two of them within fifty feet of the bedroom window. I can't stay here—I can't even sleep. They start at dawn, bulldozers and that damned bleep-bleeping, and go until dusk. Seven days a week." A huff of frustration came through the phone. "So I've listed my property. When it sells, we'll find a place where you can have your horses and your study, and I'll have a shop to putter in and maybe a studio for my painting. The hardest part will be deciding where we want to be. But we can spend time looking in the fall."

It was a dream come true—or would be when we found it. But could I trust such a dream with Remo? The December holidays with his family in Virginia had been a disaster. Remo spent half the time shut in his room wrapping gifts or whatever, and the rest of it shopping, or joining his family at the board and card games that went on incessantly in the dining room. Out of respect for his Catholic family, we slept in separate rooms. But for Remo, who cherished his family traditions, it was as if I weren't even there. To spend any time with him, I had to invite myself on his shopping trips—hardly my favorite activity. Other than that, I was expected to join the family at their games, or otherwise entertain myself. I would gladly have settled into a good book, but when I excused myself to do that, subtle stares told me I was being antisocial.

The only fun part of the trip had been driving to New Jersey to visit my mother, during which time Remo came out of his shell a bit and treated me as if I were someone he knew. He was attentive to my mother, who gave us her bedroom to sleep in, but even then he was reluctant to pay me any attention. I vowed never to go east of the Rockies with him again, and returned to the ranch with huge relief.

But that was the winter of Zamar and Bruja's locoweed deaths, and of the severe chest pains that sent me churning through muddy snow for medical help. Both episodes left me feeling vulnerable—not a feeling I was used to or comfortable with. When Remo, long distance, offered genuine sympathy for the horses, insisted on paying my medical bills, and acted as if nothing untoward had happened back East, I decided to just see where things would go.

Between then and our upcoming camping trip, two significant 'things' had happened. One was the decision to sell his home and find a place for "us." The other was a poem he had written for me but had hesitated to show me because, as he said, "It's my first poem, and after all, you're the poet." Now I sat in the dappled May sunshine at Marmo, back against a rock, re-reading the typed verses I already knew by heart:

Invitation

take my hand
come walk with me
on ancient sediment, stone
now sand

to dare explore without a plan
wild places, serpentine canyons,
depths of solitude untouched
by man

repose atop a slickrock knoll
that overlooks the country wide
smell the pinyon, touch the rock,
hear the winds
confide

and on discovery, awe, we'll feed
drink ephedrine brew
from the treasured
weed

though skies be clear
we'll not return 'til dusk descends
and shadowed spires
disappear

share all this and more with me
talk, and love, adversity

The poem was inscribed with Remo's formal signature and an elegant hand-drawn bouquet of hearts. Aside from its literary quality—which even Bruce, a major poetic talent himself, later judged as "not all that bad"—this 'Invitation' was not merely to a hike or camping trip, but to a committed relationship. As I understood it, and Remo, it was the equivalent of a marriage proposal. Lately he had amended his 'rules' by saying things like "I'm not monogamous, but I'm not interested in any-one else," and "I've never felt about any woman the way I feel about you." Although "Where are we going?" was for me still a big emotional as well as geographic question, Remo had made clear his desire that we would be going there together.

Now it was a brilliant spring evening, birds calling through Marmo's woodland. I felt an urge to climb the cliff and visit the ruin on a ledge up there—the "grandfathers' house," I called it, after a dream I'd had one night during a previous stay at Marmo. In the dream, coppery skinned boys were playing leapfrog on the ledge. As I focused, they turned into half-naked young men performing daring gymnastic stunts at its edge. Then they were hunter-warriors in buckskins holding council, standing on the ledge with bows and lances and pointing out over the valley below. Then they faded to old men seated on the ledge in a semi-circle facing south, passing among themselves an aromatic pipe. The feathers hang-ing from the pipe were white, which seemed important as I woke to the fragrance of sage.

I had felt good about the dream, which was vivid despite its timelapse dissolves. Though I hadn't known what to make of it, I felt it was a gift, and had thanked the elders—the 'grandfathers'—and asked their blessing.

Now I felt it would be right to do so again, to ask a blessing for Remo and me together, and for his health. I climbed through gratchy brush and up through a boulder chimney to the ledge, stepping over a large clump of passion-red claret cup cactus to get there. I sat and breathed with the setting sun, the last twittering birds, while time disappeared into prayer. Then Remo hooted to ask where I was. Hooting back, I stretched and stood, looking down at our little camp in the trees. The aroma of whatever Remo was cooking for supper wafted up as I descended. Polenta. Cornmeal on a Coleman stove. I smelled generations of roasting corncakes.

Next morning, we re-packed Remo's Bronco. Everything had its place, and by now I knew the basic arrangement of Coleman stove, lantern case, fuel, water jugs, cooler, Koa's food, tent, clothing, sleeping and eating necessities, all packed in the cargo space with not a half-inch to spare. "That way," Remo had explained, "the load can't shift, even on a really rough jeep trail. And," he added with satisfaction, "everything you need is within easy reach."

Remo's "everything" was enough to make me cross-eyed. Tucked away compactly and conveniently were a first aid kit, snakebite kit, water purifying kit, Bronco tool kit, spare parts box, extra fluids box, roadside hazard kit, sewing kit, shoe repair kit, tent repair kit, waterproofing kit, eyeglass repair kit, lantern repair kit, riveting kit, and a desk kit complete with several kinds of writing instruments, graphic design tools, stationery, envelopes, postcards, stamps, labels, paper clips, push pins, rubber bands, rubber cement, rubber cement thinner, scotch tape and stapler. We were as self-sufficient as a Wal-Mart store, but took up less space.

Both Remo and I were fascinated with maps. After the Bronco was packed, we pored over topo maps on Marmo's picnic table, while Remo acquainted me with the area where we were going to spend the next ten days. He had been there, briefly, twenty-five years ago. "It doesn't look like much on the map—no deep canyons, not very dramatic," he said, tracing a finger along contour lines. "But it's lovely country, and it's friendly. I found a few ruins in the two days I was there, and I think we'll find a lot more." In Remo's vocabulary, 'friendly' meant inviting, hospitable terrain, likely to have been inhabited by ancient people in times of peace.

And so we closed up Marmo and drove south, Koa alert in the middle of the front seat, Remo singing our travel song, me chiming in for the chorus—"We're on our way, our bags are packed / We're on our way, we won't turn back / We're on our way, though we don't have a dime / We're going, and we're gonna have a happy time..."

Later that afternoon we sat in the Bronco at the head of a jeep trail, while a heavy downpour turned it to clay soup. Then, after the rain stopped, we sat there some hours more, waiting for the road to dry out, munching Remo's homemade gorp. By the time we'd driven the eight rough miles to where we planned to camp, the sun was almost to the horizon, and the rain-fresh grassland, with its pink rimrock and muffin-shaped rocks, glittered and sparkled gold.

Remo stopped the Bronco in an open piñon-juniper grove, and our ears quickly tuned in to the cheerful pulse of evening birdsong. Koa, overjoyed to be released from the front seat, bounded off to explore. A pair of ravens sailed out of a large piñon and followed Koa to see what he might scare up. Scrub jays cawed, mourning doves wailed, phoebes cooed, and everywhere in the trees unseen voices cheeped and chittered and warbled. Blue larkspur, yellow buckwheat, red paintbrush, and white primrose brightened the green spectrum of grasses and junipers. Tussocks of magenta four-o-clock had wakened, and the scent of wet sage permeated everything with the fragrance of praise. A friendly place, indeed.

We set up camp near a large outcrop, the tent hidden from the trail and protected from the wind, the 'kitchen' arranged beneath a sheltering overhang. Remo rigged a rain poncho over a juniper limb for Koa's tent, then scrambled an egg, onion and cheese omelet for supper. We fed each other ripe strawberries for dessert, then snuggled into the tent and slept soundly.

In the morning the sky was clear—but not for long. By the time we set off on our first day's hike, the clouds had regrouped. No matter. We soon came to shelter in the form of a partly caved-in sweat lodge, which we guessed to be Ute or Paiute, perhaps two or three hundred years old. I was struck to think of the men who once sat hunched in this log dome, who likely had not heard of the palefaces that had arrived in huge winged canoes and were methodically clearing the land of their brothers to the east. To the people who used this structure, history was as personal as the sweat with which they cleansed themselves and renewed that history. I tried to imagine their songs.

The clouds lifted and we walked on to explore the sinuous pink rimrock bordering the grassland, one of us above, one below, Koa attending to his own interests. Communications were simple: one hoot meant 'I'm here, where are you?' Two hoots indicated 'I've found something, come see,' and three were for an emergency that so far hadn't arisen.

Remo, a veteran of such explorations, claimed to disbelieve in any kind of a 'spirit world'— even an imagined one. He merely raised an eyebrow when I told him about my grandfather dream. For him it was enough that ancient people had crafted objects that gave him pleasure to find and to contemplate. Nevertheless, I found the first arrowhead, a squat fat piece of taupe flint with oddly delicate, symmetrical tangs—almost as if it had been made by two people.

Then Remo hoo-hooted. His find was a red-and-black painted pot-shard that had been shaped into a rectangle with a hole drilled through one end, to be worn on a thong as a pendant. Knowing that such pottery wasn't local, and probably came from much farther south, helped us see the dynamism at work in this culture. They travelled, they traded, they exchanged ideas and methods over many generations, They raised children and grandchildren, who perhaps saw the world differently, yet were not quick to leave behind their land or their ancestors.

The rainstorm hit just as we discovered a series of cysts, or storage bins, under a wide ledge. A large ruin with velvet soot staining its rock ceiling indicated that the site had been used for dwelling as well as storage. While rain poured over the ledge, enclosing us in a literal shower curtain, we examined the potshards we found there. Red and black, gray and black, gray and white, plain gray corrugated. Then we just sat, listening to the lisp of falling water and staring through clear liquid drapery at gem-blue penstemons on their long stalks, nodding in the rain.

Before dawn the next morning we were wakened by coyotes yelling close by, so loud and voluble they seemed to come out of our dreams. Then the birds began singing, and there was no going back to sleep. The sky was clear, the stars fading. Why not start out before the clouds piled up again? We continued exploring the rimrock, and soon came to another row of cysts under a ledge. The stonework had been toppled by cows and there were no artifacts to be found. But all by itself in the dust under the ledge was the skull and great curled horns of a bighorn sheep. "You won't believe this," Remo said. "I don't recall this ruin, but I remember that skull. It's exactly where it was twenty-five years ago. Look—" he said, drawing from his pack a worn topo map that threatened to fall apart along its folds as he opened it. In Remo's tiny block letters, right where we were on the map, was penciled 'Ram's Head Ruin." I smiled, pleased as he was to think that no one had been in this area for a quarter century—for surely anyone else would have taken the trophy skull. Remo was full of stories about rare finds he'd left for the next trip and never seen again. We left the skull where it was.

That evening, the wind came up and began to spit rain just as we were making supper. Tired of huddling in the Bronco for meals when it rained, we took our plates of food and a rug, and cuddled under the ledge above the kitchen. The sun set beneath the rainclouds, casting a brassy glow over rippling grasses, while strong wind nudged the piñons and blew birds off their evening course home. Soon it was dark. The rain had quit, but the wind was still trying to find us. I tucked myself against Remo's chest while he held me in his arms for what seemed hours, now and then kissing my hair or caressing my face. Never had I felt so much tenderness, so deep a harmony. It was well after midnight when we unfolded ourselves from each other and walked to the tent. The stars were bright and the wind watched us, holding its breath.

So much rain was a luxury. It was good for the land, it kept the days fresh, cool and bugless for hiking, and it provided most of our water. Each morning I carried four plastic buckets to the far side of the outcrop, where a large area of slickrock was pocked with pools and potholes. Scooping carefully with a tin cup, I filled the buckets with water for cooking, bathing and dishwashing. Because of the risk of giardia from deer and cattle, our drinking water came from the five-gallon jugs we'd brought with us. Koa, of course, found his own, just as he found his own sticks and dropped them at Remo's feet—not mine. Remo, always attentive to Koa, played at wrestling sticks in the kind of male-to-male way that Koa loved fiercely.

The rain clouds were thick and low that morning, and we decided to explore the huge muffin-shaped rocks across the grasslands near our camp. They were farther away than they'd looked, however, and it was raining by the time we reached the first one. While we waited under the two-story muffin cap for the rain to stop, Remo studied the ground and located a large shard of finely-painted black and white ware. He challenged me to find a piece like it, and I did, but only a small fragment. Still, we found that my piece seemed to fit his along a single brush stroke of black paint. "Turn them over," Remo said, and the confirming surprise came as we saw that the fingerstrokes on the inside of the pot were continuous across the crack between the pieces. Remo felt inspired to find another fragment, then I found another, edgewise among stones. Though we found no more pieces of the pot, and couldn't match the ones we had by their painted zigzag designs, we fit all four pieces together by their interior fingerstrokes. One fragment held the maker's entire whorled fingerprint.

No two ruins we had found on our hikes here were similar, indicating they may have been contructed by different generations. The first one we came to that afternoon was unlike any structure we had seen. Set on a ledge and protected by the ledge above, it was shaped like a beehive and built of sandstone slabs set upright between vertical cedar logs. Its curved portion was braced by sticks and mud, and the whole fragile structure was bound by juniper roots held together by knotted loops of willow bark. From its tied-together, beehive shape, to the small stones set into its mud and the fingerprints and knucklemarks beside them, the ruin had the feeling of a child's playhouse.

I pulled myself up onto the ledge, fascinated by the delicate willow bark rings, tied in simple square-knots, dry but still intact after seven or eight centuries. "Look inside," Remo said. "Sometimes when willow bark is used, you find knots that have come loose and fallen on the floor." Sure enough, as I peered through the rounded door into the dimness, there was a knotted loop in the dust. Picking it up, I turned and held it out to Remo.

"You salted it!" I accused, jumping from the ledge into his arms. "You knew it was there!" Knowing he couldn't have known, had never been to this part of the rimrock, and laughing, both of us laughing. "You're magic. This place is magic. This ring is magic!" I said, hugging him.

Whereupon Remo, so often emotionally evasive, slipped the loop onto the fourth finger of my left hand, and with his dark eyes shining, kissed me and said, "Yes, and it symbolizes other things, too—for us." So enriched was I from the days we'd spent together, and so elated by all we'd seen, it took me several moments to realize that Remo had, in his own way, and as much as he ever could, formalized the union between us.

What children we were at heart, we who still appreciated and participated in the high cultural life of a city in the mountains. To be so fascinated by the dwellings and artifacts of an ancient community, that here among them we came to trust each other's love into a shareable future. A relationship that in Aspen might have remained a coy game until one or the other of us tired of it, here in this rich swale of desert had bloomed with simple joy and deep care.

Chapter Fifteen

Coming to Terms

I was on my way from Aspen to Horsethief, driving fast, already fearing what I might find. Bonnie had called me the night before to ask if I had heard from Stephen, who had agreed to ranch-sit for a week while I was at a writers' event. I'd heard nothing from him, whereupon Bonnie explained that she'd been working days at the Park but spending nights at the battered women's shelter in Moab, after Stephen had tried to strangle her five days ago.

Thoughts shimmered like mirages in the July heat reflected from the highway. The Stephen I had come to know was not a whole person, was two halves of himself. Neither half seemed remotely in touch with the other. Stephen of the good ideas, good words, good neighboring, was not the Stephen who smacked Bonnie to the ground, broke her glasses, and nearly broke her arm. In April, Stephen had helped me repair the garden irrigation system. I'd made him lunch, sat with him beneath the apricot, and listened to his complaints. "I've lost Bonnie's love," he said as if she had withdrawn her feelings capriciously. "She doesn't make love to me anymore. I need it, but she doesn't want it. Doesn't want me." No hint of 'Bonnie fears my violence. Bonnie tries to bolster my spirits but I keep tearing myself down and saying that's how *she* sees me.' But Bonnie had already told me her side of Stephen's story—that he smoked pot and wanted sex constantly, day and night, even during her half-hour lunch break from work, and that while she tried her best to accommodate him, often she simply couldn't find the energy.

Unfortunately, Stephen wasn't being dishonest. It was far worse than that: he was totally blind to himself. I had seen him blatantly pick fights with Bonnie, then act as if Bonnie were running Stephen into the ground instead of Stephen doing it to himself. Recently Bonnie had told me about him wrestling her service revolver from her holster again, badly wrenching her arm in the process, and driving off in his bus threatening to kill himself, and her if she tried to follow. She was convinced he meant it.

"He's always pointing a gun at himself," she said sadly. "Either a real one or the one he carries in his mind."

Now Stephen's abusive side had gotten totally out of hand. Two of Bonnie's cousins had come to visit, and the four of them had spent a pleasant weekend at Horsethief, returning to the Park on Sunday evening. But no sooner had the cousins left on Monday morning than Stephen began taking his belongings to the bus, complaining that Bonnie loved her cousins more than she loved him. When she tried to reason with him, he turned on her, put his hands around her throat, and choked her into unconsciousness. When she came to, struggling for breath, she was lying on the floor with a severely bruised neck. Stephen was gone, so was Bonnie's truck. The red bus was still parked outside.

Bonnie managed to walk to the Visitor Center for help, and was taken to town for medical treatment. Counselors advised her to spend nights at the women's shelter, and also to file a restraining order against Stephen, banning him from the Park. Her phone call to me was part of an attempt to find out where the sheriff should deliver the restraining order.

By the time I turned into Horsethief's driveway, I was almost sure there would be no need for such an order. The surprise came when I saw Michael's new pickup parked near Bonnie's old one. I had just seen Michael in Aspen, and as ever he had said nothing to me about visiting his ranch. We had been on cordial though not friendly terms for the past two months, ever since Michael had agreed to raise my pay in order to have me remain as caretaker until he could find a replacement. Michael's circumnavigation of the globe was done and he'd resumed ownership of his lodge in Aspen, which meant I could expect him to appear unexpectedly and often at Horsethief. Remaining at the ranch under Michael's thumb was not my idea of home, and I had sent him a resignation letter months ago. But I had agreed to stay, and here I was.

And here was Michael, walking out of the house as I drove in. He indicated Bonnie's truck and said it had been parked there since he'd arrived the previous evening. "The keys are in it, and there's a duffel bag of clothes on the bed in the living room. But I haven't seen anyone around," he said. My heart clutched up, and I briefly told him what Bonnie had told me. Then I went straight to the closet in my bedroom. The .22 caliber rifle Stephen had lent me after Zamar and Bruja's locoing was gone. Things did not bode well.

Michael calmly suggested we search around the rimrock of the home canyon, including its east and west arms. "If we don't find any sign of him," he said, "we can take the horses tomorrow and make a wider circle.

He's probably just out camping somewhere." That gave me something to hope for, as we hiked to the rim between east and west canyons and circled east. But the hope was short-lived. At first only a whiff on the hot July breeze, the stench of putrifying flesh soon became inescapable. As Michael searched among the outcrops on the rim, I climbed down into the east canyon above the spring to check a live trap I'd set for porcupines who'd been destroying piñons and fruit trees. Maybe, if only...

There was nothing in the trap; a shriveled ear of corn still rested in the bait-pan. Overcome by the reek of rotting flesh, I stepped back from the trap around the branches of a piñon—and there, sprawled on the sand thirty feet away, was the bloated purple corpse of my friend Stephen. The little .22 rifle lay by his side, with a notebook and plastic waterbottle. The fingers of his right hand rested on the rifle like fat roasted sausages. His face, unfortunately, was still recognizable. I tried to take a deep breath, gagged on the putridness, yelled to Michael.

Michael had no hesitation about walking right up to Stephen's corpse and studying what had happened. I stopped about six feet away. Stephen had shot himself in the temple, had doubtless died instantly. More than that I did not need to know, did not want to see, and especially did not want to have to remember. But the sight, and the stench, seared me anyway.

After ascertaining that Stephen had left some writing in the notebook, Michael said we needed to notify authorities. We drove to Dead Horse Point, where there was now a pay phone, and Michael called the sheriff's office while I asked at the Visitor Center for Bonnie. I was told she'd had meetings in town that day, and I could reach her in the evening at Seekhaven, the women's shelter.

Michael and I returned to Horsethief to await the arrival of the sheriff or his deputies. Even before we got there, I had the feeling that a monstrous presence had installed itself at the ranch. Vaguely assuming it would go away when Stephen's body was removed, I tried to relax by catching up with the neglected, overgrown garden.

The sheriff's deputies arrived at dusk, while Michael and I were eating a supper I'd thrown together. Michael guided them up past the spring to the corpse. It was midnight before they finished making their observations and measurements, and lugged Steven's remains in a body bag to the coroner's ambulance waiting outside the gate. One of the deputies said he was going to town to notify Bonnie, and asked if I cared to accompany him—which of course I did.

Following the deputy's vehicle in my car, I was again hugely grateful for Koa sitting beside me. The deputy asked me to wait in Seekhaven's entryway while he broke the news to Bonnie. Moments later she threw her arms around me, screaming "Stephen is dead! My husband is dead!" I held her as she wailed helplessly, then walked her to her room and stroked her back as she cried and sobbed face down on the bed. Later, as her wails subsided to uncontrollable weeping, she sat up and I held her. Even in the dim room, I could see her black-and-blue neck.

Still in tears, Bonnie said she needed to go home so she could feed her dog and cats and be there on time for work—adding that she would only go if I stayed with her. Relieved to agree, I realized how much I was dreading driving into the ranch in the dark.

And so we got through that first night. Bonnie, bless her soul, actually went to work that morning. And after promising I'd come stay the night with her again, I drove back to what for so long had been home. Michael had gone to town. His log note was generous toward Stephen, whom he had met only once. It even helped a little bit toward mending our friendship.

...I have a sense that Stephen's spirit will be with us for some little time, until he feels cared for and free to go on... The gentle, loving spirit of this canyon is very old. Apparently Stephen needed to come here. The old spirit has released him. We should, too. This would be a good place to die. Welcome, Stephen, and good voyages. Know that we remember your kindnesses and that you made a good difference.

Much as I appreciated Michael's words, I was finding it difficult to be so magnanimous. The normally confused feelings toward a person who commits suicide—compassion for the victim of a murder and simultaneous fury at its perpetrator—were compounded by Stephen's psychological makeup. In addition, I couldn't shake the anger I felt that he would use Horsethief, and in particular the delicate area above the spring, to stage his demise. And absurd as it was, I was irked that he hadn't kept his agreement to care for the ranch in my absence.

Aware that I was doing a poor job of standing on such deeply shadowed terrain, I went out and found the horses, and brought them in to give me strength. As I was putting out hay for them, Michael came out of the breezeway tool-room with nipping and lopping shears. Together we cleared and widened the paths to the spring and into the east canyon, past the site Stephen had chosen, all the way to the cavern pourover. The idea, it seeemed, was to be with the *place*, the east canyon, with Stephen's spirit in it. And to mindfully create paths for that spirit—to set Stephen free from his death, and from the sacred land that had braced his end. It was another sensitive gesture on Michael's part, and we both felt better for it.

As the sun sunk beyond the west rim, Michael and I agreed that I would drive Bonnie's truck to her at the Park, and Michael would pick me up there next morning and bring me back to the ranch before returning to Aspen. I put together a bag of garden veggies and some things from the freezer to make a stirfry for Bonnie and me, but my appetite vanished before I drove out the gate. The pickup's cab was rank with the metallic smell of fear, blame, sickminded despair; the steering wheel was grimy and sticky with dread. I felt—I smelled and swallowed—what it had been like to be Stephen, locked in the grip of his final intention.

Still, what I needed to do was be there for Bonnie, who was greatly traumatized despite her effort to put on a brave front. After all, she had borne the brunt of Stephen's savage attempts to destroy the dark side of himself after projecting it on her—a form of love perhaps, but one that was demonically ill from the start.

I had never gotten to know Bonnie well while she and Stephen were together. Now, over supper by candlelight, I listened as she told me of her life. How her father had left her mother when Bonnie was an infant, and had refused to communicate with his ex-wife or daughter even though he remained in the same city. How her mother was basically good to her but had no interest in leaving Denver to visit her only child. How her mother's mother—her beloved Gram —had been the mainstay and inspiration of her life, but was now going senile in a nursing home. How her first husband had abused and beaten her, had sold her possessions—even her horse—out from under her to support his drinking and drug habits. How she had come to be a ranger, how it had held her together over the years and reassured her of her dignity and worth.

I found myself filled with admiration for this spirited, tenderhearted woman, and was glad to get to know her better. Despite—or because of—such emotionally flayed circumstances, I felt honored that she valued my friendship. And cowardly though it may have been, I was grateful that she needed my companionship as much as I needed hers, at least until the shock subsided.

I knew I had to return to the ranch—not just daily, as I'd been doing to keep up with the work of the place—but for the nights as well. I had to learn to *live* there again—alone. But the 'monstrous presence' I had felt the evening we had found Stephen's body had not disappeared with the removal of his corpse. I could not shut out what I had seen. No matter what meditation I tried, I could not douse a haunted awareness of *that place, there*, above the spring. Worse, I was unable to control my dilated imagination. I lay in bed—any bed in the house—and waited, *waited* for the dragging, scraping footsteps that meant Stephen—the Stephen I had last seen grotesque on the ground—had something else to reveal to me, something more he wanted.

I was terrified. I kept the four horses—Moriah, Aquila, Shasta, and Blackie—in the corrals, and forced myself to visit them around midnight with pieces of apple, as I had previously done with such happy innocence. Their sheer bulk and gentle awareness helped. But it didn't dispel. Nor did keeping Koa by my bedside, his water dish nearby. The blessed solitude I had loved for four years had dried up and blown away, grit in the wind. In its place was isolation and fear. Even during the day, working in the garden or doing other chores, I half expected to turn and see Stephen's corpse standing there waiting for me to claim its cold, bloated friendship.

Something had to change. I accompanied Bonnie to the funeral parlor in town while she chose a container for Stephen's ashes. I went with her to the counseling office, where the help she received was minimal. But she did learn that the counselor Stephen had seen a week before his death had prescribed Prosac for him; that Stephen had given a false address and phone number to the counseling office; and that he had not returned for his follow-up appointment. She also learned, from phone conversations with Stephen's best friend Gary in Seattle, that Stephen's split personality and suicide threats had long caused concern to his friends there.

We went to the sheriff's office, where Bonnie as widow disclaimed Stephen's rifle, and where the deputy who had brought her news of Stephen's death told us that Stephen had left a note for Bonnie and one for me. He handed me mine, but warned Bonnie that the contents of hers would be upsetting, and gently advised her to wait a few years before reading what he told us were harsh and blameful words. Tearfully, Bonnie asked me if I would keep the letter for her, and having read the note he had penciled to me, with its imperative "You will forgive me's," I agreed.

Knowing Stephen had died on the dark side of himself, full of the wildly false and paranoid claims he'd made about Bonnie's unfaithfulness to him, Bonnie's rejection of him, was deeply saddening. I realized how much I wanted to think of Stephen's good side as his stronger one. But if it had been, he would be alive and Bonnie would not be a widow with a bruised throat.

And I would not be frightened of spending nights alone at Horsethief. On the night we found Stephen, I had called Remo from the sheriff's office before going with the deputy to Seekhaven. Now I called to ask him please to come stay with me for a few days and nights. Knowing how reluctant he was to leave Aspen during the summer, I expected him to refuse. But I was also thinking that if we were going to live together somewhere else in Colorado or Utah, he would have to break the Aspen habit. Charily, he agreed to come.

Once he arrived, however, he was not begrudging. We visited Bonnie and took her an apricot meringue dessert Remo made. The next evening she came to the ranch for supper—a courageous act, since she was as spooked by the place as I was. We took turns ringing the big bell, swinging its handle and clanging it deep and loud—more to release our pent-up tensions than as a rite or ceremony. Bonnie wanted to be home before dark, so we sent her off with extra helpings of pasta and dessert. I felt guilty that she faced the night alone, while I had Remo for comfort.

As for us, our dance in the hot tub had become more settled, but it was what I needed: to be outdoors at night and lose, for minutes at a time, the sense of being haunted. Later, lying in bed beside Remo, I could actually sleep; and when I couldn't, at least I was distanced enough from my fear to see how irrational it was. I took Remo up past the spring and showed him where Stephen had ended his life. Then we searched for arrowheads on the mesa, above the gully where I'd met the Anazazi boy. I sensed only his absence, and that of Tia Cojonuda.

But with Remo there, I was able to relax a little. I hadn't told him the extent of my fear, only that I felt "uneasy." He'd scoff, I was sure, to know how deeply spooked I was. But he must have sensed something amiss with me. Before getting into the Bronco to return to Aspen, he held and hugged me longer than he usually did when we parted. "Think about finding our own place," he whispered into my hair. "Think about finding our own Horsethief."

Much as I rejoiced at that, I still had to find my way back to the Horsethief under my feet. I thought I had learned to live with ghosts—the ghost of my father helping me plant seeds, the ghosts of each year's garden, of Zamar and Bruja, of Tia and her people. I had honored them and become comfortable with them. But this was different. I simply did not know how to honor the murderer in Stephen. I was as split by his personality as he had been. But I was not as helpless. I wrote:

> *My job is to stay here, to come to terms with the new big lens of the place and allow gracefully that which is my responsibility and that which is my violated horror to come into balance with each other. I am still terrified, but that terror must be part of an expanded peace. My job is to see lucidly, with unimpaired ability to walk abroad at night, this place—in all its unique capacity for intimacy.*

As might be expected, much help toward this goal came from the horses. Compassionate, noble Moriah was the horse I chose to ride out one evening to find Koa, who had for the first time in his life run away, chasing a female coyote. The coyote had been hanging around the west rim since Stephen's suicide, and though I saw no omen in that, I was terrified that my dear dog would be duped by the female and killed by others of her pack—terrified he would disappear and I would never find him. Dusk had turned to darkness on the mesa when Koa answered my calls for him to come. Suddenly he was there beside Moe's legs, panting, white teeth grinning up at me, while from a nearby ridge the lady coyote yipped for him in the dark.

I turned Moe home, begging Koa to "please stay with me," and relaxing a bit when I saw that he would. Far off on the horizon, a red flare from the long set sun remained. In thanks, and to ward off the spooked feeling I anticipated as I approached the home canyon, I began humming, humming to the rhythm of Moriah's hoofbeats, humming until the humming began to find words, humming the words until they became a song, a slow, low-pitched song, a rhythmic prayer for *peace in the land,* I was singing *peace in the land, peace in the land that I love...*

It was to become my song, then and through many circumstances later.

Little Blackie had gone from accepting a halter to wearing it proudly. One evening, riding Moriah, I led Blackie back out the driveway, as I had done before, trying to get him over the impish habit of nibbling at his halter rope. He behaved so well that I rewarded him by letting him run free. But on the way back, I had to chase him away from the mothballs I'd strewn to keep deer away from the fruit trees along the driveway. Later, still forcing myself to go out at night, still focused with fear on the site above the spring, I visited the corrals. Neighing loudly, Blackie trotted over to me, sank to his knees, fell over and lay stretched on the sand, groaning. Quickly I got him to his feet and began leading him around.

Whenever we stopped he went down. Freaked by something real now, I kept him walking, no way to leave and get help. Susan Obermeyer and her friend Annie had been due in that day, and with all my heart I prayed they would show up. After an hour of keeping Blackie on his feet, I glimpsed headlights beaming in along the driveway. Immediately Susan spelled me walking Blackie, and Annie got the boys in bed while I explained to Susan that this was a case of naphthalene poisoning, not colic. "He didn't have time to eat more than a couple," I said, "but I've no idea what damage they can do to his liver or kidneys."

Finally, around four a.m. Blackie showed signs of wanting to drink and eat, and soon afterward seemed quite recovered from his disabling, manure-spattering bout with poison. Susan went to the bunkhouse to sleep. I spread my sleeping bag on the corral sand where I had slept four months ago with Blackie—an act unthinkable since Stephen's death.

Susan, Annie, and the boys had stopped at the ranch on their way to visit the Barrier Creek pictographs in Horseshoe Canyon, west of Horsethief on the far side of the Green River. There, an isolated zigzag of Canyonlands National Park protects some of the most impressive rock art in the southwest. I had seen photographs of these humanoid, ghost-like figures, and had long wanted to view them face to face. Now I felt I needed to see them, *needed* that medicine.

We drove east, north, west, then south, 120 miles around, to get to a place that wasn't but fifteen raven miles from the ranch. Arriving at Horseshoe's rim, Susan and Annie pitched a tent by the hazy light of August's high-riding moon. I sat on a rock gazing at the sky, steeped in welcome relief, while in the tent four sleepers breathed softly, Tom or Billy murmuring in dream.

By morning, wind had herded in flocks of gray clouds, and we descended into the canyon dressed for rain. Showers pelted our faces as we gazed up at the first tall glyphs, and we were driven to take shelter and eat lunch under a venerable cottonwood. Then the rain subsided, and we walked the canyon floor from wall to wall, locating mysterious red- and ochre-painted figures on the smooth red cliffs. The boys asked what the figures meant and why they were there, while Annie and Susan studied them, interpreting some by what they'd learned from their longtime native shaman teacher in New Mexico. Through them, I learned too.

We came to the most noted part of the canyon, the 'Great Gallery' of dozens of painted and chipped figures—animals, humans, humanoids, ghosts, some tiny, others larger than life, many possessed of an eerie, mysterious presence. Two of the red-painted human shapes reminded me of the powerful figure whose spell I had come under the day the deer had plunged from the cliff. I was looking intently at one of these when Susan pointed out something I hadn't noticed. "See," she said, raising her hand to the height of the figure's chest. "See, there are two animals inside its chest—or inside its heart—and they're fighting one another. See the claws?"

I stared. There was Stephen, painted a thousand years ago by someone who understood the deadly pain of a divided self. I felt a sense of immense relief, as if a dove had fluttered into my own chest and was perched there, cooing softly. I felt anger drain out of me, and fear. And in place of them, finally, came grief. The compassion I had sought for Stephen's helplessness against himself welled into consciousness and brought tears to my eyes. I cried for him, and for all those blinded by such battlegrounds of psyche and heart.

It was dark when we drove into the ranch that night. For the first time in weeks, I did not feel afraid. Alert and aware, yes, with the awareness still directed toward the east canyon. But the sense of a menacing, monstrous presence had faded, had almost disappeared. I still wanted the horses with me, but as I fed each one, I realized I wasn't hiding behind them any more. I wanted to enjoy their company, continue training Blackie, ride Moriah and Aquila out on the mesa and sing my song. I wanted to greet Tia Cojonuda, whom I sensed had been watching from a distance, and let her know I was home.

The next evening, after Susan, Annie and the boys left, I went to see Bonnie, and was happy to learn she too had resolved some feelings about Stephen. With courage and compassion, she had accepted the blackness Stephen had projected on her, had gone into it with him in spirit after his death, as she had during his life, until she deeply understood the power it had over him—and her. If she wanted to go on loving the good in Stephen, she had also to embrace his demon. She had loved and wed and been widowed by one man, not his divided selves.

Still, it was September before Bonnie asked me to join her in the rite of spreading Stephen's ashes under the piñon where he had taken his life. She arrived fresh and lovely in a flowered skirt, blonde hair flowing around her, holding the box of ashes with only a hint of apprehension. This would, after all, be the first time she had visited that place. I led the way, and showed her where I had found him. I drew a quick breath as Bonnie swirled her skirt out over the spot and knelt down. But then it was okay, as she asked me to kneel too, and put my hand with hers on the box as she spoke directly to Stephen. She told him how deeply she had loved him, how many good things he had done, how much he was missed. Then, opening the box, she reached into it and cast a handful of ashes around her. We stood, wishing peace to Stephen's spirit, as Bonnie broadcast another handful of ashes where she had sat, then offered the box to me. Never having touched such ashes, I hesitated, then took a handful of the greasy-feeling flakes and scattered them with my blessing. *Peace in the land,   peace in the land that we love...*

And that was the state of things when, a few days later, a man who was not quite a stranger rode his bicycle through the front gate. I was in the garden harvesting beans when Koa woofed, and couldn't see through the tangled jungle until the man stepped from his heavily laden bike and pulled off his baseball cap. I recognized Tom Dodd, the friend of Michael's friends Betty and Hal, who had helped mount the big bell. "I see nobody's walked off with that thing yet," Tom joked as I came over to shake hands. "I hope I'm not arriving too early."

"Too early?" I asked, guessing he was meeting Hal and Betty again.

"Michael told me I didn't have to start work until October first, but

I thought if I came a couple weeks early I could help out and learn the ropes while you were still here to teach me."

"Oh," I said, trying to grasp Tom's words.

He saw my look. "Didn't Michael tell you I'd be coming? That he'd hired me as caretaker?"

I took a breath, thinking fast. It would be neither fair nor professional to begin Tom's tenure, if such were to be, with a rundown on Michael's communication skills.

I simply said "No. I hadn't heard a word about who might be coming. Or when."

Now it was Tom's turn to say "Oh. Well, maybe I'd better..."

"It's fine," I said. "No worries. It's good you're here—you know how this place can always use help." My mind was still racing. "Park your bike while I get us some lemonade."

A few minutes later we were sitting in the shade of the apricot, frosty glasses in hand.

"Where have you been biking?" I asked, supposing he'd parked his car somewhere and ridden down the switchbacks to the river and back up, or some such ride.

"Well, today I rode from the town park in Green River," Tom said, pushing tousled blond hair off his damp forehead. "And before that, from Seattle. And before Seattle, from La Paz, in Mexico. I've got a sailboat moored there, just a little gunk-holer, but that's where I've been living since I was here last."

I grinned, remembering his quick humor. "Glad to hear you don't like to travel much," I said. "Are you sure you can stand staying in one place?"

"I figure it'll take a year to learn the basics around here," he replied casually, resting ice-blue eyes on the garden. "Then I'll just have to see."

That evening, after Tom had unpacked his belongings in the bunkhouse and we'd had supper together, I rearranged my mind around this new state of affairs. That Michael hadn't informed me about it didn't surprise me. His attitude toward communicating with his help was a big reason I knew I couldn't stay at the ranch after Michael's voyage was over.

But neither was I ready to leave.

For one thing, I felt I still needed time to come to terms with Stephen's death. For another, I had a few pieces of writing I wanted to finish at the ranch, since once I left I would be working full time. Remo had said I could live in what he was calling "our house" in Aspen. But I couldn't imagine getting much done in that small cabin except during the winter while Remo was back East—and then I'd be working at whatever job or jobs I'd found.

When I phoned Michael from town to say Tom had arrived, Michael apologized for not letting me know about Tom. And, he added, "You can stay there as long as you'd like. I just can't pay you after October first." It was settled, then. I could eke out my savings until the end of the year, then face the culture shock of living in Aspen again while Remo was back East. Easier not to have to make two adjustments at once.

Tom told me the only thing he knew about gardening was how to use a knife and fork, so I thought that was a good place to start showing him details of caring for the ranch. Intelligent and strong, Tom was quick to learn, clever at initiating needed projects, and easy to be around. He was also disconcertingly attractive. He told me he was 'sort of' going though a divorce, but that he and his wife Kelly still spent time together. He was being pursued by another woman, but was reluctant to get into a new relationship. I was glad to hear it.

One evening after we'd been working together for several days, we got into a bottle of wine with supper and talked about our mutual attraction. By then Tom knew a lot about Remo and I knew something about Kelly. But still, there was this electricity...We both felt it, and when I told him my fantasy of co-caretaking the ranch with him, Tom said he'd had the same thought. At which we both laughed, red-faced with wine and confession. We decided we had a "hot friendship," but nothing that could intrude on Tom's relationship with Kelly or mine with Remo.

In October, with Tom installed as caretaker, Remo and I went looking for real estate. We'd already searched around Moab and farther south in Utah, but had seen nothing that made us look at each other and say Yes! Now we were going to explore the Four Corners area of southwest Colorado, tugged that way by its climate, geography, rich anthropological history, and mix of contemporary cultures. We also had friends there, the writer Russell Martin and his wife at that time, artist Karen Holmgren. They had visited us at Horsethief and persuaded us it might be the place we were seeking.

Russell, a native of the area, introduced us to real estate agents and even drove us around to look at properties. Recent rains had made clay soup of roads into remote places we wanted to see, but it was dry enough to get to one of them—and we fell in love. Forty acres of meadow and woodland overlooked a canyon stream running through one corner of the land, and afforded spectacular views of the Sleeping Ute mountain nearby and the La Plata peaks in the distance. There were no buildings, but Remo immediately began plans for a house, studio and barn. "I'm not a builder," he said, "but I can design what we need, and I'm sure Russell can steer us to a reliable contractor." We walked the entire property and camped there that night. In the morning we went to the real estate office and made an offer.

Remo suggested we go to Marmo for a few days, and he would then phone the realtor to see if the offer was accepted. Three days later we were acutely disappointed to learn our bid had been flatly refused. The realtor was sympathetic: "The owner thinks that land is going to make him rich," she said.

We reconsidered building a permanent home at Marmo, but knew the steepness of the road up to it wouldn't allow winter access. "Better we keep it as a place to visit," Remo said. "We'll look here again in the spring. After all, I have to sell my cabin first. What matters is we've found an area we like, and we agree on the kind of place we want."

As we drove into the ranch, Tom greeted us, accompanied by his handsome black lab Calvin, whom Kelly had brought during our absence. "We've got company," Tom warned with good humor, "a whole family of company." While Koa and Calvin were deciding to become best buddies, Tom introduced us to the people he called "the French family": Andre Capdot, his wife Penny, and their children—Loic, age fourteen, Jerome, age ten, and Hélène, age seven. They had met Michael in the Mediterranean harbor of Malta, where Michael had anchored his yacht next to the Chinese junk Andre and Penny were sailing around the globe. Andre spoke little English, but Penny, whose English parents had raised her in France, explained that she and Andre had become alarmed at how fast the planet was changing. "We wanted the children to experience some of the unspoiled places and peoples on Earth, before they're gone forever."

In the way that Horsethief often created instant intimacy, we were soon friends. Tom had settled Andre and Penny in the livingroom/bedroom and had taken the children under his wing in the bunkhouse. They called him "Cowboy Tom," and as he penned in the logbook, *The ranch is a better place with kids.* Andre and Penny insisted the children have a complete education, so weekday mornings were devoted to academic lessons around the kitchen table. Penny, highly artistic herself, also encouraged the children to draw and paint, write poems and songs, make costumes and act out their own plays. The ranch buzzed with activity, and we felt like a family, with Tom and Remo and I as uncles and aunt. Koa and Calvin belonged to everyone, especially the children, who gave the two gentlemen dogs all the attention they asked for.

While Remo and I had been away, the garden was struck by light frost, and Tom had heeded my advice to harvest *everything*. The root cellar was crammed with produce, the earthy smell and spell of Hallowe'en was in the air, and we decided to stage a Hallowe'en party for the French children, to whom it was an unfamiliar holiday. Meantime, our 'family' grew with the arrival of Betty and Hal. No one wanted to sit still, so we saddled the horses and went for a Hallowe'en ride to some goblin-shaped rocks east of the ranch. But the best horse event of the day came when we returned and I put Hélène on Blackie's bare back and led him around with his first rider. Blackie's calmness was a match for Hélène's excitement. "Papá," she piped, "please take my picture. I am riding a *real* wild horse!"

Then it was dusk, full moon rising, bunkhouse quaking with preparations. Masks, make-up, rattling chains and a tape of eerie Tibetan music—the singing bowls, the deep, deep horns—were readied. The adults put on their costumes and masks and hid in the darkness of the jack o' lantern-guarded bunkhouse. Remo led the kids over from the house, "to see what the scary noises are about."

Hélène, bravest, advanced first. As she stepped into the bunkhouse, her flashlight beam caught Betty's pointy-toothed, bloody-mouthed vampire mask. With a shriek, Hélène ran back out, nearly trampling Jerome and Loic, who were already running. While the rest of us feared we had gone too far, Remo talked the kids down into a frightened ferocity. They came racing back to the bunkhouse, finding and pummeling Andre in blackface behind the fridge, Penny as a bewigged and ketchup-bloodied witch behind the couch, Hal as a mustachioed bandido in the closet, and Tom, a pillow-fattened clown lurching out of the bathroom. Screams and peals of laughter accompanied poking fingers and more pummeling. We all took turns bobbing for apples, and soon fright was forgotten. Another hearty meal led to another deep sleep, while the pumpkin moon sailed coolly overhead. Before joining Remo in our bedroom, I sat for a while in the sandy corral with the horses, and encountered not a single ghost.

And so the days grew short, but remained mild. Remo returned to Aspen to have hand surgery for his carpal tunnel syndrome. He'd be back before Thanksgiving. Home schooling continued, and horse-riding, at which all three kids excelled. Hélène, it seemed, was afraid of almost nothing. Not only did she help train Blackie by riding him to my instructions, but this little blond snippet of a girl delighted in cantering Eagle, the stallion, up and down the driveway.

Meantime, Tom and Andre kept up with ranch work, while I weaned myself from it to finish my writing projects. I was feeling much angst about leaving, and Remo's notes of reassurance about our future were all that kept me from chronic panic. Then the weather turned cold and rainy, rendering dirt road conditions iffy. Penny and Andre made the difficult decision to return to their boat in Fort Lauderdale. The kids were heartbroken. Loic complained of "always having to leave my friends behind," and Jerome and Hélène wanted to "stay at the ranch forever."

Remo returned the evening before they were to leave, reporting the road still passable. Jerome and Hélène swarmed around him, begging him to save them from having to go. But Remo told them how lucky they were to be able to see the world, and asked them to send him postcards and poems and paintings to tell us where they went and what they saw and learned. That seemed to pacify them enough for sleep. But next morning, while Andre was loading their belongings into the car, Jerome hid in the house and refused to come out.

Remo went to find him, and after about ten minutes they both appeared, Jerome still tearfully stubborn. "You will forget me as soon as I leave," he told Remo, who promised he would do no such thing. "You write to me, or send me pictures, and I'll always write back and send you a surprise," he said. Finally Penny hugged Jerome into the car, and Andre called Loic and Hélène, who had spent the last hour saying goodbye to the horses. We all embraced, promising to stay in touch, and then they were in the car and this delightful, inspiring family was going through the front gate and on around the world.

The silence that descended on the canyon was quiet indeed. Remo and I looked at each other, unable to say words that weren't necessary. Koa nudged Remo's bandaged hand, and Remo reminded me he'd come to help me pack the things I wouldn't need during my remaining time at the ranch. Something in my heart cracked at this first step toward departure.

But I had collected and stored dozens of cardboard cartons in the root cellar, and now I brought them out. While I packed what I wasn't going to need from the kitchen and caretaker's room, Remo with his bandaged hand meticulously catalogued most of my books and put them into numbered boxes. Though it was painful not to have all my books accessible on shelves, Remo's system was the next best thing. For each of fifty-six numbered cartons, he made a master list of the books in it. If I wanted my favorite anthology of early English poetry, or a volume on American Indian medicine, or my college microbiology text, I could find them even in a storage unit, which is where they would soon be going.

The future was creeping all too close as we called it quits two days before Thanksgiving to begin preparing the holiday meal. Besides Remo and me, there would be Bruce, Bonnie, Duce, and Remo's long-time friend Robin Molny, an architect from Aspen. Tom would be in Denver with his family. As I made ginger pumpkin soup and the dry part of the dressing for the domestic but organic turkey we would have, I considered what to serve the evening before, when Bruce would be with us. I took a small hunk of corned beef from the freezer, to put with cabbage, potatoes, carrots and onions for a stew.

Next day while cooking, I found in the fridge two roots that looked and smelled like horseradish. Penny had asked if she could dig up a few of the spicy roots to take to the boat, and from the kitchen window I'd pointed out the horseradish patch in the garden. Now it appeared she'd forgotten them, so after biting into a root and tasting its heat, I grated them into the pot.

Bruce arrived, and we sat down to bowls of stew, Remo's figassa, salad and a bottle of pinot blanc. As always, Bruce and Remo kept the conversation and laughter level high, and I ladled second helpings for Remo and myself. After the meal, Remo went out to check the hot tub, Bruce retired to the livingroom/bedroom to read, and I cleaned up the kitchen. Washing dishes, I began to feel very strange and woozy for having had just two glasses of wine. Feeling weirder by the minute, I went and asked Bruce how he felt. "Since you mention it, I've felt peculiar since we ate supper," he replied.

"Me, too," I said, "and I'm terribly thirsty. I'd better go see how Remo is." But I couldn't find him outside, so I came back in, abandoned the dishes and went to our bedroom to lie down. A bit later, Remo came in, saying he too needed to go to bed. I got up for a glass of water, drank two, and brought one for Remo, who was staring at the ceiling. "Something we ate or drank wasn't right," I said vaguely. "I wonder if it was in the wine."

"What did you put in the stew?" Remo asked, his tongue thick.

"Just the meat and vegetables, and some dill, juniper berries, and horseradish for flavoring."

"Is that what that grated stuff was? Horseradish?" he asked. Then said, "Never mind. I'm going back outside to walk around." He bumped into the doorjamb as he left.

I tried to sleep, but my mouth was so dry and my throat so sore it was no use. With what remained of my mind, I tried to think what could have happened. Worms in the juniper berries? A druggy joke in the bottle of wine? Nothing made sense. I fetched a liter jug of spring water, drank it within minutes, but remained painfully thirsty. When Remo came in, I made him drink more water. Then, as I returned from the bathroom, he asked "Who was that woman lying here next to me?" When I said it was me, he wanted to know "Well, then who is that woman with the dead baby wrapped up in rags out by the hot tub?" I tried to say it was part of the poisoning, but Remo hushed me, saying we mustn't wake the French family. "I already woke Ken by coming in the back door," he added. I hadn't the coherence to explain, but in my stupor recalled that Remo had never taken any social drug besides alcohol. This 'trip,' whatever its cause, must be far weirder for him than for Bruce or me, I thought, and worried about his heart.

Finally I slept, and when I woke it was daylight. Remo was asleep beside me and I heard Bruce in the kitchen. I went into the bathroom and peered in the mirror at my dilated pupils. I looked, and felt, as I had once before, when Rob and I had tried anti-seasickness patches before a sailing trip, and I had used two instead of one. The active ingredient had been belladonna.

Bruce was chipper enough, but his pupils were dilated too. I told him about the seasickness patches, but it didn't bring us any closer to understanding what had poisoned us. I sipped some tea and munched some bread—things I trusted—and while Bruce finished doing dishes I carefully seasoned the dressing for the turkey, stuffed the bird and put it in the oven.

By then Remo was up, if not coherent. As I went out to feed the horses, he was asking Bruce if he had seen the paintings on the ceiling of our bedroom—the mountains, the Indians with their teepees, the cars that had driven off the cliff? At least he's alive, I thought gratefully.

When I returned to the kitchen, Bruce was scolding Remo. "You mean you put your bandaged hand in the *toilet*?" It turned out that while Remo was reaching for a Kleenex on the back of the toilet, his nail clippers dropped from his shirt pocket into the bowl. "I had to use that hand," he said defensively. "I was holding myself up with the other one."

Still somewhat woozy, I continued dinner preparations. Remo went out to soak in the deserted hot tub and Bruce read and kept the fireplace going. By midafternoon, Remo could distinguish that there were no paintings on the bedroom ceiling—only stains from the leaks in the roof. He was well enough to start making some of his special dishes for dinner.

Around four, Bonnie arrived with Robin, and soon after came Duce. We told them about the night's misadventures, and I was staring out the kitchen window at the garden when Bonnie asked what I'd put in the stew. Something went *click*. "Oh my god," I said suddenly. "I could have killed us." Everyone crowded around as I pointed out the window. "See those long rust-colored leaves in that bed?" Uh-huhs ensued. "That's horseradish," I said. "Now look *directly* beyond it. See that big brown sprawly plant?" More yeahs and uh-huhs. "That's datura. That's what we ate and that's what poisoned us. I'm sure of it."

I explained about Penny wanting to dig up some horseradish roots—and suddenly hoped we'd eaten all she had dug. It would be terrible if the French family, the kids in particular, had to suffer what we'd been through, especially at sea. I also explained that I'd smelled and tasted a root before using them, and that it had tasted like horseradish and hadn't smelled like datura. "Datura root smells like rotten leather," I said, and Bonnie agreed. Finally Duce suggested maybe both kinds of root had been in the fridge, and I'd tasted only one. "I think you're right," I said, and we let the matter go.

With Stephen no longer with us to offer good words, and his absence a hole, I asked Robin to speak for us as we gathered around the table. "We are thankful for many things," he said slowly. "For food. For health. For freedom...friendship...love. We thank the earth for its gifts and the sky for its inspiration. We ask for the wisdom to know we have enough and the compassion to share it. We remember our history and ask blessings on our future."

And so another remarkable Thanksgiving passed. Remo stayed several more days to help with packing, and to celebrate my birthday. On that December evening, as he had done for the past two years, he found a moment when I least expected it to present me with himself, nude, sporting a large red bow on a special part of his anatomy. That had always led us to the hot tub, and this night was no different. It was beautiful, and comforting in the unthinkable grief of leaving the ranch, to be immersed in warm desert water, under brilliant cold stars, and to be held in love and silence.